G000022440

The State of State Theory

The State of State Theory

State Projects, Repression, and Multi-Sites of Power

Davita Silfen Glasberg, Abbey S. Willis,
and Deric Shannon

LEXINGTON BOOKS
Lanham • Boulder • New York • London

Published by Lexington Books
An imprint of The Rowman & Littlefield Publishing Group, Inc.
4501 Forbes Boulevard, Suite 200, Lanham, Maryland 20706
www.rowman.com

Unit A, Whitacre Mews, 26-34 Stannary Street, London SE11 4AB

Copyright © 2018 by Lexington Books

All rights reserved. No part of this book may be reproduced in any form or by any
electronic or mechanical means, including information storage and retrieval systems,
without written permission from the publisher, except by a reviewer who may quote
passages in a review.

British Library Cataloguing in Publication Information Available

Library of Congress Cataloging-in-Publication Data

ISBN 978-1-4985-4248-7 (cloth: alk. paper)
ISBN 978-1-4985-4249-4 (electronic)

∞™ The paper used in this publication meets the minimum requirements of American
National Standard for Information Sciences—Permanence of Paper for Printed Library
Materials, ANSI/NISO Z39.48-1992.

Printed in the United States of America

Contents

1 Power and the State   1

2 Breaking the Theoretical Stalemate: State Projects and
a Multi-Site Model of Power and the State   37

3 State Projects and Economic Intervention: Balancing
Political Forces   59

4 State Projects and Heteronormativity: Framing
and Selectivity Filters   79

5 State Projects and Social Movements: Racial Formation
and the State   95

6 State Projects and the Human Right to Shelter: Balancing
Political Forces and Intersecting Relations of Inequality
and Domination   117

7 State Projects and the Human Right to Food: Direct Action
and Balancing Political Forces   127

8 Intersections of State Projects, Multi-Sites of Power,
and the Welfare State   137

9 Where Do We Go From Here? Implications and Steps Forward   155

Bibliography   165

Index   193

About the Author   201

Chapter 1

Power and the State

INTRODUCTION

In this global moment of austerity, multiple crises, and various antagonist movements across the globe arguing for alternatives (Shannon 2014), we struggle to make sense of the nature and role of the state. Indeed, rollbacks on social programs achieved through labor-based struggles throughout Western Europe demonstrate quite clearly some of the limits to reforms won *within* the capitalist state. The landscape has changed to such a large extent that most of Europe's ostensible "socialist" parties are locked into pro-capitalist, pro-austerity policies, fitting them hand-in-glove with global capitalism's drive for accumulation. At the writing of this book, the only class-based party alternative to arise in Europe is Greece's far-left Syriza, and even they seem to be capitulating to the European Union and global financial institutions as they engage in the realpolitik of running a capitalist country within a global capitalist political economy.

Because of these large-scale state failures, nestled within this reality have been a number of movements from below, outside (and sometimes against) the state. Movements such as the Arab Spring, the various Occupy encampments, and more recently the explicitly stateless democracy of the women's movement and other extra-institutional actors in Kurdistan (see especially Dirik 2014) have appeared on the global stage with an unexpected ferocity and staying-power, transforming from occupations of public space into movement formations that intervene in daily life. And like most social movement contestations, these groupings have led to a number of instances of rethinking how power is organized in our daily lives. From anti-sexual harassment squads in Tahrir Square, to "Occupy Patriarchy" and "Black Lives Matter," to eco-feminist stateless confederalism in Kurdistan, each of these movements

1

developed their own analyses, not just around labor, the politics of the state, and social class, but recognizing patterns of multiple sites of power that must be addressed in efforts for social transformation.

It appears, then, that the sociopolitical issues of our time demand a rethinking of state theory. If we recognize that there are multiple sites of power in our institutions and daily life, it becomes clear that traditional theories of the state leave many questions unasked: How do we explain the relationship between the state and society that produces the main social organizing principles of race, class, gender, and sexuality and their varied intersections?

Theorists of the state have explored the question of the relationship between the state and society for decades, producing a lively debate among proponents of contrasting models, most of which have, however, remained embedded in an exploration of *class*-based issues. But how do we understand issues that are not specifically class-based? Moreover, at issue in much of the debate has been a quest for recognition as the only valid model by each of the competing model proponents. It has often been the case that they were all looking at the same policy (the New Deal legislation) framed in very different terms, and arriving at very different conclusions as to what caused the legislation to emerge, and what it means. We have consequently been left with a spirited debate over decades with no progress in sorting them out: Which one was right, and which ones were wrong, and why? We argue that the issue is not that one of them is correct and the others not, but rather that each is looking at a specific corner of the bigger picture and arguing that they see the whole. Instead, we argue that each model is actually offering something of value that needs to be incorporated into a model that makes room for the validity of these seemingly competing pieces of the larger picture. They are, in fact, not necessarily competing, but rather offering a piece of that bigger picture. How do we fit these pieces together so they make sense and become useful in understanding the broader (class-based and beyond) relationship between the state and society? We suggest a model here of multi-sites of power (MSP) to do this, braiding the salient contributions of each of the competing models by organizing them around conceptual tools.

Clearly the state has organizing patterns around multiple systems of inequality and an MSP approach to state theory can highlight that. It is increasingly important to do so in the contemporary period given the wide berth of state projects surrounding multiple sites of power and their intersections. In order for sociologists to understand, describe, and analyze these processes, we need not build an entirely new theory. Rather, we argue that we can re-tool Jessop's (1990; 2008) concepts of state projects, the balance of class forces, and selectivity filters to rise to the occasion of analyzing state power and the state-society relationship as it exists across a broad range of systems of inequality.

But these ideas can be expanded even further. In order to empirically demonstrate the utility of our MSP approach to state theory, we focus in this book specifically on race, class, gender, and sexuality and, of course, their intersections in state policy. But a rigorous MSP approach to the state should also have the capacity to account for structured inequalities constructed around ability, age, notions of normalcy—any number of relations of domination that exist in human society. Future studies might do just this, expanding the MSP approach to state theory by applying it to as yet unexplored territories.

We also make the argument that an MSP approach to state theory, in part because it is a *critical* state theory, should not shrink from borrowing from theoretical perspectives typically ignored by sociological state theorists. Of particular importance in this text are our engagements with queer theory and anti-state forms of anti-capitalism, such as anarchism. This provides sociological state theorists with a powerful set of tools for analyzing the state-society relationship.

In order to sort out and identify the relative contributions of the competing models and how we might build on and incorporate their strengths to widen our view, we will need first to explore the various models that have dominated the scholarly conversation for decades. One caveat: scholars in the United States and scholars abroad use different taxonomies to compare and contrast competing models, but these tend to overlap a great deal. We will use the taxonomies more common in European scholarship to organize those more often used in the United States to facilitate a common understanding of the contrasting vocabularies as we explore the question of who's in charge.

We will begin this theoretical exploration with an examination of the very concept at the core of this question: the state. What is "the state"? We will follow this with a comparative analysis of the prevailing models in a critical assessment of what each offers and what their limitations are.

WHAT IS "THE STATE"?

Contemporary conceptualizations of the state borrow heavily from Weber ([1921] 1978, 54), whose definition of the state derived not from its theoretical function but from how it was organized and how it deployed its legitimation of authority and coercion and its use of force: "a compulsory political organization with continuous operations will be called a 'state' insofar as its administrative staff successfully upholds the claim to the monopoly of the legitimated use of physical force in the enforcement of its order." In this sense, then, the state is an array of institutions comprised of personnel whose specific duties are to dispatch and enforce its goals. The state enjoys a monopoly to enact rules and laws, and enforces these with its monopoly of force and authority, all within a territory defined by boundaries. Note that the state's ability to do so is predicated on its legitimation by those over whom it exercises its authority. Thus, the state is the organization of political positions and the structure of political relations in society. Note that the state is different from the government, which refers to the people who occupy positions within the state. Individuals may come and go in a government, and as such specific policies may change in part because of individuals' personal styles, perspectives, party affiliations and other allegiances, interests, and so forth. However, the structure of political relations (electoral processes, policy-making processes, and relations between the government and corporations, labor, consumers, and others) remains intact no matter who occupies positions in the state.

The Weberian conceptualization of the state tends to focus on its internal political dynamics and suggests a salient success of the state to assert its legitimacy over time; that is, it focuses on the ability of the rulers to assert and reassert the authority of the state in a "top-down" perspective and tends to ignore the response of the ruled. Thus, it tends to move aside as marginal or irrelevant the significance of factors like social movements from the ruled that challenge or resist pressures from the state to abide. But history is replete with evidence that states do not enjoy absolute consent indefinitely, and thus the notion of legitimation raises questions of the mechanisms by which the entity of the state develops and enforces its legitimacy, and how it maintains consent of the ruled. Understanding that the state may not always enjoy absolute rule and consent, what mechanisms do the ruled use to challenge that legitimacy and what factors affect their efficacy? How does the state maintain a tender balance between consent and coercion even as it may confront challenges from below?

Moreover, the Weberian conception of the state, defined by territorial boundaries, raises questions of the relationship of multiple states: How might the state's legitimacy be challenged by external forces? That is, the state presumably does not exist within a vacuum, but rather in relation to other states. The implication is that the tenuous balance of consent and coercion within the state is echoed in its external relations to other states. How, then, does the state balance its internal processes of consent and coercion with these external processes?

Much state theory builds on Weber's notion of the state, and differentially struggle with how to respond to the questions it raises, making different assumptions about the nature of the state. But all appear to view the state in structural or institutional frameworks. In that context, political agents or actors operate in a structural or institutional setting which differentially constrains or provides discretion of negotiated order. Jessop (1990; 2008) refers to this setting as "strategic selectivity," insofar as the structures and institutions of the state shape, frame, and are amenable to some perspectives, strategies, and agendas more than others, providing opportunities for recognition and negotiation to some but not to others. Any notion of "free will" of political actors becomes bounded in this way by the structural selectivity posed by the organization and function of the state.

Some theorists, particularly feminist theorists and poststructuralists, dispute the very notion of the state as a structural or institutional entity. Beyond the structures, they argue, "the state" must be understood in terms of cultural repertoires of meaning, meaning-making, and discourse. We will examine these in greater detail later, and suggest ways to incorporate their insights into a fuller understanding of the state. For our purposes here, however, it is worth noting that these theorists raise a challenge to view the state not only as a disembodied structure, but as a process and relationship as well.

The challenge, then, for theorists of the state: "they must give rather more attention to the processes through which the state is conceived of on the one hand, and the relationship between such conceptions and the institutions, processes and practices of the state on the other" (Hay and Lister 2006, 14).

We now turn to an examination of how different perspectives grapple with questions of the state and its relationship to society.

PLURALISM: THE STATE AS OBSERVABLE BEHAVIORS

Pluralist theory covers a broad range of thinkers, and itself is not really a theory of the state but rather a theory of power that has important implications for how we understand the state (Laborde 2000; Smith 2006). Contrasting variants have emerged in the United States and in Great Britain. In the U.S. version, pluralism became, as Merelman (2003, 18) noted, a legitimating framework to justify the power of existing leaders because it equated the ideals of the Declaration of Independence with a presumed reality. Because pluralism was a strong apologetic for existing power structures and a model asserting that the ideal of democracy was in fact what existed, the model dominated political and social theory for many decades. In fact, Daniel Bell (1960, 402) asserted that pluralism was no longer debatable, but was indeed accepted as fact when he declared the end of what he considered ideology. He says, "in the Western world . . . there is rough consensus among intellectuals on political issues: . . . [including] political pluralism."

Pluralist theory asserts that the state is the embodiment of power in a capitalist political economy. It stands above influence from the pressures applied by all interest groups, presumably including economic interests (see e.g., Bentley 1967; Truman 1951; Dahl 1961; 2000; Lipset 1981). The state thus acts as the neutral arbiter, weighing all competing interests to legislate in the "common good," striking some balance between the competing demands of these interests. The pluralist analysis places economic interests on a par with noneconomic interests, as if all were equal in power and strength in their ability to influence the state and to get their respective agendas addressed.

Pluralists argue that the state is not a monolithic, unified structure but rather a fragmented structure of dispersed, diverse, and competitive groups and elites representing a wide range of interests (Dahl 1963). They compete in the political marketplace for support from voters, all of whom are equal regardless of their economic resources, education, race or ethnicity, religion, gender, or age because all have one and only one vote to spend in that marketplace. Thus, the state is a stable system balanced by competition between elites who are held in check by countervailing political interests (Galbraith 1983; 1985). The masses would be able to hold elected officials accountable with the threat of voting them out of office if these elites did not adequately pay attention to their interests. Indeed, political analysts often appeal to this notion of the potential for "voter rebellion" when they report on elections: voters are often viewed as "fed up" with elected leaders who remain insensitive, politically out of step, or unresponsive to the common good or to voters' interests. For pluralists, then, power in the state is dispersed among the millions of individual voters, all of whom have an equal amount of power in their single votes.

Furthermore, the political interplay between elected elites themselves contributes to stability in the system, because policy-making procedures typically require a majority of them to agree to pass a bill. This is because all elected elites are equal: each has one vote in the legislative process, and none of them has enough power to unilaterally push their agenda against the will of the others. Therefore, all elites must negotiate with the others to form coalitions in decision-making, thus modifying their points of view and their level of aggression in pursuing a single-minded agenda. Such an arrangement ensures that all interests will eventually get addressed, as elites make deals with each other in agreements: "you support my issue, and I'll support yours."

Political stability and balance, then, continue to be assured by a consensus of values: the assumption is that everyone knows and accepts the rules of the game to include electing leaders from among a slate of candidates who usually run for office with a political party, with the presumption that once elected, these elites will dispatch their duties fairly and in the common good. Political participation thus is defined as voting rather than violent insurrection, mass rebellion, or revolution. Assassinating leaders who displease the electorate is unacceptable; impeaching such elites, recalling their elections, or waiting until the next election to vote them out of office are. Even when individual voters' preferred candidates do not get elected, the winner of the election is accepted by all as legitimate because all eligible citizens had a chance to participate in the process. Perhaps next time, those whose candidate lost the election will have greater success. In the meantime, the masses are expected to rally behind the winner unless and until such time as that leader proves unworthy.

Here, potential interests remain important elements of political stability: the threat of the mobilization of latent interests against incumbent elites with whom voters are displeased is seen as sufficient for ensuring that they do not ignore voters' interests or the common good (Truman 1951). Elites will not trample on the interests of the oppressed if there is the real possibility that the oppressed will become galvanized to oppose them and vote them out of office.

Scholars in Great Britain adopted a largely similar variant of pluralism in the 1950s through the 1980s to analyze British politics (see Finer 1966; Richardson and Jordan 1979; Jordan and Richardson 1987a; 1987b; Jordan 1981; see also Smith 1990). They argued that the byplay of interest groups defined Western European politics, much in the way that U.S. scholars had described politics there. As such, policies could be seen as a reflection of the relative strength of interest groups at a particular point in time, but that none dominated the process absolutely or indefinitely. Indeed, some scholars have drawn a somewhat finer line, arguing that there are interest *domains* in which some groups may dominate more than others, but only within that domain, rather than across all interest domains to dominate in the state overall (Jordan and Richardson 1982).

Pluralist analyses of the state, particularly in democracies, have chiefly evolved in examinations of the United States and Great Britain, and this makes them too vulnerable to criticisms of ethnocentric or parochial bias. However, even as a model of the state in the United States and Great Britain, it remains problematic. While the pluralist model of power structure may be consistent with the basic principles and ideals of these nations, it does not necessarily describe what actually occurs. There are several important analytical points to be considered.

One key element of the pluralist argument of system stability is the threat of "potential interest groups" emerging to pressure the state for attention. While this concept is appealing in its attempt to demonstrate dispersed power, it is quite imprecise: How do we know when there is sufficient threat as to alter the behavior of existing groups or of political elites? How much of a threat is necessary to capture the attention of existing groups and political leaders? How do we measure these? For example, the firearms industry in the United States maintains a highly active and well-funded lobby (the National Rifle Association, or NRA) to help them maintain their economic position with as few restrictions on their activities as they can manage. How do we evaluate the effect that "potential interest groups" might have on how aggressively they pursue their interests? Can we reasonably say that they refrain from seeking exclusion from gun control regulations and legal restrictions against its commodities, and that elected leaders refrain from supporting firearms interests, because of the concern that their actions *might* antagonize a growing number of people (how many?); that leaders of these aggrieved parties *might* emerge; that they *might* locate funds to support their own lobbying and resistance; and, *if* enough people have enough time and energy to devote to the resistance, that a potential group *might* coalesce, oppose the current advantaged status of the industry, and might even seek to reduce the industry's advantage in the United States and abroad? Political leaders and economic interests like the NRA and the firearms industry may indeed harbor some apprehension that such groups might develop (and some certainly have), but how much? Enough to say that potential power was exercised? How do we know that this potential actually affected the behavior of the firearms industry and of political leaders?

In addition, the very concept of stability or equilibrium presented by pluralists is questionable. Equilibrium may in fact exist in the state and society without providing for all substantial interests. And can we necessarily assume that even if substantial interests are not being met, it is because to do so is in the best interests of the "common good"? For example, it is possible to achieve "racial balance" in schools and in jobs by pursuing racial diversity among the student bodies and employees that are reflective of the proportions of different racially defined groups in the populatio?. At the same time, however, there may still be a high degree of inequality and discrimination in the programmatic tracks students are enrolled in, the differential wages personnel receive, the mentoring either may or may not receive, and the informal differential treatment people receive in these settings. Can this still be construed as equilibrium in the system? Is this persistent inequality in the "common good"? For that matter, what exactly is the "common good," and who decides? Do all interests and all constituents have a say in formulating that definition? Whose definitions prevail and why? Is there a pattern to whose definitions are given greater legitimacy, and whose are ignored? These are important empirical questions to explore, as they suggest a critical evaluation of pluralism.

Furthermore, while the pluralist model recognizes the vast array of interest groups that may exist, this does not mean that power in the state is dispersed (Marsh 2002). That is, pluralism implies that all interest groups and all voters are equal: no one enjoys absolute power all the time. At any given time, everyone has a chance to be heard and to have their interests addressed. We might for the moment agree that a principle of "one person, one vote" provides some basis for assuming that perhaps voters have equal ability to affect the outcome of elections. But this does not address the question of which people are perhaps not "eligible" to vote and are therefore less able to have their interests met because they do not have even this one ballot to cast. Such is the case, for example, for the homeless, children, and convicted felons in many states in the United States (Manza and Uggen 2008).

Moreover, are all interest groups of equal ability to affect decision-making in the state to their advantage? Pluralists do not rank groups' relative power or identify the elements that might make some more able than others to have such an effect. In particular, pluralists do not examine the differential resources to which various interest groups might have access and that might therefore affect how much influence they may have. One would be hard pressed, for example, to say that the War Resisters' League in the United States has the same ability to affect the state's decision-making about military buildup and going to war against other nations as the major corporations among the Department of Defense's contractors.

The presumption of the equality of all interests and groups further ignores how extensively economic institutions, particularly corporations, permeate all facets of society. The economy, and most people, rely substantially on the wealth and health of corporations to provide good-paying jobs (or any jobs at all), goods and services, and tax revenues to enable the state to provide for many of the services corporations do not. This is a position that is not enjoyed by noneconomic actors. The dominance of corporate actors is thus likely to make their interests loom more significantly than many others, and to render some interests invisible or unimportant by contrast. The pluralist model does not take this into account.

Similarly, this presumption of equality between interest groups does not take into account how strongly structures of oppression such as patriarchy, heteronormativity, and racism frame and pervade society. Maleness, heterosexuality, and whiteness have historically implied "normal" in the United States, rendering women, LGBTQ (lesbian, gay, bisexual, and transgender and queer) people, and people of color as "the other" and thus symbolically annihilating them (Tuchman, Daniels, and Benet 1978). To the extent that males and whites have historically dominated society and the political agenda of issues to be publicly debated, their interests are likely to be framed as "the common good," while interests of women, LGBTQ people, and people of color are more likely to be framed as "special interests." Schattscheider (1975, 34–5) once observed that "The flaw in the pluralist heaven is that the heavenly chorus sings with a strong upper-class accent. Probably about 90 percent of the people cannot get into the pressure system." One could also note that the chorus also sings with a decidedly male, heterosexual, and white voice as well.

The question of the likelihood of all interests getting addressed sooner or later is heavily based on the assumption of the neutrality of the state. But "the state" is composed of elite individuals who make decisions affecting every-one's lives in fundamental ways. These individuals, as human beings, have previous status positions in society that shape their personal sets of interests, based on such things as class, race, gender, religion, age, and other axes of difference. They are unlikely to eschew these completely as they step into public office; to expect that they could do so is unrealistic. They carry their personal histories and relationships with them, such that their prior interests and connections may certainly affect how they view issues or even *recognize* various interests at all. Moreover, state managers may have their own inter-ests in maintaining their privileged power positions, and this may be likely to affect their decision-making in ways that may certainly address their own interests but not necessarily be in the interests of the "common good." This also begs the question if there even *is* a "common good" within hierarchical institutions such as the state.

Pluralists argue that it may very well be that some interests are not getting addressed *at this point in time*, but that the masses accept this because they share in the consensus of political values and rules of the game and goals. However, this mitigates the notion that the rules of the game have previ-ously been set by those already in power and are therefore likely to reinforce their ability to maintain that power to the detriment of others. If there does appear to be some consensus of the rules of the game, how is it that most people come to accept these even when the outcome may be inconsistent with their own interests? How do people perhaps come to view the interests of the privileged in society as deserving their advantage, and they themselves undeserving?

Finally, pluralists largely emphasize electoral politics as the arena of political behavior and power, and the means by which the masses may hold accountable the elites whose decisions fundamentally affect individuals' lives. Setting aside for now the question of how much power electoral par-ticipation may offer individuals to hold even elected elites accountable, there are substantial nonelected elites who also make important decisions that so affect people's daily existence. For example, there are many among political elites who are not elected and whom it would be difficult if not impossible to hold accountable by voting, such as members of the Supreme Court, Pen-tagon officials, and cabinet officers in the United States; or Departments or Ministries of Foreign Affairs or military leaders in other nations. To be fair, pluralists would argue that such individuals are appointed by leaders that the masses do get to elect; but the critical point here is that, once appointed, these individuals may not be held directly accountable through voting, and some, like Supreme Court justices who are appointed for life, cannot be so held accountable at all.

Even more to the point, there are many economic actors and groups whose decisions affect people's daily lives in the most basic and significant ways, and yet are completely untouchable by voting. For example, corporate chief executive officers and their boards decide when to downsize, when to close production, how much to pay people who work for them, where to operate, and what products to make and services to offer. Financial institutions decide who gets access to money and investment capital and who does not. These decisions substantially affect people's life chances; but the decision-makers are not held accountable by voting whatsoever. How are they controlled? How might we hold them accountable? How might their power be restrained? What are the mechanisms which the citizenry can use to influence them? More to the point, how does this power affect the structure and relations of the state? Pluralism does not address these questions.

This critique of pluralism does not mean that voting behavior is irrelevant in the study of the state and its relation to society. But it does suggest that the pluralist vision by itself is limited, and that voting may be one of the many factors to be considered when evaluating the questions of the state. And many scholars, from a wide array of theoretical vantage points, have shifted their focus from power in the state as dispersed and a function of behavior in decision-making, to an examination of power as concentrated in institutional structures of the state. This leads them to ask very different questions.

ELITISM AND STRUCTURALISM IN THE STATE

Two broad categories of state theories contrast sharply with the pluralist focus on behavior and its assertion of power as dispersed and decentralized in a neutral state: Marxist theories (business dominance, capitalist state structuralism, and class dialectic perspective) and statist theory (particularly state-centered structuralism). The focus of these theories is on structure rather than behavior, and they assert power as centralized; however, they do not necessarily share a rejection of the assumption of the neutrality of the state, as will be evident below.

Marxist theories of the state reject the stratification model of the relationship between the state and society offered by pluralists and instead begin with the assumption of antagonistic classes whose conflict is built into the structure of society. There are several contrasting models of Marxist theories of the state, but each contains an implicit, and at times, explicit, analysis of the relationship between the state and a capitalist political economy.

Interestingly, although much of the spirited debates that have occurred between the models we will examine in this section are derived from analyses of Karl Marx and Frederick Engels's work, they themselves never offered a fully developed theory of the state. But they did assert some observations that have stimulated much of the contemporary debate. In particular, Marxist scholars have long debated the meaning of a single sentence in *The Communist Manifesto* (Marx and Engels 1967, 18): "The executive of the modern state is but a committee for the managing of the common affairs of the whole bourgeoisie."

This quote raises several pertinent questions: Does the state act as the coercive instrument of the capitalist class? If it does, what is the process by which that happens? If it does not, what IS the role of the state in modern capitalist society?

BUSINESS DOMINANCE AND ELITISM IN THE STATE

Business dominance state theorists, for example, have consistently focused on the relationship between the state and economic or class actors that reproduces largely capitalist class relations through the state's authority to create policy and the huge dominance of capital interests over the state (Akard 1992; Burris 1992; Clawson, Neustadtl, and Weller 1998; Hooks 1990; Prechel 2000; Skidmore and Glasberg 1996).

The earliest variant of a theory of the state in which economic interests control or dominate the state is instrumentalism. Theorists using this model did not frame their analysis in terms of class struggle. Rather, early instrumentalists offered a "capture" theory of the state in which capitalists virtually captured key positions of the state apparatus to use the state as their tool to legislate in their own interests (Burnham 1943; Mills 1956; Weinstein 1968; Miliband 1969; 1983; Domhoff 1970; Scott 1991; Dye 2002). In this scenario, a cohesive group of elites rules the state; they circulate easily from one strategically central institutional realm to another (identified primarily as the corporate economy, the military-industrial complex, and the state itself), thereby blurring institutional distinctions and solidifying their control of the state. These elites are impervious to the demands of the nonelites, and reinforce and reproduce their ranks from within.

Capitalists captured the state by running and getting elected to office, such as Governor David Rockefellar of Virginia, Governor Nelson Rockefellar of New York, President John Fitzgerald Kennedy, Senator Ted Kennedy of Massachusetts, Representative Joseph P. Kennedy of Massachusetts, Governor DuPont of Delaware, Governor Jeb Bush of Florida, and Presidents George Herbert Walker Bush and George W. Bush. Each of these men were scions of major industrial capitalist families. Alternatively, individual capitalists may capture the state to make it their instrument by consciously and deliberately applying their considerable economic power to bear on the state itself.

While this scenario would seem plausible, and many examples would seem to be readily available, the fact is that few capitalists ever actually captured the state outright, a criticism that more recent theorists took to heart. Indeed, some argued that capitalists actually would have an easier time getting their interests met if they did *not* sit in the command positions of the state: such blatant and obvious power grabs would quickly lose legitimacy. These theorists offer instead a view of business dominance rather than the more extreme view of individual capitalists consciously and deliberately capturing the state. In this more recent variant, capitalists do not own the state or capture its key positions. Instead, they dominate the state by sitting on important advisory groups like the Council on Foreign Relations, heading regulatory agencies, and using Political Action Committees in electoral and legislative processes (Useem 1984; Domhoff 1990; Prechel 1990; 2000; Akard 1992; Burris 1992).

Moreover, more recent research explores what appears to be the increasing diversity of the presumed power elite, particularly among gays and lesbians, women, and people of color (Zweigenhaft and Domhoff 1998). Indeed, many in the media have pointed to the election of Barack Obama as president of the United States in 2008 as evidence that the nation had entered a "post racial" society, suggesting that the increasing diversity of the power elite was eroding its previous strangle-hold on power and the state. However, although the research does show this increasing diversity among the power elite, the authors reject this means that anything has changed at all, noting that even these "newcomers" share the same class characteristics as the more traditional power elites, attending exclusive schools and enjoying access to resources that the poor and the working class do not. There are still very few women and people of color serving in elected positions of power and as chief executive officers of major corporations. As such, the power elite remain firmly drawn from among the most economically privileged in society (Zweigenhaft and Domhoff 2006). But the evidence of increasing diversity in the power elite, however small thus far, points to a weakness in the business dominance model, to the extent that it challenges Mills's (1956) assertion of omnipotence of the power elite.

The Council on Foreign Relations is an important advisory committee to the president on foreign policy. Its membership is heavily corporate, and thus their world views and perspectives regarding national interests are shaped by their corporate and capital accumulation interests. Since the president relies heavily on the analyses supplied by the CFR, corporate viewpoints and interests are likely to shape presidential pronouncements of foreign policy, including whether or not to sign international treaties and accords, go to war against another nation, or invest huge proportions of the federal budget into Department of Defense projects.

Regulatory agencies are commonly headed by people drawn from the industries these agencies are supposed to govern. This is because regulators often oversee complex industries such as nuclear power, banking, and communications. Individuals from within these industries are presumed to possess important expertise regarding how they operate, what issues they must confront, and what particular problems might arise. However, their ties within the industry make their independence as regulators questionable, and the fact that most of them cycle back into the industry from which they arose when their time is done as regulators (and commonly at a more lucrative position than before) makes it unlikely that they will enforce regulations the industry views as particularly harmful to its interests.

Finally, Political Action Committees may not buy a political candidate outright, but their contributions to political campaigns do buy them access to legislators, and gives them a stronger voice in shaping legislators' viewpoints, perspectives, and priorities. These mechanisms of corporate participation in the processes of decision-making thus enable capitalists to dominate and influence the state. Importantly, that dominance occurs not by capturing the decision-making positions themselves, but by providing key resources to those that do (Clawson, Neustadtl, and Weller 1998).

Although not conspiratorial, the business dominance position implies that business leaders operate on the basis of a clear, fairly unified conception of both corporate and capital accumulation interests and the policies necessary to address those concerns. Given sufficient threat to their interests and adequate mechanisms granting them access to the policy formation process, business leaders consciously organize the political and economic resources of the corporate community around successful passage and enactment of pro-corporate policy. This analysis also implies that the state is the locus of power; this is why capital accumulation interests find it so necessary to capture or dominate it. The state exists in a capitalist society.

The instrumentalist and business dominance perspectives suggest that individuals make a difference: if the individuals who occupy the important seats of power or the key organizational mechanisms of influence were to change, the state would presumably legislate to protect other, noncapitalist interests. That is, if labor leaders were to get elected to Congress and the White House, or to take control of the Council on Foreign Relations and the regulatory agencies, and to become the largest, most important Political Action Committees, legislators would have to accede to labor interests instead of capital accumulation interests.

This analysis discounts the role of political socialization in the production of policy in the interests of corporate concerns. The legitimation process facilitates the general acceptance by the wider population of the belief that societal interests and business interests are one and the same: "What's good for General Motors (or WalMart) is good for the United States," or "The business of the United States is business." As such, legislators and policy makers are likely to frame their perspectives in corporate terms because the dominating ideology with which most people are socialized in the United States filters and frames perspectives in such terms. Blatant seizing of the policy-making process or decision-making positions is not necessary if the dominant ideology legitimates such interests as the common good anyway.

Finally, the business dominance and instrumentalist analyses ignore the working class's role in policy making and the effect resistance may have on those processes. They imply that the working class tacitly accepts without resistance what capital accumulation interests and actors force the state to do, even if it is not in the workers' interests. However, history is replete with instances of resistance, which have at times facilitated the production of policy that business interests found abominable, such as the right of workers to collectively bargain. That resistance could have the effect of thwarting or at least defying oppression is a significant challenge to the instrumentalist and business dominance positions.

CAPITALIST STATE STRUCTURALISM

Capitalist state structuralists, in contrast, have emphasized the notion that the state is not simply situated in a capitalist society, but is instead a *capitalist* state. State policies are forged by the structure of the state itself and its position within the larger capitalist economy. State managers are constrained by the imperatives of the capitalist political economy to create and implement policies that reproduce the conditions of capital accumulation and to manage the conditions that create accumulation crises. State managers have no choice but to legislate this way: were the state to somehow operate outside of these structural parameters, it would court economic crises, which in turn would create political legitimacy crises that state managers can ill afford (Poulantzas 1969; Mandel 1975; Wright 1978; Valocchi 1989; Block 1987; Glasberg 1987a; 1989; Glasberg and Skidmore 1997). Moreover, because the state is the structural unification of contradictory class relationships, it remains free from direct control by class-based organizations. Pro-capitalist state economic intervention is not, therefore, produced by the participation of business organizations and corporate actors in the policy formation process. Rather, policy is a product of the contradictory relations of power embedded within state structures themselves. It is an expression of the state's underlying, capitalist structural bias.

Capitalist state structuralists and business dominance theorists agree as to *what* the state does: it legislates to secure the conditions of capital accumulation and in the interests of capitalists. But they disagree as to *why* the state does so. Instrumentalists and business dominance theorists argue that the state legislates this way because state managers are either capitalists themselves or they are dominated by such interests. Capitalist state structuralists argue that the state legislates as it does because state managers simply have no choice: their range of alternative actions is restricted to only those decisions that will not threaten capital accumulation or risk economic collapse and hence loss of control of the polity and their position of political leadership. This does not require dominance of the state by corporate interests.

In fact, capitalist state structuralists argue that the state is "relatively autonomous" from individual competitive capitalists; the fundamental requirements of capital accumulation at the core of the capitalist political economy delimit the state's range of discretion, not competitive individual capitalists. In contrast to the instrumentalist and business dominance perspectives, capitalist state structuralism implies that the structure of the state is impervious to changes in personnel: regardless of the types of individuals in the state apparatus, the state is structurally constrained to operate for the benefit of the capitalist class. What's good for General Motors or WalMart is good for the United States not because everyone has been politically socialized to accept that this is true or because the capitalists have seized control or dominance of the state to make this so, but because it simply *is*.

Capitalist state structuralism shares a view of the masses with instrumentalism and business dominance analyses in its discounting of class struggle as a factor in policy-making processes. But where instrumentalist and business dominance analyses focus on corporate elites and their role in the state to the exclusion of an examination of resistance from below, capitalist state structuralist analyses acknowledge that such resistance might occasionally occur but minimize its importance. Class struggle is viewed by capitalist state structuralists as highly mechanistic, devoid of class consciousness. The state's role is to preserve the organization and coalescence of the capitalist class by arbitrating and cooling out the divisive structural contradictions and antagonisms within that class and to cool out antagonisms between capitalists and the working class. For example, the state uses regulatory policy and anti-trust legislation to reduce conflicts between capitalists that might threaten the underlying conditions of system-wide capital accumulation and therefore the general health of the political economy, if not the welfare of specific capitalist individuals. The state similarly chills potentially damaging antagonisms between labor and capital by institutionalizing class conflict with such mechanisms as legislation guaranteeing labor the right to collectively bargain with capitalists. Another example of the state's ability to institutionalize and control class conflict is the Taylor Law in the United States that forbids workers of "essential services" such as police, firefighters, sanitation workers, air traffic controllers, teachers, and the like from striking. Workers who go on strike risk losing two or more days' pay for every day they remain on strike or may even lose their jobs. This anti-strike clause weakens labor power and reduces the potential of class conflicts to damage the conditions of capital accumulation.

While the capitalist state structuralist model explains *why* the state operates in the interests of capital accumulation, it does not specify *how* the state accomplishes this. It does not provide a description of the mechanisms by which the state produces policies in the interest of the capitalist class without being run by that class. Is there some overt process by which new members of the legislative body are socialized or come to understand that they must legislate this way? What mechanisms remind legislators that they must operate in the interests of capital accumulation? Is it a conscious observation by legislators that they have no choice but to address capital accumulation interests?

Further, capitalist state structuralism does not define the mechanisms on which the "relative autonomy" of the state might hinge. The concept is not operationalized in any empirically useful way. Were one to explore the question of the state's relative autonomy, there is little direction in the theoretical model to guide how to measure or document it or to evaluate its relativity. Relative to what? How much or how little relativity might be construed as autonomous? The capitalist state structuralist model itself does not clearly identify what the mechanisms of "relative autonomy" might be, or how to empirically evaluate these.

In addition, if state policy making is centered and shaped by the imperatives governing capital accumulation, how do we explain noneconomic policy making? For example, what guides the development of civil rights legislation, women's rights legislation (particularly reproductive rights), gay and lesbian rights, the Americans With Disabilities Act, and legislation protecting endangered species, just to name a few. Capitalist state structuralism does not provide a mechanism to explain the production of policy that is not presumably driven by capital accumulation interests. Moreover, if state policy is compelled to comply with the requirements of capital accumulation, how is it possible that such interests do not always gain their objectives? How do we explain the production of state policy that would appear inconsistent with capitalist class interests? For example, how do we explain the passage of workers' rights legislation (including worker safety and health policy, minimum wage policy, the right to collective bargaining, and so forth)? Indeed, this is a problem shared by the instrumentalist/business dominance model: If capitalist class actors and interests do dominate the state, how is it possible that they at times fail to thwart policy that contradicts their interests?

Finally, capitalist state structuralism and instrumentalism/business dominance theory share a similar focus on the internal structure of the state as a
national structure. This focus tends to treat the state in isolation of its global
context, and thus omits an analysis of the external or international forces
that might affect the state. Yet there is some evidence that such forces may
indeed matter. For example, when Mexico nearly went bankrupt in 1982,
an organized banking community largely from the United States refused to
negotiate the nation's loans until the International Monetary Fund imposed
some very strict austerity conditions on Mexico's domestic policy. Among
these conditions was the devaluation of Mexico's currency, the privatization
of key industries that had previously been owned by the Mexican state, and
sharp curtailing of social welfare expenditures in favor of devoting substantial proportions of the national budget to paying their debt to private banks in
the United States (Glasberg 1987b). Thus, the Mexican state managers lost
control of their own domestic policy making to international forces outside
their own state structure. The capitalist state structuralist model does not provide a theoretical mechanism for exploring this.

STATE-CENTERED STRUCTURALISM

In contrast to both business dominance and capitalist state structuralist
theories, state-centered structuralist theories argue that the state is the site
of *bureaucratic* political power. The state is neither necessarily capitalist
in nature nor subject to capitalists' demands. As an institution, the state has
interests separate from the demands of external groups or economic pressures. Thus, it is possible for state managers to create policy to which all
interest groups might actually object. State policy is shaped neither by the
class backgrounds of its personnel nor by the nature of the capitalist political economy, but rather by the imperatives of bureaucracies. The state, as a
bureaucratic and political structure, is separate from the economy. As such,
state policy is shaped by past policy precedents, political and party needs,
and state managers' interest in expanding their administrative domain and
autonomy. In sum, the state is impervious to mechanisms of intraclass unity
identified by business dominance theory and unaffected by the "capitalist
nature" of state structures assumed by capitalist state structuralists (Skocpol
and Ikenberry 1983; Skocpol 1985; 1992; Amenta and Skocpol 1988; Hooks
1990; 1991; Amenta and Parikh 1991; Amenta and Halfmann 2000; Chorev
2007). It is also, according to this perspective, impervious to pressures from
below.

Here, the state is once again depicted as neutral relative to competing interests as it was in the pluralist model. The state is, in this model, a structure that

transcends the pressure and influence these interests might exert, regardless of the resources these interests might control and regardless of the structure of the economy. But instead of describing the state as legislating in the interests of the common good, state-centered structuralists argue that the state legislates in the interests of the bureaucracy itself, including the interests of bureaucratic agencies to expand their bureaucratic realm of power and of political parties to enhance their legislative power. However, this characterization of the state as a class-neutral or class-transcendent structure raises questions concerning the past backgrounds, allegiances, and interests of state managers themselves. Who are the state managers, and what are their class backgrounds? How do they shed their past class allegiances and interests when they become state managers? Is it possible for state managers to fully divorce themselves in any meaningful way from their class backgrounds and experiences?

This analytical model does leave more room for analyzing and perhaps understanding the production of state policy that is not governed by capitalist class interests or the need to strengthen the conditions supporting capital accumulation. Here, ostensibly noneconomic policies such as reproductive and civil rights, gay and lesbian rights, the rights of people with disabilities, endangered species protection acts, environmental laws, and the like may be understood as the product of party politics or the interest of some bureaucratic agencies to expand their administrative sphere.

Further, is it realistic to expect state managers to ignore altogether the requirements of the political economy to remain viable? If state managers are guided by their political party and bureaucratic interests, is it reasonable to expect them to discount the effects of their decisions on the health of the economy? Might their policy decisions based on bureaucratic and party interests threaten the very administrative domain they presumably seek to expand if these decisions in fact undermine the economy?

Finally, state-centered theory shares a focus on elites with instrumentalist and business dominance theorists. Where instrumentalist and business dominance theorists focus on economic and corporate elites, state-centered structuralists focus on political elites among state managers as separate and distinct from economic elites. This focus omits an analysis of the role of resistance and challenge by the masses or the working class. What is the role of resistance from below?

CLASS DIALECTIC PERSPECTIVE: BRINGING CLASS BACK IN

Proponents of the class dialectic perspective disagree with the assertion that the state remains impervious to pressures from below. Instead, they complicate the analysis of state policy formation by examining the role of labor in addition to the state and capitalists in the decision-making process. In this model, class struggle processes affect the state and its policy making. As such, social movements through organized resistance can in fact apply substantial pressure on the state to legislate in their interests or otherwise address their needs, even if these needs are not entirely consistent with those of capital accumulation interests (Zeitlin, Ewen, and Ratcliff 1974; Zeitlin and Ratcliff 1975; Whitt 1979; 1982; Esping-Anderson, Friedland, and Wright 1976; Levine 1988; Eckstein 1997; Jackson 2008). Resistance from below is most effective, then, when working-class interests are organized and workers are mobilized into social movements and able to create mass disruptions (e.g., with labor strikes) (Jenkins and Brents 1989; Quadagno and Meyer 1989; Quadagno 1992). When the state cannot legally and institutionally mediate class conflicts, it may resort to its sole legitimate use of force and violence to repress labor unrest and mass disruption. But the state actually resorts to the use of force and violence relatively rarely, because such physical coercion risks a legitimacy crisis. More often than not, before working-class organizations can create mass turmoil, the state will seek instead to mediate and cool off conflicts through legislation designed to co-opt labor interests without seriously eroding capital accumulation interests (Witte 1972; Schmitter 1974; Galbraith 1985; Levine 1988; Swenson 2002).

This analysis might help explain what previous models could not: how is it possible for capitalists and capital accumulation interests to fail to gain their objectives every time if they are either so powerful or if their interests are so embedded in the state structure itself? The class dialectic model suggests that this is possible because capitalist and capital accumulation interests are not all-powerful; they are subject to organized struggles from below, and so is the state. Were they impervious to resistance, workers would never be expected to gain their objectives at all. Yet a casual observation of the development of labor law in the United States and elsewhere suggests that capitalist class interests do not always fully dominate the state and the policy-making process.

Does that mean that when workers' interests gain advantage in policy making by the state capital accumulation interests necessarily lose? Not at all. The state on occasion may produce policies which benefit labor while simultaneously supporting and legitimating the broader political economy (Quadagno 1992). State policy in this model is the mediation of labor and corporate conflicts and is linked to dynamic struggles between business and labor that is played out in the state. The policies which emerge out of these struggles organize labor into institutionalized forms such as trade unions (as opposed to the more generalized industrial unions that represent all workers in a single, large union) amenable to capitalist interests.

For example, far from acceding entirely to labor interests, labor laws in the United States allow for the right to collective bargaining and the formation of labor unions, but impose restrictions such as no-strike clauses and binding arbitration to the deal. Workers enjoy safety and health protections by law, but must often bargain for extensions of these as contractual issues. And although workers have won a federal minimum wage policy, there is no guarantee that their wages will be any higher; since minimum wages are set by a political process rather than tied to inflation, it is possible for the standing minimum wage to be far below poverty levels. To gain sufficient wages above the legal minimum, workers must negotiate contractually with employers. And to get federal mandates to define the minimum wage at higher rates, workers must often struggle against the dominating influence of corporations and small businesses alike, who typically apply their considerable resources to influence policy makers.

While the class dialectic model does introduce the role of an organized working class and resistance to a model of the relationship of the state and society, it is less specific as to the mechanisms that might animate dynamic class relations which might produce policy that is inconsistent with capital accumulation interests. What sparks class conflicts enough to erupt in struggles over policy? When do antagonistic interests mobilize into action, and why? What are the conditions that might be necessary and sufficient to make interests become action? Specifically, under what conditions does the working class assert its interests? Under what conditions is it more or less successful in pressing for state redress of their grievances?

The class dialectical model also shares the focus of other models on economic and class-based policy. How do we explain noneconomic struggles over policy? Since not all struggles over policy necessarily play out between capital accumulation interests and worker interests, or between the affluent and the poor, how do we understand the dynamics that animate conflicts over other policy domains? How do we explain gendering policies, or policies affecting and defining the racial formation process?

Finally, the class dialectic model shares the implication of other models that the state is an object and an arena of struggle between accumulation and nonaccumulation interests. What it does not address is the question of how various participants in the dialectic come to define the structures and processes, how they come to share a common view (if they do), what affects the processes of perspective, and how these processes and relations might affect the state itself.

Moreover, the class dialectical perspective shares the limited frame of other state theories, in that it remains focused on the internal structures and dynamics within specific geographic boundaries. This raises the question of the possible role of external forces beyond national boundaries. Since no state

exists in a vacuum, but instead shares physical space if not necessarily political and economic interests, the ability of other states to affect the structures,
processes, and relations of power within states becomes of interest.

GLOBALIZATION THEORY

There are several models of the relationship between the state and society
that adopt a global perspective. These challenge the assumption of much of
state theory that the state is insulated from external forces; some even question the very notion of the "boundedness" of the state as defined by national
boundaries.

For example, those observers using a hyperglobalist perspective (Reich
1991; Ohmae 1996; Brecher, Costello, and Smith 2000) argue that the world
of the twenty-first century is markedly different from the world at the end of
the previous century. In previous decades the global economic landscape was
dominated by nations. By the twenty-first century, the power shifted from
nation-states to private corporations who now rule the global economy. Corporations thus render the world "borderless" insofar as they may transcend
national boundaries as they seek the cheapest labor costs and the fewest legal
and regulatory restrictions on their ability to extract ever-higher rates of profit
and wealth.

In this view, then, the state becomes far less salient and powerful: corporations have the ability to ignore national borders as they freely mobilize productive and financial capital across national boundaries and this undermines
the state's preeminence in governing as a nation-state (Gray 1998; Greider
1997). Ironically, the state itself has been its own hand servant in the mitiga-
tion of its power by sharply reducing corporate tax burdens and entering into
international trade agreements that loosen corporate constraints imposed by
production regulations, trade restrictions, taxation, labor rights laws, environmental laws, and product safety regulations. In particular, the erosion of
corporate tax revenues means a sharply decreased ability of the state to maintain social spending for such public goods as education, healthcare, housing
and nutritional supports, police and fire services, and the like. In this way,
globalization implies the demise of the nation-state that state theory generally presumes. Or, at the very least, suggests an external force that calls into
question the validity of theorizing a state insulated from the rest of the world.

The thesis of hyperglobalization is certainly not one shared by all globalization theorists. Skeptical theorists (Hirst and Thompson 1999; Rugman 2000;
Wade 1996; Zysman 1994) argue that the twenty-first-century landscape
hardly looks so different from that of previous decades. The global economy,
they argue, is actually less integrated now: there may be international trade

agreements that can potentially undermine the range of state power in some respects, but trade and investment remains increasingly concentrated within the Global North and Japan, all but leaving out the developing nations. And nation-states and their national borders are alive and well, and strongly asserted as nation-states jockey for economic as well as military and political supremacy. For skeptical theorists, then, the nation-state remains a viable entity, even if permeable to a degree by external influences.

In fact, complex globalization theorists (Dicken 2003; Held et al. 1999) reject the notion of the static fait-accompli of the demise of the state implied by hyperglobalist theorists; instead they posit globalization as an ongoing process. They do not disagree that trade and investment is increasingly concentrated in the Global North and Japan; but they argue that the increase in trading clusters such as the European Union and the North American Free Trade Agreement are part of the overall, wider process of globalization. That is, nations wanting to participate in these trading clusters are under pressure to align their internal policies with those in the trading bloc, which commonly means relaxing protectionist policies. This makes nations more accessible to the rest of the world (see Breslin and Higgot 2000). The distinction here between complex globalization theorists and hyperglobalization theorists is subtle but important: they agree that the world is indeed different in the twenty-first century; but "whilst the *level* of integration is similar, the *nature* of integration is not. This is because it is much deeper, including not only the trade of goods and services between countries, but also the production of goods and services in other countries" (Marsh, Smith, and Hothi 2006,174; emphasis is original). The world is hardly borderless; instead there is significant inequality in the world economy, such that production and extraction of important resources occurs largely in the developing nations in the Global South while wealth and profit accrue to the postindustrial nations in the Global North (see Dicken 2003). Moreover, owing to state policies and practices, capital flows across borders in ways that the majority of humans cannot. Witness, for example, the tragic refugee crisis in Europe and the Middle East: while oil flows easily from the Middle East, refugees fleeing war and violence are met with severe dangers of crossing the Mediterranean, and refusals by many states to allow them safe passage and asylum (or any passage and asylum at all). Note, as well, that states like Germany first opened its borders to accept refugees (and pressured others in the European Union to do the same), and then quickly reversed itself and closed its borders. This implies that the state has hardly ceased to exist as an important institution; rather, the role of the state has undergone a transformation (Cerny 1997; Scholte 2000). Power has undergone a multidirectional shift: both externally (to international organizations such as the EU and NAFTA and to international social movements), internally from below (from domestic social movements), and above and beyond the simple rubric of external/internal relations (from market relations with supranational corporations). States thus compete with each other in the arena of international markets and economies, to the detriment of exerting its power on domestic issues such as wealth and poverty (Cerny 1997).

While these globalization theorists have all focused on the material and structural position of the nation-state in global relations, and the implications this may have on the salience of the state, they do not examine how ideas may shape and frame the state. Ideational globalization theorists (e.g., Hay 2000; 2004; Hay and Marsh 2000) are less concerned with whether or not levels of trade and investment are creating a more or less globalized world; rather, they presume what sociologists call the Thomas Theorem (1928): it does not matter whether or not such processes of globalization are in fact occurring; if those in charge of making policy in the state believe that globalization is a formidable force to contend with, it will shape and frame their decision-making as if it were, and the consequences of that decision-making in policy will be very real, regardless of whether policy makers were correct or not in their assessment. In this way, ideas themselves may be generating policy, which affects state power. For ideational globalization theorists, the power of ideas is implied to be the chief explanation for state policy in the global setting, with little regard for the social, economic, and political frameworks or settings from which they arise. But it does introduce discourse and meaning-making as an important, perhaps necessary, element (if sufficient factor) to consider when examining the relationship of the state to society and all that shapes and frames power in that relationship.

THE STATE AS RELATIONS OF POWER, MEANING-MAKING, AND DISCOURSE

While elitist and structuralist models of the state's relationship with society have dominated the literature, there are several bodies of literature that have begun to shift the conversation by highlighting what these models have ignored: gender, sexuality, racialization, globalization, and culture, power, and discourse. Feminist theorists have likewise looked at the state and the ways that it is implicated in patterns of gender inequality. There have been debates about whether patriarchy or the capitalist class relation should be considered "primary" in its treatment in social theory, while some feminists have argued for a more intersectional approach. These latter feminists, influenced by black feminism, argue that multiple relations of power operate in society and intersect in complex ways, both within our institutions and our daily lives. A longer treatment of the specifics of these theories will be presented in chapter 8.

Taken together, these contrasting perspectives that make up the extant body of feminist state theory scholarship suggest that the state plays a role in far more than just the management of class relations and the reproduction of conditions that reinforce capital accumulation and systems of class oppression. It is also an active participant in power processes and struggles (including resistance and the state's response to that resistance) of gendered oppression. It is, in short, a patriarchal state, but one that is subject to alterations prompted by challenges from below (see Connell 1990).

POSTSTRUCTURALISM

Pluralism, business dominance theory, and class dialectic theory share a tendency to locate power within specific institutions like the economy or the state. Poststructuralist theory, particularly as developed by Foucault (1980), posits power as behaving quite differently: here, power is not located within specific institutions like the state and capitalism but is rather dispersed throughout social life. As such, the state itself is not so much a static structure but rather a contested terrain of meaning-making and discourse of power (Foucault 1980; 1991). According to Foucault (1980, 60), "nothing in society will be changed if the mechanisms of power that function outside, below, and alongside the State apparatuses, on a much more minute and everyday level, are not also changed." His work on "governmentality," then, explores the techniques and mechanisms used to shape and frame the behaviors and perspectives of the population, which create a fiction of "free will" while constraining that freedom through social policy (Foucault 1991; Gordon 1991).

Charting histories of punishment, sexuality, and madness, for example, Foucault found that the bodies of knowledge that we created over time had productive power: those discourses had the power to create specific identities and social relationships. He noted the historical development of factories, prisons, and schools and the disciplinary techniques each used to create certain types of people, and that these institutions borrowed repertoires and techniques from each other so that they shared similar disciplinary techniques. This created a highly disciplined and managed social body, accustomed to control. Likewise, his work on sexuality (Foucault 1987) showed how the development of sexual identities actually had the power to manage and discipline desire, as well as pathologize entire bodies of people.

Poststructuralists were thus faced with the need to create new ways to conceptualize power and how it operates in the social world, thus implying a reconceptualization of the state. Deleuze and Guattari (1987), for example, developed the concept of the "rhizome" to describe power operating as a root-like structure throughout the social world, with multiple points of connection.

In this conceptualization, power has no "base" (as it does in elitist and struc-turalist state theories) but is complex and multidimensional. This model for analysis offers a metaphor for the Foucauldian conception of power as diffuse and not centrally located within specific institutions like the state.

Poststructuralists, then, turn from examinations of the structures of the state itself as the seat of power to an exploration of discourse and cultures of meaning-making. Laclau and Mouffe (1985), for example, conceptual-ized society as a dialectical web of intersecting repertoires in which dis-courses shape and frame and modify each other. As such, Laclau and Moffe conceived of society as lacking a focal structure such as the institution of the state. They rejected "the state" as the controlling central *structure* that dictates individuals' identities, where they fit in the larger society, and how they are to function; they argued, instead, for "the social" as the controlling, ongoing *process* of discourse, meaning, and negotiation by which identities are articulated, formed, and modified over time. What matters, then, is not the state as a thing, but rather the relations of power.

Important to this conceptualization of the process of articulating identi-ties and the emergence of dominating social repertoires and meanings is Gramsci's (1971) notion of hegemony. Hegemony refers to the process by which dominating members in society may assert, enforce, and maintain their supremacy by framing their social, moral, economic, political, and cultural values as normative, buttressed by ideologies of inexorable "common sense," the "natural order of things," or as "ordained by God." This normative lens narrows discourse to a range of possibilities that remain consistent with the dominants' interests, not because they inhabit key structural positions in soci-ety but because they dominate the discourse by ideologically framing other values as impossible. Discourse analysis, then, highlights and foregrounds not only what is obvious and observable (behaviors and structures), but more importantly what is omitted or demonized as "the other," what is silenced and what is preempted as even thinkable, in the process of creating the fiction of agreement and social unity (see e.g., Laclau 1996).

The state in this configuration is not a singular, central structure of power or a structural sum of several institutions, but instead a decentralized, ongoing process in which repertoires and practices derived from ideologically defined "traditions" and "customs" define and redefine identities. The state becomes an arena for that process, "both a site and an outcome of political practices; an ongoing project to 'hegemonize' the plurality of its apparatuses and society itself" (Finlayson and Martin 2006, 163). The state does not define power and politics, but is rather an arena of discursive rationalities and meaning-making, and itself a product of that process of hegemony. It is important to note here that the notion of the state as a hegemonic battleground is not alien to elitist and structuralist theories of the state (see e.g., Nash 2002); but they do not foreground that notion as a central, defining characteristic of their analysis, as poststructuralists do.

QUEER THEORY

Queer theory puts poststructuralism rigorously to use in its attempts to outline the ways people have come to be placed into identity categories and the historical ways identities have been constructed, as well as what gets left out when we rely on these simple identity models for discussing nonnormative sexual and gender practices. Since the idea of "sexual orientation" has been organized around gendered sexual practices (such as hetero-, homo-, and bisexuality, which are categories that assume sexual orientation and that desire can be reduced to the gender of the identified person and the object(s) of their affection), queer theorists stress that we cannot isolate oppression around sexuality from gender. Further, people are disciplined and identities are constructed in often similar ways due to nonnormative sexual *and* gender practices. This opens up queer investigations beyond solely sexual orientation identity models such as lesbian, bisexual, and gay, to include the experiences of nonnormative gender practices and performances like transgender, drag, genderqueer, etc., as well as an investigation into sexual practices that are not necessarily organized around or reducible to gender (e.g., polyamory, BDSM, and sex work).

One of the ways that investigations into state projects and heteronormative oppression have been articulated by researchers is through the concept of sexual citizenship (see e.g., Evans 1993). Sexual citizenship troubles the assumed divide between the public and private spheres, which typically relegates the sexual to the private sphere—thus outside of the purview of public policy and state initiatives. This functions as a selectivity filter that can serve as a barrier to sexual minorities having their grievances heard in the formation of public policy. But public policy, as researchers have demonstrated, can curtail access to full citizenship rights for sexual minorities. This demonstrates how the public/private divide is not static, but rather oscillates on the whim of the state, causing the "private" to become very "public" when the state shines its light on the bedroom.

Perhaps one of the most obvious examples of this is in state projects around kinship—especially marriage. Indeed, access to marriage and the state benefits that come with it seem, at the outset, to be a very basic requirement for full citizenship—particularly where kinship intersects with state policy. Married partners have access to over one thousand legal rights, denied to non-married persons/partnerships (e.g., immigration and residency for partners from other countries; joint parenting and adopting; benefits such as Social Security and

Medicare; joint insurance policies for home, auto, and health; wrongful death benefits for a surviving partner and children). Yet, marriage laws in most countries restrict the institution to opposite-sex dyadic partnerships.

Further, in the United States, one can see how state projects around kinship and marriage have historically been shaped by oppressions that become embedded in governing structures. For example, anti-miscegenation laws prohibited marriage between white and black people. Likewise, before the Civil War, slaves were not allowed to marry at all. And before the year 2000, no gay or lesbian couples were legally recognized in any state in the United States. Slowly, however, this has been changing as a result of changes in the balance of political and institutional forces around gay and lesbian struggles for access to marriage.

Many states began seeing large mobilizations in support of same-sex marriage, challenging the state's right to limit these legal partnerships. For example, in Connecticut, Love Makes a Family mobilized community resources around this support, staging protests, organizing letter-writing campaigns, and holding educational and community events to teach the public about the concerns of lesbians and gays who wanted access to marriage rights (http://www.lmfct.org/). The state, in turn, under Bill Clinton, signed the Defense of Marriage Act (DOMA) into law to roll back some of these efforts. DOMA defined marriage as a legal union between one man and one woman for the purpose of all federal law. Thus, while individual states could allow legal marriages within their state's borders, other states did not need to recognize these unions and federal laws and benefits were denied to same-sex marriages (see http://www.domawatch.org/index.php). As we see with racialized and gendered discrimination, cultural and ideological frames of "normalcy" come into play in these public policy debates. That is, opponents of same-sex marriage mobilize arguments that same-sex relationships are "abnormal" or "unnatural" in order to frame the debate in ways that fundamentally alter the lens of the debate from discrimination and exclusion to "natural" and "normal" cultural and ideological frames of reference that exclude same-sex partnerships. This becomes further complexified by queer theoretical models that argue for the legitimacy of all consensual nonnormative sexual and romantic practices (Rubin 1984).

Indeed, even the legalization of same-sex marriages in the United States continues to exclude multi-partnered and non-monogamous relationships or families of choice which may not be based on romantic involvement and/or relationships, as well as removing other forms of recognition such as domestic partners or civil unions, thus forcing marriage as the sole legitimate form of sexual/romantic relationship recognized by the state. This reinscribes the assumption that the highest order of love and affection should be limited to couples and their offspring, in effect limiting which configurations of people who care for each other get recognized as "family." This is because of the assumption that dyadic, monogamous relationships are "natural" and "normal" despite the existence of many different kinds of multiple partnerships that fall outside of this normative, patterned expectation. Thus, queer theorists often point to the concept of "normal" itself to critique how we have come to police the sexual and gender practices of others, as well as ourselves (see especially Warner 1999).

This has led to research into the ways in which the state creates legal barriers to free sexual expression of all kinds. Again, since queer theoretical perspectives include investigations into all sexual minorities, then sexual and/or gender practices that fall outside of our heteronormative assumptions, but may not necessarily be organized around gender (as in LGBT models), are included in queer research. This allows us to look into the ways that the state legislates against practices such as BDSM, sex work, and non-monogamy.

For example, in the United Kingdom, it is not legally possible to consent to bodily harm. Thus, any consensual sexual act involving bodily harm is an actionable offense according to the state. This policy led, in one case, to a man being convicted of aiding and abetting in his own assault (see Sadist 2006, 180). Similarly, in Italy, anyone willingly causing "injury" to another is subject to legal penalty. Likewise, in Austria the law allows for consent in bodily injury except where it offends "moral sensibilities". In the United States, laws surrounding sexual practices differ widely depending on the state, and sometimes even the county and/or city, in which they occur.

As we saw in the debate over same-sex marriage, cultural and ideological frames of "normalcy" are often employed in the disciplining of consensual sexual practices such as BDSM. As well, ideas of moral rightness and correctness are mobilized to defend normative assumptions about sexual and/or gender practices from cultural, as well as legal, change. And these frames are used to keep attempts to limit state-involvement in nonnormative sexual practices out of public debate.

While there has been a rise in BDSM community organization (sometimes referred to as the "leather community" or "kink") and attempts have been made to mobilize political and economic resources around changing the legal status of various BDSM practices, this particular struggle has not made much inroad into public debate. Part of this might be due to the ways that sexual identity has been constructed in our society. Indeed, "BDSM" is typically not even considered a "sexual orientation" due to the fact that it is not organized around gender and is not considered immutable. This can lead to the mistaken assumption that people who engage in BDSM practices are not actually sexual minorities because there is not a culturally available identity category for them. Thus, the discursive frames that have been historically created in the history of sexuality can also serve as selectivity filters for what gets discussed and what gets ignored in state policy. As well, the concept that a form of sexuality must be an "identity" (often understood as "immutable") in order to be recognized and protected under the law becomes an interesting question, as does how antidiscrimination laws end up becoming part and parcel of the discourse which produces (and disciplines) particularly-sexualized people (Zylan 2009). In this way, the state acts as both an actor (for its role in discourse and meaning-making) and an arena of struggle over legislation. As well, notions surrounding equality and domination can preclude some communities from involving themselves in a given struggle, such as the fight for the legal right to free sexual expression as it relates to BDSM practices. Because of this, BDSM has caused a split in feminist theorizing and organizing about the nature of the claims surrounding these practices. Some feminists, for example, have claimed that BDSM represents the internalization and eroticization of a culture based on coercion and control. Therefore, to these feminists, BDSM itself is a practice which reinforces the structured domination so common in patriarchal societies. However, other feminists, often referring to themselves as "sex-positive" feminists, argue that power is not so simple and that consensual sexual practices that "play" with power can actually lead to a deeper appreciation for, and understanding of, the complex ways that power operates in our world. These internal disagreements also have effects on the ability of communities to seek support from other social movements in their attempts to affect changes in state policies as they change the balance of institutional political forces.

Similar processes can be seen at work in struggles over social viability for people who transgress our binary understanding of gender. Indeed, notions of "normalcy" and "naturalness" are mobilized to delegitimize the demands of transgender people, intersex people (people born with reproductive or sexual anatomy that does not seem to fit the "typical" definitions of female or male), and nonbinary and genderqueer people (those who completely fall outside of our binary construction of gender). Similarly, some feminists have rejected claims made by transgender people based on essentialist notions of what it means to be a "real" woman (see e.g., Raymond 1979), while many feminists accept that if gender is a social construction, then "womanhood" is a social category available to people who might be assigned male at birth.

While many of the legal claims made by gender-variant people have been centered around simple social viability (e.g., access to public bathrooms, personal gender assignment on legal identifications, etc.), the gender-variant community has also struggled to get protections under nondiscrimination laws. Such laws have successfully been passed in thirteen states in the United States and there are proposals for such bills in twenty states. These have come as a result of successful challenges to state policy by the gender-variant community and their allies.

An interesting feature of these debates has been the ways that medicalizing discourses have served as selectivity filters within policy discussions. The DSM (the Diagnostic and Statistical Manual of Mental Disorders utilized by psychologists and psychiatrists) lists "gender identity disorder" (GID) as a mental illness. This effectively frames the problem around those notions of "mental illness" rather than questioning the utility of our binary construction of gender in most modern societies (despite evidence of societies with much more flexible notions around gender and many different available categories for gender than just "woman" and "man"). Interestingly, GID replaced homosexuality in the DSM. Whereas homosexuality has become somewhat acceptable in the United States in a particularly homonormative way, gender-variant people became the "bad queers" in opposition to the "good gays."

At play here, then, are the selectivity filters used to frame gender-variant people as "mentally ill" as well as the balance of institutional and political forces being effected by ruptures in progressive movements, such as feminism, which might be seen as natural allies in the fight for transgender rights. Thus, the medicalizing discourses used to treat gender variance as an "illness" that might be "cured" limit the ability of social movements to pressure the state to protect gender-variant people from discrimination. Likewise, ruptures in movement alliances can weaken the ability of gender-variant people to mobilize resources in order to struggle for social viability and protection from discriminatory practices.

Like feminism, part of the struggle of queer movements is toward weakening the selectivity filters that create barriers to inclusion in state policy (as well as maintaining criticism toward how inclusion in state policy reifies the discourse of sexual orientation as "natural" rather than a historically specific form of producing particularly-sexualized people). Similar objectives are at work in movements that attempt to affect state policy around racialized oppression.

CRITICAL RACE THEORY AND THE STATE

Research in critical race theory parallels many of the issues raised in feminist state theory and suggests a similar challenge to state theory that focuses exclusively on economic and class relations and oppression. For example, analysts using racial formation theory (Omi 2001; Omi and Winant 1990; Haney Lopez 1996; Ignatiev 1995; Winant 1994; 2000; Calavita 2005) emphasize that conceptualizations of race as a matter of biology has no meaning. Instead, they argue, "race" is *socially* constructed, the product of ongoing political struggles over its very meaning and its implications for people's political, social, and economic rights (Stevens 1999). This analysis implies a role of the state in the process of socially constructing race, since the state is involved in much policy-making and political maneuvering relative to racialized issues.

At the very least, the state has clearly been an arena for battles over rights, sparked by a claims process by civil rights movements. Much like the gendering claims process described by Peattie and Rein (1983), the racial formation claims process involves a struggle over shifting the line between the "natural" or biological and the artificial or political. How much of racial inequality and oppression is simply a matter of biology, wherein one race (whites) is inherently, genetically superior and all others genetically inferior (see e.g., Herrnstein and Murray 1994), and therefore immutable and nonresponsive to reform policy? How much of racial inequality and oppression is more a matter of social constructions that can therefore be challenged and altered with political struggle and legislation? Historically, civil rights movements around the world have set such claims processes in motion and challenged the racial regimes that are "steeped in discriminatory or exclusionist traditions" (Winant 2000, 177–8), much like feminist claims processes have challenged gender regimes.

Contemporary racial theory has had difficulty explaining persistent racial inequality and oppression that legislative reform by the state should have been expected to eliminate. For example, ethnicity-based theories (see Smith 2001) of race, which view race as a culturally rooted notion of identity, expect integration, equal opportunity, and assimilation to be the antidotes to prejudice and discrimination: the more contact we all have with one another, the more we will understand, appreciate, and accept one another as equals. However, ethnicity-based theories of race are limited by the fact that despite civil rights legislation, serious structural obstacles persist to limit the success of legislation which may have mandated the social and political rights of individuals to be included but did not mandate the substantive economic resources necessary for accessing to those rights (Massey and Denton 1993; Lipsitz 1998). Furthermore, the notion of assimilation was predicated on people of color willingly assimilating to white dominant cultural norms, a prospect that was less than appealing to many. The result of this limitation of ethnicity-based theory is the production of analyses that blame people of color themselves for adhering to a race-consciousness harming their ability to assimilate (Thernstrom and Thernstrom 1997), or that reassert the importance of defending a "national culture" threatened by immigration and integration (Balibar and Wallerstein 1991; Taguieff 2001).

Class-based analyses of race saw racial conflict as an arena in which class-based struggles were played out: limited resources and opportunities drove a wedge between members of the same class who were differentiated by their membership in different racial groups and pit them one against the other (Bonacich 1972; 1976; Reich 1981; Gordon et al 1982; Wilson 1996a). These analysts expected class consciousness to override the racial divide, and legislation like affirmative action to correct the effects of prior discrimination. However, that class consciousness has not evolved to transplant race-consciousness; indeed, as gainful employment opportunities become scarcer, growing competition causes whites to increasingly seek to protect the invisible privileges of whiteness (McIntosh 1992) and to resist affirmative action programs, making it more difficult to recognize their common class position with people of color.

Where ethnicity-based and class-based analyses of race and racial inequality focus on individuals in racial groups or the groups themselves, racial formation theory focuses on the state and political processes that socially construct the meaning of race. Rather than being an immutable, stable construct of clearly defined categories and dimensions, race becomes an ongoing, shifting process in which meanings, identities, dimensions, rights, and oppression are constantly contested and reformulated politically. Racial formation processes are subject to the discursive and interpretational perspectives and actions of a wide range of actors, from individuals to groups and social movements, as well as to structures and institutions, history and politics, both national and international. Here, the state is both an arena and an actor, engaged in these struggles over legislation and meaning.

Like much of the gender and state literature, the literature of racial formation and the state tends to de-emphasize the state's use and sanction of violence in the reproduction of systems of racial inequality and oppression in the racial state (see e.g., James 1996; 2000). Racial state theorists (Goldberg 2002; Niemonen 1995) instead view the state as a racial state to the extent that it is simultaneously a structure and an actor, both the arena of conflict between dominant and subordinate groups and a significant actor in those conflicts (Hall 2003). The state frequently uses racial profiling against people of color in policing, for example, as has been painfully evident in highly publicized patterns of excessive use of police force and violence (up to and including widespread shootings and killings by police) against unarmed people of color on the streets; and the state has historically tolerated lynching of African Americans at the hands of white vigilantes, allowing acquittals of lynchers by all-white juries. Jury selection processes that routinely reject the seating of jurists of color have been challenged in many states as racist and therefore unconstitutional in denying people of color the right to due process and a trial by a jury of peers. This practice of jury selection continues today, contributing in no small way to the overrepresentation of African Americans and Latinxs in jail and on death row. In essence, when the state sanctions racism in court proceedings and in policing, it is in fact participating in an institutionalized lynching. And when state policy denies convicted felons the right to vote for life, it is compounding the violence by disenfranchising a substantial segment of the population of color, ensuring a hardening of systems of racial inequality that reinforces white privilege (Uggen and Manza 2002).

Yet, as powerful as the racial state is, it is nonetheless, like the patriarchal state, not inexorable or monolithic. Wilson (1996) argues that the state's role is frequently "paradoxical" in that it largely protects, legitimates, and reproduces the dominant racial relations of oppression, but also can be seen to occasionally use its power and resources to mitigate that oppression and address the concerns and interests of the oppressed. The racial state, then, is subject to pressures from below to alter and change the form and content of racial formation processes. This becomes evident in the ebb and flow of racial formations state projects.

Racial state theorists thus describe a state in a racist society; in contrast, racist state theorists more pointedly argue that the state is, in fact, a racist state in that it presides over and participates in an institutionalized structure of systematic racialized oppression (Feagin 2006; 2010; Cazenave 2011). In this conceptualization, racist oppression is historically built on and reproduced by the very structures that organize social, economic, and political institutions, buttressed by the state's reliance on ideological frames justifying continued inequality as "natural," inexorable, or a reasonable response to an inherently pathological population. However, these ideological frames are subject to counterframing from below. The question then becomes *how* counterframing becomes sufficiently salient as to effectively challenge the racist state's ideological frames to chip away at its oppressive impulses.

THE STATE AND CHALLENGES FROM BELOW

So far, we have seen that the focus of most elitist and structural state theories has largely been a top-down emphasis on rulers within "the state." The class dialectic perspective critiques the implication that the ruling class has absolute or at least dominating sway over the state by introducing the notion of resistance from the working class, but it tends to ultimately conclude that even these struggles result in policies that remain consistent with ruling class interests. Challenges to the class-centric focus of this literature have come from feminist theory, critical race theory, and queer theory; challenges to the tendency of the literature to examine "the state" within its territorial boundaries have emerged from the globalization literature. What is missing so far is an analysis of how and why resistance from the bottom up may compromise elite interests, and how these may affect the structure and relations of the state, and even challenge the very assumption of the salience of the state itself. That is, while the power of economic, gendered, and raced dominants in society is formidable in advantaging and privileging them and oppressing others, their power is not absolute. Indeed, nonelites may pose a countervailing force. Nonelites may resist, challenge, subvert, and otherwise alter power relationships and the policies that emerge from governments, prompting change from the bottom up through large-scale social movements. We will take up this literature in great detail in chapter 5. Suffice it to say at this point that we view social movements as an important element affecting the balance of political forces, and therefore something that must be incorporated into the model of multi-sites of power.

We are now faced with the challenge of how to develop a framework that incorporates the valuable insights of these many and disparate literatures that facilitate our ability to examine the state's multiple sites of power and multiple oppressions. It is to this challenge that we turn next.

Chapter 2

Breaking the Theoretical Stalemate

State Projects and a Multi-Site Model of Power and the State

Proponents of primarily class-based theories of the state have debated vigorously for decades without resolving which model is the most accurate. Taken together, the models do illuminate significant structures, processes, and relationships affecting state power and policy making. Many sociologists have increasingly called for an analytical framework for reconciling the strengths that each perspective of the state-society relationship might have to offer (Jenkins and Brents 1989; Prechel 1990; Gilbert and Howe 1991; Hooks 1993; McCammon 1994); others note that attempts at convergence across theoretical models (as well as across literatures and disciplinary silos) is already occurring, even if not definitively achieved (although questions have been raised as to whether convergence is even possible) (see, e.g., Lister and Marsh 2006). We add, furthermore, that there are whole areas of social and political policy making relative to oppression that are not adequately covered by the dominant class-based models of the state and society relationship. How do we explain the dominance of patriarchal, racialized, or heteronormative policy making with the existing theoretical frameworks these models offer? Is it sufficient to simply replace the existing concepts of class domination with concepts describing gendered, racialized, or heterosexist domination? We argue that the answer is no: while some analyses have in fact tried to do just that, the concepts do not lend themselves easily to such a simple transplant. What is needed is a model of the relationship between the state and society that allows for an analysis of multiple oppressions and how they intersect and overlap in policy and everyday life. Again, we call this model the "multi-sites of power" (MSP) approach to state theory (for a theoretical overlay of this perspective, see Glasberg and Shannon 2015).

As we noted in the previous chapter, several analysts have explored the relationship between gendering and the state (Abramovitz 1996; 2000; Brush

2003; Curran and Abrams 2000; Gordon 1994; Haney 2000; Mackinnon 1989; Orloff 1993; 1996; Zylan 2000); between racial formation and the state (Calavita 2005; Feagin 2001; Goldberg 2002; Haney Lopez 1996; Ignatiev 1995; Marable 1983; Omi 2001; Omi and Winant 1990; Winant 1994; 2000; Yanow 2003); and between sexuality and the state, particularly in the exploration of sexual citizenship (Ackelsberg 2010; Evans 1993). However, we remain without a conceptual framework that blends these literatures, as well as literatures concerning social movements and resistance to the state, in a broader explanation of the relationship between the state and society. What are the elements that such a framework would need to include? We recognize that we cannot simply add racial, class, gendered, and queer theories of the state and society and stir. These elements are interwoven in an intricate web of patterns of domination and resistance, as accurately described by the Combahee River Collective (1977) and built on by Crenshaw's (1989) critical legal scholarship on intersectionality.

In order to explore the relationship of the organizing principles of race, class, gender, and sexuality with the state, we need to understand them within a capitalist, gendered, heteronormative, racialized, and imperialistic society. By that we mean that we might build an understanding of systems of power that privilege whiteness, maleness, normative sexualities, and private capital accumulation in the context of a "free" market economy that is holistic rather than centered on a single relation of domination (most often, in the literature on state theory, class). How, then, do we construct a theory of the state that at once recognizes and incorporates the insights of class-based state theory as well as feminist state theory, theories of racialization, queer theory, and social movement theory, so as to more fully understand the relationship between the state, on the one hand, and society and power processes that affect and define that relationship, on the other hand? How do we construct MSP approaches?

STATE PROJECTS OF RACIAL FORMATION, GENDERING, SEXUALITY, AND CLASS RELATIONS

We begin with the assumption that "the state" is not reified here as simply a monolithic and unchanging structure with a coherent and inexorable agenda. Rather, we treat the state as an institutional structure and actor that participates in an ongoing interactive relationship with the forces and interests in society, and as an arena of discourse and struggle. Processes of that interactive relationship may affect not only various interest groups in society, but also the state itself (Pringle and Watson 1992). The state, then, becomes a fluid product of these interactions, rather than a "given" that can be anticipated to necessarily act to maintain and reproduce capitalist, patriarchal, heteronormative, or racist relations, even if it can be found to do so in a given society. The point is not *whether* the state necessarily reproduces these relations by design or by structural constraint, but rather *how* that may happen *if* that is, in fact, the observed pattern. Thus, gendered, racialized, sexual, and class inequalities may be embedded in the state, and the state embedded in the inequalities; we suggest an agenda that seeks to explore the conditions under which this embedding occurs.

The use of the term "structure" here is not meant to suggest the state is ossified into an unchanging and unchallengeable entity. By structure we mean the organization of social relations (see, e.g., Landauer, as quoted by Kuhn 2010, 214) and institutional arrangements that comprise the state. While these may together over time reproduce patterns of racialized, class, sexual, and gendered privilege and disadvantage, it is not a priori assumed to be obligated to do so. The state as a structure is construed here to be permeable and fluid, able to affect and be affected by organized struggles from below as well as from elites. This does not necessarily mean an adoption of a pluralist assumption of equality of all interests. Some interests may certainly be better positioned to increase their likelihood of affecting the state. Nor do we mean to suggest that the state itself should be conceptualized as organized governance free of critique, as anarchists have consistently argued that as an institutional whole, the state is a form of illegitimate hierarchy. Rather, we argue for the need to examine the conditions under which the likelihood of privileged interests are actualized, and the conditions under which those interests that are less advantaged may tip the balance to affect the state—or in some cases, perhaps, create extra-institutional means to replace gaps in state policy and planning. Thus, we propose an analytical framework that borrows from and builds on Jessop's (1990; 2008) strategic-relational approach and his concepts of state projects, selectivity filters, and balance of forces, but altering those concepts in unique ways for an MSP analytical framework.

STATE PROJECTS

In Jessop's approach, policies are not isolated, singular initiatives to be studied divorced from their historical relationship to other policies. Rather, policies are elements of larger state projects, which are sets of state policies and/or agencies (as opposed to singular, unrelated policies and/or agencies) unified around a particular major issue, however transitory that unity may be. The concept of "state projects" does not denote a centralized state with a clearly defined goal motivating decision-making. Rather, the concept is used to indicate a process in which the state itself is both an arena of struggle and an actor that, above all other actors, has the unique authority to codify social constructions into legalized norms and to enforce these in ways that shape cultural repertoires and social behaviors, but which is simultaneously subject to resistance and modification from below. State projects, then, are not necessarily only produced and reproduced by the state, but are also the production of struggles between the state and political forces over the contested terrain that is state policy.

Although neither preordained nor determined by a single actor or force, policy is not random; Jessop (1990; 2008) argues that more recent policies build on, or are shaped by, prior policies (see also Quadagno 1992). But neither are state projects absolute: they involve dynamic and ongoing claims processes in which social constructions of gender, sexuality, race, and class may be maintained, challenged, or altered. State projects are thus animated by the push and pull of political forces in a claims process that produces an ongoing dialectic of policy making and implementation, as well as social practices and repertoires over time. State projects, then, are best understood in the context of the dynamic factors that may affect the interplay of political forces and future policy and social behavior. Although Gramsci (1971) emphasized such hegemonic processes to militate largely in support of capitalist class interests, he did recognize counter-hegemony efforts from below. More recently, Jessop suggests as well that hegemony may be challenged, resisted, and redirected from below. And, we argue, this dialectical conceptualization of hegemony may be mobilized to understand *gendering, racial formation,* and *sexuality* in state projects as well, accounting, again, for multiple sites of power *and* complex processes of contestation. Further, we might also consider contestations to state power that are *non-hegemonic*, that seek to pluralize, add multiplicity, and use extra-institutional means to either directly challenge state power, or to exist alongside it (Day 2005).

The dynamic factors at play in this process include the following: 1) organization, such as the extent to which interests are unified and the extent to which they may develop networks and coalitions (Domhoff 2009; Dye 2002), within and between competing interests; 2) access to and ability to mobilize resources (Prechel 1990; 2000; Clawson et al. 1998); 3) structural relations, including the state's power arrangements of capitalism (Poulantzas 1969; 1978), patriarchy (MacKinnon 1989; Hartmann 1976; Connell 1999; Brush 2003), racism (Stevens 1999; Goldberg 2002), and heteronormativity (Ackelsberg 2010; Phelan 2001; Seidman 2001; Evans 1993); 4) relative structural condition of the economy (O'Connor 1987); 5) constitutional constraints on policy creation and implementation, existing regulations, and precedence in implementation (Skocpol and Ikenberry 1983; Skocpol 1992; Hooks 1993; Haney Lopez 1996); 6) opportunity (or perception of potential) for interests to create alliances and take action (Eckstein 1997; McAdam and Snow 1997; Tarrow 1998); 7) relative autonomy of state actors and agencies (Poulantzas

1969; Vallochi 1989); 8) and unity and organization within and between state agencies (Amenta and Halfmann 2000). These dynamic factors and conditions undergo a dialectical process with selectivity filters that frame and shape perceptions of issues and policy solutions (including previous policy precedence and mobilization of bias).

State projects of economic intervention generally involve legislation, Supreme Court decisions, and federal budgetary allocations that seek to secure the conditions of capital accumulation. These commonly address not only issues concerning the economy itself (such as taxes, inflation, recession, and markets) (see, e.g., Devine 1983), but also those issues concerning class relations more generally. Policy initiatives in economic intervention state projects include labor laws governing the rights to collective bargaining (Levine 1988; Weinstein 1968), strikes (McCammon 1994), and the material conditions of workers (Sheak 1990); deregulation of industries (Glasberg and Skidmore 1997); and bailouts of large corporations and industries (Glasberg 1987a; 1987b; Glasberg and Skidmore 1997). In such state projects, then, the state participates in the social construction of classes and class relations, and reproduces class inequality.

State projects of gender formation and sexuality include policy initiatives and issues articulated by the executive, policies and budgetary decisions passed by the legislature, constitutional provisions, determinations, and rulings by the judiciary (including the Supreme Court), and implementation of policies directly and indirectly affecting the social construction of gender and sexual practices by administrative agencies. Such policies include military policies and practices such as "Don't Ask, Don't Tell," and marriage and family law, including same-sex marriage, divorce, child custody, adoption, and domestic violence laws (Bartfeld 2000; England 2000); social services, such as Aid to Families with Dependent Children and Temporary Assistance to Needy Families (Edin and Lein 1996; Kammerman 1984; Roschelle 1999); affirmative action and equal rights laws, such as Title IX, equal opportunity for women in the labor force, and the enfranchisement of women in the political process (Ruggie 1984; Piven 1990); abortion laws (Luker 1984; Petchesky 1984); laws forbidding some sexual practices (Richardson 2000); zoning laws in the construction of "family" and kinship patterns; and sexual assault laws. These policies, as entries into the state project of gendering, affect the social construction of gender and sexuality insofar as they participate in shaping and defining the meaning and social significance of sex, gender, and sexualities, thereby affecting the life chances of both men and women, and of heterosexuals as well as those who are gay, lesbian, bisexual, or transgender—and the many other sexual and gender practices that defy simple identification or that are excluded by the dominant markers of identity (i.e., "man," "woman," "lesbian," "bisexual," etc.).

Much of the gendering and sexuality state project has served to create and reinforce a social construction of gender and sexuality in a patriarchal and heteronormative society, such that women remain subordinate to men politically, socially, and economically; and sexual and gender minorities are denied full citizenship and all the rights attendant to that status (leaving aside, for now, the desirability of the strategic goal of formal equality under the existing institutions) (Waites 2005). However, there clearly are policies enacted and implemented by the state that alter the social constructions of gender and sexuality such that women's social, political, and economic positions in a patriarchal society, and thus their life chances, are improved, as are those of gender and sexual minorities generally.

Similarly, state projects of racial formation contribute to the social construction of race through legislation, policy implementation, and judicial determinations governing such issues as slavery, segregation and integration, civil rights (including enfranchisement of African Americans in the political process), affirmative action, multilingualism, and immigration. These policies, as entries into the state project of racial formation, affect the social construction of race insofar as they participate in redefining the meaning and social significance of race, thereby affecting the life chances of both whites and people of color and, in some contexts, playing a role in defining what it means to be "white" or excluded from that dominant category (Ignatiev 1995).

Much of the racial formation state project has served to create and reinforce a social construction of race in a racist society, such that people of color remain subordinate to whites politically, socially, and economically (Brown 1995; James 2000; Quadagno 2000; Neubeck and Cazenave 2001). However, there clearly are policies enacted and implemented by the state that alter the social constructions of race in such a way that the social, political, and economic positions of people of color in a racist society, and thus their life chances, may be improved (Fording 2001).

Several researchers have pointed to the role of the state in reinforcing racist stereotypes that reproduce racial inequality. For example, Marable (1983) has forcefully argued that the racist state has served to underdevelop African Americans in the United States through a combination of constitutional amendments, Supreme Court decisions, and institutionalized cultural practices, including Article I Section 9 of the Constitution defining slaves as three-fifths of a human being, voting restrictions based on race, chattel slavery, sharecropping, segregated educational institutions, etc. (see also Omi 2001; Omi and Winant 1990; Wilson 1996a). More recently, welfare reform, with its provisions concerning workfare, has reproduced racist social constructions in that its implementation has primarily harmed women and children of color. This is because women of color face far more limited opportunities than white women in the labor market as a result of institution-alized racist assumptions about work ethic, intelligence, and ability. The state refused to acknowledge racism in the economic institutions as it aggressively enacted and implemented a draconian welfare system of benefit denial and short eligibility definitions. The state thus contributed to and reinforced a racially constructed (and gendered) inequality (Lieberman 1998; Quadagno 2000; Neubeck and Cazenave 2001).

Taken together, these policy implementations and interpretations serve to reiterate a social construction of race in a white racist society, such that people of color generally remain subordinate to EuroAmericans politically, economically, and socially. Yet, as we saw in the gendering and sexuality state projects, there are obviously policies enacted and Supreme Court deter-minations handed down that alter the content of the social construction of race so that the life chances of people of color are improved.

The question is: What shapes these state projects over time? Jessop's concepts of selectivity filters and balance of class forces are useful here, par-ticularly if those concepts are altered in such a way as to account for multiple sites of power, including, but not limited to, class.

SELECTIVITY FILTERS

Selectivity filters function to mobilize bias in that they act as a lens through which actors perceive, understand, and act on issues. Some notions and perspectives are filtered in and others are filtered out of the policy-making process. As such, these filters have a mediating effect that frames and shapes not only perceptions of and discourse about issues, but also the emergence of policy solutions. Selectivity filters go beyond individual policy initiatives and are integral to the dialectic process. The reflexive interplay between selectivity filters and the relations of political forces reverberates through the implementation of that policy and sets the stage for later policy creation, modification, and implementation. These filters include larger state projects, which provide a framework—past policy precedents of state projects influ-ence the viability and content of future policy initiatives, precedents, and discourses that frame debates and perspectives.

Several analysts have incorporated the notion of the role of framing in social movements (Gamson 1992; Benford 1997; Oliver and Johnston 1999): How do actors themselves come to define and understand issues, structures, processes, and strategies? What is the role of culture, ideology, and discourse in setting the parameters of analysis and action? This suggests an important question for theories of the state: How does the process of framing affect state-society relationships and policy making?

Cultural and ideological frames, as well as prior legislative precedence, act as selectivity filters biasing policy creation and implementation, although these may be challenged by the processes and dynamics of political forces. Cultural frames that dominate class-based and economic state projects begin with the assumption of capitalist relations and "free" markets as inexorable givens. Similarly, the cultural and ideological frames which the claims processes of gendering, sexuality, and racial formation state projects are commonly predicated upon contain an underlying assumption of the inexorability of biological determinism. For example, the structure of language and its usage contains hidden assumptions about gender and sexuality, such that men and heterosexuals are reinforced as the norm of human existence and are appropriately superior and dominant; women, gay, lesbian, bisexual, and transgender individuals are symbolically annihilated (Tuchman, Daniel, and Benet 1978) and represented as the other, invisible, or inferior and subordinate (Sorrels 1983).

Similarly, when identity is the frame through which we articulate sexual politics, people who do not fit neatly into available categories for gender and sexuality can be written out of policy. For example, since our ideas about "sexual orientation" revolve around gender, policy debates about marriage edge out multi-partnered relationships and other nontraditional kinship patterns (see Warner 1999; Conrad 2010). Language, then, acts as a cultural selectivity filter biasing and reinforcing patriarchal and heteronormative assumptions undergirding policy initiatives and the state gendering and sexuality projects. Other cultural selectivity filters that may contribute to the reinforcing of patriarchy and heteronormativity include gendered definitions of appropriate and inappropriate behavior and aspirations, such as motherhood norms (Schur 1984; Zylan 2000), father-as-breadwinner norms (Curran and Abrams 2000), appearance norms (Barthel 1988; Wolf 1991), and sexual orientation norms (Blumenfeld 1992; Duberman 1993). Such norms and language assumptions often find their way into policy, including those defining who may marry whom.

Cultural frames also include institutional traditions that become routinized as "normal." These include practices that privilege the nuclear, heterosexual, middle-class family form wherein the male adult is rewarded as the dominant force and the breadwinner and the female adult is subordinated as the primary caretaker and unpaid domestic laborer; in cases where the female adult participates in the paid labor market, the cultural expectation is that she remain the primary caretaker with the responsibility of domestic labor (Hochschild and Machung 1997). Notably, this gendered frame shifts when it intersects with class, so that welfare reform and workfare policies frame poor women with children as responsible only if they work outside the home in the paid labor market. The state penalizes women (and their children) who do not conform to the norm of poor mothers as breadwinners by denying them welfare benefits beyond a maximum of two years. Examples like this, where there are intersections of the multiple sites of power that the state intervenes in, are important to keep in mind. That is, we are not suggesting a state theory that treats multiple sites of power as singular nor are we proposing an "additive" model, where multiple oppressions are mixed together haphazardly. Rather, we propose overlapping and intersecting multiple sites of power that are historically, culturally, and geographically contingent—thus, selectivity filters and processes of framing can and will change depending on the site(s) of power, their intersections, their time, and their location.

Class and gender further intersect, as economic institutions reiterate this cultural framing of family structures and roles by maintaining gendered definitions of "men's jobs" and "women's jobs" in segmented labor markets, defined by vague extensions of perceptions of each gender's "natural" abilities: women typically as helpers and caretakers, men typically as leaders and physical and mental laborers (Federici 2012; James 2012; Kessler-Harris 1980; Reskin and Hartmann 1986; Reskin and Roos 1990; Padavic and Reskin 2002). Economic institutions also reinforce the notion of male superiority and privilege by maintaining differential wages for men and women, even when they do the same work (see www.statab.gov).

Educational institutions often reiterate this theme in the differential treatment of boys and girls within classrooms (Sadker and Sadker 1988; 1994; Boggiano and Barrett 1991) and in tracking of majors and areas of study (Gaskell 1984; Peltz 1990), as well as in more subtle gendered transmissions of information in textbooks' content and form (Ferree and Hall 1990). Religious institutional structures commonly privilege males as the legitimate leaders and women as subordinate supplicants (Renzetti and Curran 1992). Taken together, these institutional patterns act as selectivity filters to frame and bias policy creation and implementation. Witness the difficulty of introducing or passing an equal rights amendment (Mansbridge 1986) and pay equity or comparable worth policies (Greenberger 1980; McCann 1994; Padavic and Reskin 2002).

These patterns of gendering and sexuality in cultural institutions, which act as frames biasing policy creation and implementation, are further supported by the ideological underpinnings of patriarchy and heteronormativity, particularly through notions like "anatomy is destiny." This ideological prism identifying sexism and (hetero)normative sexualities as "natural" becomes a contested terrain itself in the dynamics and processes in the balance of gendering and sexuality forces.

Past legislative policies and implementations have tended to have the overall effect of acting as selectivity filters biasing the framing of newer policies so as to reproduce previous gendering and sexuality patterns. Examples include legislative policies and court determinations reinforcing heterosexual and monogamous marriage as the only legitimate relationships; no-fault divorce laws that impoverish women by routinely denying the need for alimony because of the courts' failure to acknowledge the reality of discrimination in the labor market; and family wage policies based on the assumption of the male as the breadwinner.

Cultural and ideological frames also form institutional selectivity filters biasing and shaping the racial formation state project. For example, language functions to reinforce white superiority by privileging whiteness as the standard of normal. This is evidenced in the common use of the term "nonwhite" as well as in the use of qualifiers such as "black Senator" when the incumbent of a position is black. The very word "race" is defined as a biological category defining human differences, such that physical attributes such as color of skin, texture of hair, or shape of lips or eyes, or socially constructed attributes such as language (i.e., Spanish) or geographical location (particularly Asia, Africa, and Latin America) are presumed to indicate different subspecies of humans. These subspecies are then hierarchically arranged, with whites at the top of the hierarchy and all others arranged below (Herrnstein and Murray 1994). Pejorative racial epithets and stereotypes used to describe people of color thus underscore assumptions of biological inferiority. While there clearly exist such pejoratives and stereotypes describing white ethnics, these are not based on immutable biological characteristics, but rather on perceptions of ethnicity as changeable cultural choices (Hughey 2014; Moore 1995; Wilson 1996a).

Racist stereotypes describing people of color as less intelligent, less committed to the value of education, more violence-prone, and less hard-working than whites become institutionalized in the labor market, where people of color are far more likely than whites to be unemployed and poverty-stricken (Wilson 1987; Kirschenman and Neckerman 1991; Glenn 2002). In addition, people of color are also more likely to be underemployed in menial, lower-autonomy, lower-paying, dead-end jobs in the service sector or in nonmanagerial blue-collar jobs. Even when people of color do find employment in managerial jobs, they face a glass ceiling beyond which it is extremely difficult to rise (U.S. Department of Labor 1991; Benjamin 1991; Feagin 2006; Turner, Fix, and Struyk 1991; Cose 1992; Tomaskovic-Devey 1993; Feagin and Sikes 1994; Glenn 2002; Neubeck 2006).

Racist cultural stereotypes are reiterated in educational institutions, where children of color are highly likely to be segregated into school systems with inadequate budgets and facilities (Kozol 1991; 2005; Hannah-Jones 2014). African American children are disproportionately tracked into classes for the "educable mentally retarded" and white children far more likely to be tracked into programs for the gifted and talented or college-bound (Edelman 1988).

Textbooks and other materials tend to be written for a predominantly white Anglo student body, with the historical and cultural contributions of people of color largely ignored or accorded such brief coverage as to imply that these are unimportant, and that only whites have done anything significant and positive (Apple and Christian-Smith 1991; McCarthy and Critchlow 1993). Stereotyped themes are reinforced in cultural media consumed widely, replicating the stark tropes echoed in other institutions (Hughey 2012a; 2006). White racist ideologies and culture together act as selectivity filters reinforcing a framing of racial formation biasing policy formation and implementation, much as patriarchal and classist ideologies and frames reinforce gendered and class-based policy.

Selectivity filters, then, act as significant prisms through which actors perceive, talk about, and act on issues that in turn affect the shaping and implementation of policy. However, the power of selectivity filters is not necessarily inexorable. The degree of salience of these filters is affected by political relationships and processes, or the balance of political forces.

BALANCE OF POLITICAL FORCES

Where Jessop talks of the balance of *class* forces, we expand on his notion to one of balance of *political* forces in developing our MSP approach to state theory. We do this because gendering, sexuality, and racial formation forces are similarly at work affecting state projects, just like class forces. By gendering forces we are referring not to men's interests versus women's interests, but rather to socially constructed sets of interests that may privilege one gender over others (in a patriarchal society, this is likely to mean cisgender men's privilege relative to others) as opposed to those that seek to produce greater equality regardless of gender[1]. Similarly, when we speak of the balance of sexuality forces, we do not mean heterosexual interests versus homosexual interests; instead, we are referring to socially constructed sets of interests that may privilege those with normative sexual practices over sexual minorities of all kinds. We would not be surprised, then, to find heterosexuals seeking greater equality in citizenship and rights for gay, lesbian, and bisexual members of society, for example. And when we refer to racial formation forces, we do not mean groups or interests defined by the physical or cultural characteristics culturally constructed to have biological significance. Rather, we are referring to socially constructed sets of interests that may privilege one racially defined group over another (in a white racist society this is likely to mean white skin privilege relative to people of color) as opposed to those who seek to produce greater equality regardless of racialized social categorizations defined as "race." Thus it may very well be that one will find people of color as well as whites in each set of racial formation forces.

The notion of "balance" of gendering, sexuality, or racial formation forces refers to the processes and dynamics of struggle between such sets of interests to redefine the social construction of gender, sexuality, and race. The conditions and dynamics affecting these forces, we argue, are similar to those affecting the balance of class forces as conceptualized by Jessop. Furthermore, the concept of a balance of political forces expands on the class-centric focus of Jessop's (and much of sociological state theory) conceptual framework to make room for analyses of class formation as well as gendering, sexuality, and racial formation, and the intersections of these. Hence, it becomes important to explore the balance of *political* forces (of both oppression and resistance) before, during, and after the implementation of policies and projects and the selectivity filters that operated to frame public and political discourse are these multiple sites of power. Here the state becomes an actor and the state project an arena of contested terrain, both of which are subject to resistance from below as well as dominance from above. The state thus can become an agent of oppression as well as an agent and object of change. Thus, as the German anarchist, Landauer (Kuhn 2010) noted, the state is a *social relationship* among people—again, a dynamic site of contestation, interrelation, and change.

The balance of political forces is conditioned by the relative level of unity within groups as well as among groups (Weinstein 1968; Levine 1988; Quadagno and Meyer 1989; Fraser and Gordon 1994; Peattie and Rein 1983); the relative level of unity within and among state agencies and branches (Skocpol 1992); the resources accessible to groups (McCarthy and Zald 1987); the ability of groups to mobilize such resources (McCarthy and Wolfson 1996); the ability to apply mobilized resources created by actual opportunities or perceptions of the potential threat to create mass turmoil or disruption (McAdam, McCarthy, and Zald 1996); condition or health of the economy; structural positioning of groups and state actors in the political economy; and relative autonomy of state actors. Selectivity filters shaping and framing issues and perceptions of viable solutions are conditioned by prior policy precedents (Skocpol and Ikenberry 1983; Skocpol 1985); party politics; ideology and culture; and ability of groups and state agencies and branches to mobilize bias. The resolution of the dialectical process between the balance of political forces and selectivity filters moves policy initiatives toward policy creation. Once policies are created, the dialectic between the balance of political forces and selectivity filters reverberates through the process of translating de jure policy into de facto implementation and cultural practice. The resolution of that dialectical process shapes the policy as an entrant into the larger state project and becomes part of the selectivity filters that frame subsequent policy initiatives.

For example, the ability of women in a patriarchal society to struggle against the social construction of gender as it appears in gendering state projects and in institutions, and the ability of men to reassert their dominance, is conditioned by the balance of gendering forces. That is, women are more likely to gain passage and implementation of advantageous state policy when there is greater unity of perspective among a large number of women (and often aided and abetted with the support and participation of men in coalitions with women) who are organized in formal organizations and networks. They are more likely to become organized when they perceive or face an imminent threat to their life chances. For example, increasing participation of women in the paid labor market (either by choice or by economic necessity) is more likely to prompt greater demands for pay equity, family leave policy, legal protection from sexual harassment, equal opportunity and access to education, training and jobs, enforcement of child support awards, etc. This is especially so when women are their own sole source of income and benefits, or when they are the sole or primary source of such support for their families.

Such efforts to gain advantageous legislation and implementation of policies and programs are more likely to succeed when men are less unified in their opposition to challenges to patriarchy, or when crises in other institutions increase the legitimacy of women's demands. For example, periods of severe downsizing, deindustrialization, and recession force increasing numbers of men out of work, and subsequently necessitate greater participation by women in the paid labor market in order to provide income for their families. Other examples of the enhancement of women's power in the balance of gendering forces have occurred when men's dominant cultural or institutional position became diminished. Such was the case during the 1983 copper mine labor strikes in Arizona, when court injunctions forbade men from picketing, thus necessitating the organizing of women to continue the strike efforts (Kingsolver 1989). Similar processes became apparent during World War II, when men were increasingly pulled from assembly lines to fight overseas, at precisely the point in time when dramatic increases in industrial production were necessary to support the war effort. Women's participation in munitions factories, tank and submarine factories, and other industrial settings became increasingly vital. Likewise, the severe and protracted recession of 2009–2013 has meant a necessary shift in the domestic division of labor in which unemployed men at home must take on childcare responsibilities while women, more traditionally employed in the service sector where there is more, although lower-paying, employment, attempt to provide economic support for their families. That new productive role for women shifted the line between the natural and the artificial and altered the claims process (see Peattie and Rein 1983), and thereby altered the ideological selectivity filters biasing policy.

Supreme Court decisions have also played a role in the dialectics of gendering state projects. For example, the 1973 Roe v. Wade decision gave
women greater control over their bodies by granting women the right to an
abortion anywhere in the United States. That decision has been the object of
fierce struggles in Congress and in individual state legislatures ever since.
These struggles have been animated by the dialectical push and pull of the
balance of gendering forces between those framing the issue in an ideology
of "anatomy is destiny" defining women's proper, biologically determined
role as mothers and those framing the issue as a matter of women's individual
civil rights (Luker 1984; Petchesky 1984). Both sides of the struggle are well-
organized and networked, with antiabortionists represented by Right to Life,
Operation Rescue, and the Christian Coalition, among others; and pro-choice
proponents represented by the National Abortion and Reproductive Rights
Action League (NARAL), the National Organization for Women (NOW),
and others. These organizations have been variably effective in accessing
and mobilizing resources, raising considerable funds, lobbying legislators,
organizing PACs and petition drives, buying advertising space in print and
broadcasting media, and organizing widely viewed rallies and demonstrations. Such mobilized resources and political processes give the gendered
group forces access to legislators to frame and influence the creation of abortion and other gendering policy.

Furthermore, each of the gendered interest groups has created opportunities or invoked the threat of the potential to create mass turmoil. Pro-choice
proponents have frequently organized massive demonstrations in major cities, and in Washington, DC in particular, drawing hundreds of thousands of
participants and suggesting to legislators that there is widespread support
for the right to abortion access and that failure to uphold that access could
result in political disaster for members of Congress (witness, e.g.,, the popular bumper sticker, "I support Roe v. Wade . . . and I vote!"). On the other
hand, the Christian Right has emerged in the 1980s and 1990s as such an
organized and influential force in the Republican Party that it has adopted an
antiabortion plank in its platform. In addition, members of Operation Rescue
and other similar organizations have engaged in demonstrations blocking the
entrance to abortion clinics, thereby harassing patients and doctors entering
clinics. Moreover, there have been increasing attacks against abortion clinics,
such as bombings, shootings, murders, and harassment of clinic employees at
their homes and in other public places. These actions produce or threaten to
produce mass turmoil at sites where abortions are performed and make access
to the right to abortion increasingly difficult (Mason 2002).

Antiabortion proponents have also become relatively adept at accessing the
judicial system to chip away at the implementation of the right to abortion
access. The result thus far is that although Roe v. Wade remains a powerful

force in defining women's rights, it has undergone increasing restrictions. In its 1989 Webster v. Reproductive Health Services decision, the Supreme Court allowed individual states the right to determine its own abortion policy restrictions, a move that has focused much of the struggle at the individual state level. Each state essentially produces its own set of restrictions, including requirements to secure the permission of the parents or guardians of a minor seeking abortion, refusals to allow Medicaid to pay for the abortions of poor women (showing here, quite clearly, where class and gender intersect in this state project), and the banning of certain abortion procedures; some states have even attempted to legally assign the status of personhood on fetuses and thereby provide them with the same protections as citizens, although these attempts have thus far not succeeded. Legal restrictions to abortion contribute to the state gendering project in that women who cannot afford to pay to end unwanted pregnancies or women who live in states that restrict access to abortions may find themselves unlikely to be able to access educational or employment opportunities because of the high costs of childcare, healthcare insurance, and child rearing. The result at both the state and federal levels is a gendering that reiterates the subordination of women, particularly women of color and poor women (Roberts 1997), as more become increasingly dependent either on the state itself or on their husbands or partners for economic security (again, illustrating an important *intersection* of social relations).

The ability of people of color to gain advantageous policy is shaped by a claims process similar to that in gendering processes in which the line between the biological or natural and the socially constructed notions of race are shifted. This process is conditioned by the balance of racialized forces. People of color are more likely to gain passage and implementation of advantageous state policy when there is greater unity of perspective among a large number of people of color (and often with the support of whites, an indication of a lack of unity among whites) who are organized in formal and informal organizations and networks to address racism and racialized inequality. They are more likely to become organized when they perceive or face an imminent threat to their life chances. For example, increased incidents of police brutality and violent hate crimes targeting people of color have elicited organized protests and demands for legal and legislative action—particularly in the recent Black Lives Matter protests around the United States, as has mounting evidence of continued segregation and discrimination in schools (Kozol 1991), labor markets (Wilson 1996b), credit access (Glasberg 1992; Squires 1994; Ross and Yinger 2002; Beeman, Glasberg, and Casey 2010; Hughey 2012b), housing, policing (Alexander 2012), and the location of toxic waste sites (Bullard 1983; 1993; Bryant and Mohai 1992).

Such efforts to gain advantageous legislation and implementation of policies and programs are more likely to succeed when whites are less unified in their opposition to challenges to white superiority, when there is disunity between state branches or agencies, or when crises in other institutions increase the legitimacy of the demands of people of color. For example, the Constitution's usage of *freedom from* (as opposed to *freedom to*) supports a notion of negative freedom rather than positive freedom: "Positive freedom involves the creation of conditions conducive to human growth and the development and realization of human potentials. . . . Negative freedom is freedom from restraints and from government intrusion" (Wilson 1996a, 29).

The emphasis, then, on "freedom from" creates a cultural filter protecting slavery, discrimination, and racism, rather than equality of life chances. This cultural filter remained intact until the Supreme Court altered its patterns of decision-making from an emphasis on equal treatment to one of fair and equitable outcomes, signaling disunity between state branches and agencies. That disunity created an opportunity for an alteration in the balance of racially formed forces, such that an organized civil rights movement could become more empowered to press an agenda of resistance and challenge to racism in the state and society. Civil rights organizations also became highly sophisticated at networking, such that black churches, student organizations such as SNCC, labor unions, and other organizations such as CORE and the NAACP commonly operated together in developing strategies to challenge institutional racist practices and traditions (Morris 1984). Moreover, the balance of political and institutional forces was further affected by the ability of civil rights groups to create mass disruption through boycotts, sit-ins, marches, other demonstrations, organized protests (McAdam 1982) and riots (Piven and Cloward 1977).

Since the 1980s, with the civil rights movement in a more quiescent, less militant period of abeyance than in the 1950s–1970s, backlashes and challenges to the shift in the balance of racially formed forces have intensified and redeployed into seemingly nonracial (i.e., class or economic) policy arenas such as welfare reform and attempts to repeal or undermine affirmative action (Lieberman 1998; Quadagno 1994). Indeed, many heralded the 2008 election of President Barack Obama as the beginning of the "post-racial" society, signaling a frame that racism was no longer an issue in the United States (Bonilla-Silva 2013). The effect of the return to "unbiased" or "neutral" concepts like freedom from Big Government, competitive individualism, and seniority, in a context of a less-active and vigilant civil rights movement and a more organized, resource-rich and motivated backlash movement, framed in the belief that we have entered a "post-racial" society, has been a perpetuation of racism, delinking the crucial *intersection* of class from race.

In sum, then, state projects and the policies that combine to form them are affected by the dynamic processes of the balance of political forces, requiring an MSP approach to state theory to account for these overlapping and intersecting dynamic processes of struggle.

POLICY FORMATION AND IMPLEMENTATION

How would these concepts of state projects, balance of political forces, and selectivity filters help us analyze the state's relationship to society? What would an extension of these concepts to analyses of gendering, sexuality, and racial formation look like? What, then, does the MSP approach to state theory entail? We can organize the factors suggested as important by the prevailing theories of the state to identify the significant dimensions of the balance of political and institutional forces and of selectivity filters. In particular, such factors include (1) organization (including the extent to which classes, gendering forces, sexuality forces, and racial formation forces are unified and the extent to which they may develop networks and coalitions, as well as these same factors within competing groups); (2) access to and ability to mobilize resources; (3) structural conditions (including the health of the economy, constitutional constraints on policy creation and implementation, existing regulations, and precedence in implementation); (4) opportunity (or perception of potential) for groups to create mass disruption or turmoil; (5) relative autonomy of state actors and agencies; (6) and unity and organization within and among state agencies.

The dialectical process between the balance of political (class, gendering, sexuality, or racial formation, or intersections of these) forces and selectivity filters does not end with the passage of a single policy; but rather the dialectical process reverberates through the implementation of that policy and in the subsequent development of social repertoires and cultural practices. These then set the stage for later policy creation, modification, and implementation and cultural practices within the larger state project, which then become part of the selectivity filters that frame subsequent social behaviors and policy initiatives. Individual policy initiatives thus are framed by the larger state project and prior precedents set by existing policies within that project. The introduction of such initiatives triggers a dialectical process between the balance of political forces and selectivity filters.

State projects are animated, then, by the balance of political and institutional forces in the claims process, producing a dialectic process of policy making and implementation, as well as social practices and repertoires over time. Dominant class, racial, sexuality, and gendered interests may be challenged, resisted, and redirected from below in this process. Taken together, then, the concepts of state projects, balance of political forces, and selectivity filters provide us with useful tools for developing an analytical framework for understanding the relationship between the state, society, and oppression (and resistance). The notion of "balance" of gendered, sexuality, or racial formation forces refers to the processes of struggle among such sets of interests to redefine the social construction of gender, sexuality, and race. The conditions and dynamics affecting these forces are similar to those affecting the balance of class forces as conceptualized by Jessop. Furthermore, the concept of a balance of political forces expands on the class-centric focus of Jessop's (and much of that of sociological state theories') conceptual framework to make room for analyses of class formation as well as gendering, sexuality, and racial formation, and the intersections of these multiple sites of power. It also becomes possible to incorporate standpoint theory (Smith 1999), so that analyses of state projects may emerge from the points of view of those from below rather than necessarily beginning only with the state and its policies from above.

INTERSECTIONS OF RACE, CLASS, AND GENDER AND STATE POLICY

Some observers have begun working on questions concerning the intersections of race, class, gender, and sexuality with the state. For example, McCall (2001) found that configurations of inequality are indeed not simply dimensionalized inexorably along gender, racial, and class lines, but that the intersection of these along with variations in geographic place has a significant effect on inequalities. She argued that this insight must have an effect on the formulation of anti-inequality policies enacted by the state. While her approach is indeed a refreshing departure from literature that focuses on one or the other of the crucial organizing principles in isolation of the others, her analysis treats these as independent variables whose patterns should enter into the formulation of state policy to address them. What remains to be examined is the interaction between these organizing principles, their intersections, and the interaction between these and state policy. That is, the state may affect as well as be affected by the intersections of race, class, and gender—and, we would add, sexuality. Hence the need for the MSP approach to state theory.

Glenn (2002) explores the intersections of racialized, class, and gendered oppressions in the state's development of immigration and labor policy between the end of Reconstruction and the beginning of World War II. The state wrestled with the meaning of free labor and citizenship at a time when the abolition of slavery deeply altered the nation's social construction of labor, and huge waves of immigrants fueled the Industrial Revolution and challenged the notion of who was a rightful citizen. The struggles over the redefinition of these twin state projects pitted blacks against whites in the Southern United States, Mexicans against Anglos in the Southwest, and

Asians against white planters in Hawai'i and produced what she termed "unequal freedom" among workers based on their gender and their varying racialized categories. These struggles also framed the shape and scope of worker resistance to that oppression.

In contrast, other analyses recognize the need to place race, class, gender, and sexuality at the center of the analysis within the context of the society in which they occur as well as in the larger, global context. For example, studies of colonialism highlight the powerful role of military action and economic practices and sanctions in control of nations (Sharma and Kumar 2003; Ferdnance 1998). This required the subjugation of women, people of color, and labor on a grand, global scale. Connell (1997, 1523) noted that racial and sexual issues were intertwined in the North Atlantic expansion and immigration policies that gave rise to "a growing fear of miscegenation, a hardening color line, contempt of the colonizers for the sexuality or masculinity of the colonized, and fears of racial swamping." Contemporary imperialism is more subtle but just as powerful as the internal and external colonialism of Europe and the United States. It takes the guise of humanitarian and economic aid. But the end result continues to be power and control over indigenous populations and reproduces systems of inequality.

The concepts of balance of political forces (of both hegemony and oppression as well as of resistance and challenge), selectivity filters, and state projects are useful analytical tools for exploring the production of racial formation, gendering, sexuality, and class formation state projects, and the intersections of these. Of course, this frame could be extended into any contemporary state project, from debates about same-sex marriage and kinship, to the militarization of the domestic police force and their role in quelling dissent, to the encroaching surveillance state propped up by recent legislation such as Obama's 2012 National Defense Authorization Act. The field is ripe for these kinds of holistic analyses—particularly after the economic crisis of 2008 and the resulting struggles by social movements against inequalities in a variety of forms. In this book, we put the theory to use particularly examining political economy, racialization, sexuality and kinship forms, as well as the intersections of race, class, gender, and sexuality in the context of housing (a set of state projects that directly led to the economic crisis of 2008), food and agriculture, and the welfare state.

MULTI-SITES OF POWER

Our suggestion of the use of the concepts of state projects, selectivity filters, and balance of political forces to frame our understanding of the relationship between the state and society underscores the need to expand and reconceptualize critical state theory from one focused purely on class to one that includes gendering, sexuality, and racialized processes and relations. Literatures in state theory, feminist state theory, race theory, queer theory, and social movement theory share some parallel notions of the relationship between the state and society, but remain isolated from (and in some cases with some traditions within feminism and queer theory, antagonistic toward) each other as literatures. We suggest that it would be useful to braid the insights and elements of these into a framework that helps us understand the broader relationship between the state and society as it shapes the main social organizing principles of racial formation, class, gender, and sexuality that structure social life. More importantly, we suggest that the notion of the balance of political forces conceptually facilitates an analysis that can begin from the standpoint of the oppressed and build toward an understanding of state projects as dynamic processes of both oppression from above and resistance from below.

We also emphasize an understanding of the state as a multidimensional structure that includes not only the legislature, but also the judiciary, the executive, and administrative state agencies vested with the power to implement and interpret policy on a day-to-day basis. Moreover, the state is also an actor, subject to the same forces and conditions affecting other groups engaged in policy formation and implementation processes, including unity and disunity among and within agencies and institutional organizations, resource mobilization processes, and access to opportunities to create disruption. Such an approach will help us to explain class-based as well as gendered, sexuality, and racialized policy areas by using Jessop's concepts as organizing conceptual tools. These concepts allow us to identify the relationship between the state and class relations as well as that between the state and gendering, the state and sexuality, and the state and racial formation. We can begin then to articulate the conditions under which some policies are more or less likely to develop at particular points in time and some interests are more or less likely to gain power and have their interests addressed.

We emphasize that state projects are not discrete, individual projects that are isolated from each other. Indeed, there are many places where economic state projects intersect with racial formation state projects (such as immigration policy), gendering state projects intersect with racial formation projects (as in affirmative action policy), or sexuality state projects intersect with gendering state projects (as in marriage policy). Additionally, there are policy arenas where all three state projects may intersect, as is the case in the welfare "reform" of the 1990s and warfare and homeland security policy in 2003. In the case of welfare reform, what appeared to be an economic issue (work as the antidote to poverty) operates as an entry into gendering state projects where gender is socially constructed relative to class: poor women are socially constructed as good mothers only if they work in the paid labor force and leave the care of their young children to others; middle-class and affluent mothers, in contrast, are socially constructed as good mothers only if they remain dependent on their male partners and stay at home to care for their own young children. Moreover, such welfare reforms are also part of the racial formation state project since they largely affect women and children of color more harshly than whites, and imply that the "problems" besetting welfare are somehow a function of a racialized culture of poverty. The point is not to assert an isolated nature to state projects. Rather, we advocate recognizing that individual policies do not randomly occur while bearing no relation to other policies, but rather are entries to larger state projects. We also suggest that state projects themselves are not isolated from each other. An area for further research should involve an examination of the articulation among these state projects. Similarly, further research should involve an examination of how multiple sites of power intersect and what state policy "does" at those intersections—making these intersections their own unique sites for elaboration rather than assuming they are just the sum of their parts.

Where we might go with state theory, then, is toward a holistic analysis that accounts for developments in sociology outside of state theory's canon. However, as we have argued, we think we might also draw much from existing literature on state theory—particularly Jessop's concepts as we have outlined above. We live in exciting times, during upheavals that span the globe (Shannon 2014), where the state's physical presence in the form of police violence, iron cages which are increasingly privatized (yet intimately connected to the state in the form of criminalization and conviction), and military adventures all over the world is made visible to anyone with an internet connection and a will to search out information. We believe that these conceptual tools could form a crucial part of analyzing, evaluating, and critiquing this historical moment with a sociological lens.

In the chapters that follow we will explore the elements of this multi-site model of power and the state. Each case chapter will foreground a particular aspect of our larger model, but it will also include the other elements of the model as well. That is, although each chapter will emphasize a particular element of the model, it will not do so exclusively. We are highlighting elements in each chapter to illustrate how they work, and we will then pull them all together in the final case chapter. In this way, we will build the pieces of our model toward the fuller framework in the last chapter.

NOTE

1. NB: parts of this chapter could be read in a way in which "women" seems to necessarily refer to "cis women" (and likewise, "men" seems to refer to "cis men").

It might also be read as contrasting "women" and "men" with "transgender people." In some ways, this could have the effect of suggesting that the category "women" is exclusive to cis women, thereby reproducing cisnormativity (likened by excluding trans women). An additional example emerges later in this chapter when we write about abortion solely in regard to "women" even though abortion is a medical service that people who are not women might also access (e.g., trans men). An additional result of this is the possible implication that the category "women" does not include trans women or other genders. While we are aware of the dangers of reproducing cisnormativity as well as the hypocrisy of doing so in a chapter about the state's reproduction of heteronormativity, for now, we'll leave the terminology as is (for ease of explanation), but will address cisnormativity and the effects of a rigid gender binary further in chapter 4 which focuses on heteronormativity.

Chapter 3

State Projects and Economic Intervention

Balancing Political Forces

Scholars often examine policies in isolation of their antecedents, failing to connect the dots between seemingly unrelated policies. The concept of state projects, in contrast, places what appear to be individual state policies and practices into a larger context: each policy is actually understood to be a piece of a broader framework, one in which the related policies together form a state project. In addition, the state project is not inexorable or dictated from the top down; rather it is an ongoing process, animated by relations of political forces and challenged from below. This does not suggest that all political forces are of equal ability to affect the process; but all enter into the process in some way, and it is their varying abilities, along with selectivity filters that let some voices in and keeps others out, that shape and frame state projects. In this chapter, we will foreground the process of balancing political forces as we trace out the state project of economic intervention.

Here, we ponder how we arrived at the Great Recession of the turn of the twenty-first century, and how that economic tumble has been "resolved." How did we get there, and where is it going, and why? We argue that the recession was hardly an unexpected blip or anomaly, but rather a part of the wider state project of economic intervention. Ironically enough, economic intervention is conventionally framed as attempts by the state to occasionally intervene in the functions of the market to prevent or address serious economic "events" such as recessions, depressions, and major market disruptions. Thus, in order to understand the Great Recession, we must connect the dots going back decades to draw out the links of the state project, and to delineate the balance of political forces that set the parameters of these policies.

THE AFTERMATH OF THE GREAT DEPRESSION:
GLASS-STEAGALL AND BANK REGULATION

Prior to the Great Depression of the 1930s federal oversight and regulation of the banking industry was minimal, if present at all: at this point the state assumed a laissez-faire position, on the unquestioned assumption that the "free" market would discipline the industry. Financial institutions were thus free to engage in business as they saw fit, unfettered by state intervention, and therefore able to engage in wildly speculative investments (including high-risk short sales of stock and enormous loans to single corporate borrowers), and often overexposing their assets in the process. The casino mentality that dominated the industry ultimately ignited the watershed economic free fall of the stock market crash, runs on banks by panicked customers, and a deep economic depression that sent severe economic shock waves far and wide.

In an attempt to gain better control over the practices of an industry that was the nation's economic wellspring, Congress passed the Banking Act of 1933, commonly referred to as the Glass-Steagall Act. This bill established the Federal Deposit Insurance Corporation insuring the savings accounts of individual depositors up to $100,000, thereby protecting individuals' life savings should a bank collapse; although this certainly provided a safety net for millions of people, the goal of Glass-Steagall was to restore consumer confidence and provide a safety net for banking institutions. On a broader, perhaps more important level, the bill restricted the activities that classes of banks could engage in, establishing different market niches for each class of bank. That way, large commercial banks would not overrun smaller mortgage or savings and loan institutions because they could not compete in the same market niche; and no single bank could so dominate the industry, or the economy, to the detriment of all. For example, no individual financial institution could lend more than 10 percent of its available assets to a single borrower, thus limiting the bank's risk and exposure to the fate of that one borrower (Federal Reserve Bank of New York 1933). Here, the state project was to provide stability to the economy through intervention by protecting banks from each other, in an effort to prevent ruinous hyper-competition in pursuit of private profit. The state viewed this intervention as a rare intervention into the free market, because of the failure of that free market to avert the massive crisis of the Great Depression.

Not surprisingly, from the very start the industry railed against the restrictions the bill introduced. The restrictive language of Glass-Steagall was strong, which banks clearly resented. But in practice the defined market niches were more liberally interpreted by federal banking regulators over time. The gap between de jure legislation and de facto practice allowed large commercial banks to actually expand their range of discretionary business and increasingly etched away at the industry's much-hated fetters imposed by the Glass-Steagall Act. Yet banks continued to balk at being regulated.

It wasn't until 1978 that a real opportunity to tip the balance of political forces materialized for the financial institutions in their pursuit of the repeal of Glass-Steagall to deregulate the banking industry. And notably, it was an opportunity borne of a crisis generated in no small part by the banks themselves, stewarded by state policies; the opportunity did not just happen or materialize out of thin air.

THE CHRYSLER BAILOUT

By 1978, Chrysler Corporation was in dire trouble. The erstwhile auto-making giant was hemorrhaging revenue, profits, and market share; its stock value was plummeting; and it owed an overwhelmingly huge amount of capital to its many lenders. When it pleaded with its lenders for debt relief and further support once again, the financial institutions collectively refused to lend the firm so much as another dime. The firm—and its hundreds of thousands of workers—now faced the unimaginably grim probability of bankruptcy.

Why did Glass-Steagall, which was supposed to prevent such crises, not prevent this one? Recall one of Glass-Steagall's conditions: no single bank was permitted to lend more than 10 percent of its available assets to any one borrower. While this ensured that the bankruptcy of a borrowing corporation would not also bankrupt a bank that had devoted the bulk of its available assets to that one borrower, it also set the stage for the balance of political forces now facing Chrysler: the regulation forced banks to form lending structures, or consortia, in order to collectively provide for the huge borrowing needs of major corporations and governments since no bank by itself had anywhere near the amount of capital needed. These lending consortia technically violated the legal restriction against bank collusion, but the 10 percent restriction necessitated their existence. When banks joined together in a lending consortium, each provided the amount they legally could, essentially "chipping in" the share they could afford. That spread the exposure and risk of each individual bank, enabled major corporations and governments to access the finance capital they needed to do business, and ensured the safety and security of depositors. When Chrysler faced bankruptcy in 1978, its lending consortium was composed of a total of over 325 financial institutions (Glasberg 1989). The existence of lending consortia structurally empowered the industry, particularly the largest commercial banks, in a way that violated the spirit if not the letter of Glass-Steagall: it gave the banks the ability to wield the power of pulling their collective purse strings, which they did to great effect in their pursuit of the repeal of Glass-Steagall when Chrysler stood on the brink of bankruptcy, setting in motion a battle between Congress and the banking industry. The process of the balance of political forces was rarely so exposed as now.

Congressional leaders pleaded with Chrysler's banks to bail out the automaker with more loans and the purchase of Chrysler's stock in order to prevent the economic shock waves certain to reverberate widely and deeply throughout the economy. Chrysler's bankruptcy posed every probability of thrusting the entire nation (and quite possibly beyond) into a very deep recession, or worse. Consider what the bankruptcy of a major firm in a central industry means: not only would a major employer itself go out of business, so too would much of its supplier industries. In the case of an automaker like Chrysler these included industries like rubber, steel, aluminum, glass, textiles, and electronics. When entire towns are dependent on major corporations as essentially the only major employer, bankruptcy of these firms is catastrophic: it would mean the municipalities themselves would head into severe economic recessions or depressions, prompting massive unemployment and bankruptcy of smaller local shops and deep cuts in municipal services, including education, police, fire departments, sanitation and public works, elder care and the like. In the case of Chrysler, not only was it a major—if not the only—employer in many towns and cities; so were its supplier industries. A Chrysler bankruptcy would surely bankrupt not only the towns where Chrysler was the main employer; towns and cities that grew and prospered primarily because of the presence of the corporations in its supplier industries would go bankrupt as well. The resulting massive widespread unemployment would inflame economic woes nationally because disposable income and consumers' ability to spend would dramatically decline.

Few members of Congress would have constituents who would be spared from the effects of such an economic catastrophe as Chrysler's bankruptcy. Banks sensed a key opportunity to tip the balance of political forces in their favor and they did not hesitate to seize the moment: they steadfastly refused to budge, leaving Congress terrified at the horrendous prospects they faced and ready to negotiate with banks (U.S. Congress 1979). What would it take to get the banks to agree to keep Chrysler afloat?

Needless to say, the banks did not have to think twice as to the price they wanted: they would agree to exchange Chrysler's debt for equity (something Congress wanted but banks balked at accepting) if Congress agreed that they would deregulate the banking industry. Congressional leaders were furious at this audacious quid pro quo demanded by the banks, and many viewed it as explicit extortion. Banks did not seem to worry that they would appear to be callously holding the national economy hostage; they remained focused on the goal of repealing Glass-Steagall. They were prepared to continue staring Congress down until Congress blinked first. Finally, after much heated exchange, Congress and the banks agreed to the deal: Chrysler was rescued from the brink of financial collapse, workers' jobs were presumably saved, and Congressional members avoided having to answer to frightened and angry constituencies as to why they allowed jobs to be destroyed (U.S. Congress 1979). More importantly, financial institutions had succeeded in resetting the balance of political forces as they gained an elusive but much-sought goal: by 1982 much of the hated regulatory restrictions had been removed or substantially relaxed, allowing banks to significantly expand their range of business. Bank deregulation would now set the stage for a free-for-all in the industry where there were no protections for smaller banks from the excesses of and domination by the larger ones.

Much of the debate in Congress over deregulating the banking industry's investment in Chrysler was framed in the larger state project of economic intervention. The 1970s and 1980s were a time of retrenchment in which several industries were deregulated, including telephones, trucking, and railroads. The concept that animated this round of deregulation was a resurgence of laissez-faire (neoliberal) economics: get the state out of the way so private industries could operate in an environment in which the "invisible hand" of free-market competition disciplined the firms. By separating the state and the economy, the assumption was that uncompetitive firms would fail and disappear, and more efficiently run, profitable firms would prevail. Size never figured into this equation (except in Congress's definition of major corporations as "too big to fail"); Congressional leaders never considered that larger corporate entities would pose prohibitive barriers to entry to the industries by smaller, independent firms. Congress also did not have any discussions examining why the banking industry was uniquely different from any of the industries previously deregulated.

Financial institutions are the only organizations whose role in the economy is to absorb all excess finance capital not presently in use (i.e., sitting in savings accounts or pension and trust funds) and invest it for growth. Banks alone thus determine who may access this capital and who may not. The problem is that this arrangement of finance capital allocation is organized around the distribution of a unique resource: finance capital. Unlike any other resource, finance capital is the only resource necessary to purchase all other resources required to do any other activity, whether it concerns business or governance. Moreover, unlike any other resource, there are no alternatives to finance capital: those who need it must somehow access it or be completely unable to do business or to govern. And unlike any other resource, finance capital is distributed not by a single provider but by a collective of hundreds, and sometimes thousands of providers working together and organizing their decision-making to the benefit of the providing group even if that comes to the detriment of the user. Finance capital is also the sole resource that is only borrowed rather than purchased once and used; as such, finance capital forms a relationship between provider and user that is long-term and poses long-term and far-reaching consequences for the borrower. That unique quality of finance capital places its controllers in an incredible position of power relative not only to other industries but to the state as well (Glasberg 1989), and has tremendous power to influence the balance of political forces.

Unfortunately, when Congress considered whether or not to deregulate the banking industry, they failed to grasp an understanding of finance capital as a unique resource and an extraordinarily powerful base for its providers; they did not perceive banks to be unique at all, but viewed them as they did any of the other industries previously deregulated. Indeed, much of the debate centered on deregulatory precedence that had already been set when Congress deregulated so many other industries; they saw no defensible reason not to also deregulate banks, especially after having made the promise to do so in exchange for saving the economy from the economic disaster of a Chrysler bankruptcy (Glasberg and Skidmore 1997).

With deregulation in place, banks proceeded to move full speed ahead with practices they were previously forbidden to do. But instead of spurring economic growth and wealth, bank deregulation unleashed a slew of previously forbidden activities in the banking industry that Congress would soon have to revisit. The state project of economic intervention was hardly over, and the balance of political forces would be tipped once again.

CORPORATE WELFARE, BANK DEREGULATION, AND THE SAVINGS AND LOAN BAILOUT

Without the controls of Glass-Steagall, large commercial banks were now free to compete for business with smaller savings and loan institutions, investment banks, and insurance companies. Previously established market niches no longer defined which markets each would serve, allowing the larger, better-endowed banks to make inroads on the markets of these other financial institutions and compete for business with greater resources. And all financial institutions could now conduct riskier investments in an attempt to augment the assets at their disposal in this unequal battle for market share and financial assets.

Savings and loan institutions, for example, were previously restricted to offering low-cost mortgages as their only business. But now, under deregulation, they could invest in junk bonds, high-yield but extremely high-risk investments that previously were not allowed. Banks could now invest heavily in speculative investments of home and commercial constructions; these constructions did not necessarily have buyers, but banks assumed they would when construction was completed. Savings and loan institutions, in particular, were overexposed in this market: under Glass-Steagall, their market niche of providing low-rate mortgages meant their returns on investments would be meager and occur over an extended period of time (usually thirty years), and were restricted in the interest they could pay on customers' savings accounts. Bank deregulation meant they could now offer much greater interest rates on customers' savings accounts in order to attract them away from the larger commercial banks and generate more cash on hand to invest in the speculative real estate market. But that meant they were paying out higher rates in the short term than they were getting paid on old mortgages in the long term, and this created a severe cash flow gap (U.S. Congress 1990). It didn't take very long before this gap ran up against the overheated real estate market, which by now was so saturated that there were not enough buyers, resulting in homes and commercial space remaining empty and on the market. It quickly became evident that speculative investments in construction was a horrible gamble that was not going to pay off.

Neither did the binge of junk bond purchases that savings and loan institutions used to try to boost their assets as quickly as possible to support their speculative investments. It didn't take long before their junk bond investments became so out of control that whole banks began to go bankrupt. By 1984, junk bonds accounted for nearly 22 percent of the bond market (U.S. Congress 1989); by 1989, 183 savings and loan institutions owned $14.4 billion in junk bonds, 91 percent of which were concentrated in thirty thrift institutions in California, Florida, New York, Texas, and Missouri (*New York Times* 1989). And so was born the savings and loan crisis of the 1980s, when thousands of these institutions went bankrupt.

The collapse of the savings and loan industry reanimated the state project of economic intervention and sent Congress to do the unprecedented: they bailed out the industry *as a whole*. Bailing out major corporations was nothing new to Congress: they had already bailed out over 450 major corporations since World War II, including many Department of Defense contractors like Lockheed and major industrial giants like Chrysler because, unlike small businesses, major corporations and Department of Defense contractors were "too big (or too important) to fail." They were so huge as employers and important as economic (and political) actors that the state could not afford to allow the "invisible hand" of the market to discipline them and let them go bankrupt.

But while Congress was no stranger to bailing out major corporations, they had never before bailed out an entire industry; and they had never before bailed out any corporate entity with a blank check. Every corporate bailout before this had been well-defined by a specific amount; but the savings and loan bailout was achieved with no such defined limit: the ultimate cost of the bailout was initially estimated to be $500 billion over more than forty years, with subsequent estimates of the total cost somewhere closer to $1 trillion before it was over (Hays and Hornick 1990, 50). And the definition of "too big to fail" now was expanded to mean not only how many people are employed and how much the firm contributes to the economy, but now to also mean "too centrally important an actor" to be allowed to fail (Glasberg and Skidmore 1997). Congressional leaders believed they had no choice but to bail out banks because these institutions collectively hold the resources everyone needs: families in need of mortgages and student loans, corporations in need of major investments and loans, and governments in desperate need of deficit financing. Without banks everyone is subject to massive economic depression. No other firm or industry can claim so central an importance to the common interest. Never was the existence of corporate welfare, the state subsidization of private profit making, made more apparent. The state project of economic intervention became enmeshed in corporate welfare. And the balance of political forces did not have to be as boldly expressed as it was during the hearings for Chrysler's bailout; the collective power of the financial industry had already been established in the institutional memory of Congress, whose members did not need to be reminded of that power.

Notably, the corporate welfare of the savings and loan bailout was not accompanied by any attempt by Congress to rein back in the excesses that they had unleashed with bank deregulation. Instead, the bailout allowed larger commercial banks to buy the assets of the failed savings and loan banks while the United States absorbed the losses, thereby accomplishing the same acceleration of increasing concentration of assets in fewer and fewer hands, a process that was already well under way in all other industries. But in this case, the process was achieved with Congress's extension of corporate welfare to the savings and loan industry, underwriting the risks of private profit making for the benefit of private finance capital beneficiaries at the expense of smaller, less powerful members of society. And the increasing concentration of the banking industry meant the surviving members of the industry would become larger and more powerful, and therefore more difficult to allow to fail in the future.

It is hardly a mere coincidence that this latest incarnation of corporate welfare was undertaken during precisely the same historical "mean season" (Block et al 1987) in which social welfare programs of the War on Poverty collectively came under severe attack. The culmination of that attack was codified in "welfare reform" of the Personal Responsibility and Work Opportunity Reconciliation Act of 1996 that harshly cut how much money and the amount of time over a lifetime one could collect benefits on the erroneous assumption that welfare recipients (and their children) were lazy, refused to work, and made a conscious lifestyle of living off the public dole. The assumption was that a loss of benefits would "motivate" otherwise indolent recipients to finally get a job. This assumption ignored the fact that more than two-fifths of the recipients did have jobs; they simply had jobs that paid so poorly that they remained below the poverty line. And it ignored the fact that a significant proportion of the poor were children, not able-bodied adults; children were hardly in any position to secure employment. The policy sent millions into deeper poverty, hunger, and homelessness. Welfare reform hit poverty-stricken people of color, particularly single mothers and their children, hardest, as dwindling job opportunities were more readily accessible to white applicants (Neubeck and Cazenave 2001; Neubeck 2006). The increase in corporate welfare came at the expense of social welfare; private profits, particularly of financial institutions, trumped the rights and needs of the poor, the working class, people of color, single mothers, and children, and threatened to further tip the balance of political forces in favor of finance capital— again, illustrating the *intersections* of multiple relations of inequality, indeed, multiple sites of power, in this long-term process of state economic projects.

CHALLENGING THE BALANCE OF POLITICAL FORCES: THE COMMUNITY REINVESTMENT ACT

While the story so far might suggest that financial institutions collectively always have the upper hand, resistance notably was not absent in the battle over the balance of political forces during the 1970s and 1980s. While banks were busy gaining traction for bank deregulation, community activists were fighting back from below to get the state to engage in economic intervention specifically on their behalf. In the past, individual, small, local community organizations struggled to fight banks, or to appeal to the state for help for economic development, to limited effect. By the late 1960s, they began to organize into a much larger, national network, pooling their efforts and their limited resources and sharing information and skills. Their efforts resulted in the establishment in 1970 of the Association of Community Organizations for Reform Now (ACORN), which became a powerful network: by 2010 (when the organization was defeated by an extended effort by conservative forces), ACORN's membership included 850 neighborhood chapters in seventy-five cities in the United States, Canada, Peru, and the Dominican Republic (http://www.acorn.org/).

One key piece of legislation that they were able to achieve was the Community Reinvestment Act (CRA) of 1977, a piece of legislation that actually empowered community organizations in their struggle against the banks. CRA enabled community organizations to prevent banks from expanding their business with new branches or new business ventures without opening their books to these organizations for scrutiny. If the banks' books demonstrated a failure to invest in the communities in which they already had branches (a practice referred to as disinvestment, or redlining) they would not be allowed to expand. At that point, banks would have to enter into negotiations with the community organizations to develop agreements to reinvest in the local, underserved communities. The use of CRA challenges to bank expansions worked (Bostic and Robinson 2005; Immergluck 2004; Schwartz 1998; 2000; Squires 1992; 2003; Shlay 1999), bringing over $35 billion in reinvestment to previously underserved communities by the time Congress took the unprecedented step of bailing out the savings and loan industry.

Not surprisingly, financial institutions were furious at this new, effective weapon of the previously weak to challenge their position in the balance of political forces, and they sought to find ways to circumvent the provisions of CRA. The strategy they developed to subvert CRA set the stage for the housing foreclosure crisis that sent the economy reeling by 2008.

PREDATORY LENDING, FORECLOSURES, AND THE BALANCE OF POLITICAL FORCES

The challenge banks faced was how to at least appear to be "good economic citizens" in the communities where they currently did business, if not actually acting as such. That required some ability to show they were reinvesting in previously underserved communities so community activists could not prevent their desired expansions. The cynical strategy they adopted has now come to be understood as predatory lending. Banks aggressively pursued mortgage placements in poverty-stricken communities with subprime lending, using practices that stretched the limits of acceptable practice, and often firmly beyond those limits into strictly illegal practices.

While the term "predatory lending" is now widely used to describe banks' behavior, the concept has not been clearly defined. In general, predatory lending involves the extension of credit that ultimately injures the borrower, usually by depleting the assets the borrower has previously amassed in home ownership; in the extreme, it results in the borrowers losing their entire equity in a foreclosure (Goldstein 1999; Bradley 2000). Predatory lending practices may involve one or more of several techniques of subprime lending. Prime-rate lending is credit extended only to the lowest-risk borrowers. Subprime lending is credit extended at rates higher than the prime rate. Not all subprime lending is predatory: indeed, almost everyone who borrows money accesses credit at interest rates above the prime rate. Subprime lending extends credit to borrowers with risk factors such as poor credit ratings, and therefore carries higher interest rates to offset the higher risk such loans pose. Its stated purpose is to "reward consumers trying to get out of debt and improve their credit by allowing them to build equity in their homes and to transition into prime loans as their credit improves" (Bradley 2000, 160).

The assumption of subprime lending is that the higher interest rates charged are justified by the level of risk posed by the loan. This higher interest rate is applied to all borrowers without discrimination and it carries terms and conditions similar to those applied to prime lending. In contrast, predatory lending is a subcategory of subprime lending, in that it harms rather than helps the borrower with interest rates well beyond the risk posed, is differentially applied to borrowers based on social characteristics (such as class, race, or age), carries terms far more punitive than those applied to prime lending, and is structured in ways that generally erodes and destroys the equity position of the borrower rather than helps to build it.

Not all predatory lending is illegal, even if it does result in the loss of borrowers' property. Predatory lending that is not specifically illegal includes such practices as shifting and bundling unsecured consumer debt (such as credit card debt) into mortgages; application of extraordinarily high annual interest rates, points, and closing costs, well beyond that justified by the risk; single-premium credit insurance; balloon payments on adjustable rate mortgages that result in dramatically higher monthly repayments requirements after an initial period of affordable rates; mandatory arbitration clauses; repeated refinancing, frequently resulting from high-pressure sales tactics; application of daily interest on late payments; highly aggressive, often abusive collection tactics; prepayment penalties; failure to report good repayment track record on borrowers' credit reports; and failure to provide clear and accurate loan balance information.

Lender practices that are illegal but still common include failure to disclose loan terms; failure to provide a Good Faith Estimate; failure to itemize all charges; kickback and referral fees to mortgage brokers, real estate agents, and contractors; balloon payments on loans with less than five years maturity; requirements of advance payments; interest rates that rise after default; knowingly structuring loan payments the borrower cannot afford; falsifying loan applications, including forging signatures on loan documents; charging fees significantly higher than the market rate; requiring credit insurance; and changing loan terms at closing (see Bradley 2000).

Subprime lending increased dramatically, especially in the 1990s and into the next century: the number of financial institutions specializing in such lending rose during the years of 1973 to 1999 from 104,000 to 997,000 (U.S. Department of Housing and Urban Development 2000). Furthermore, between 1994 and 2003, the total dollar value of subprime loans rose from $35 billion to $332 billion (Lord 2005). Between just 1994 and 1998, the total dollar value of subprime loans in the United States rose more than 500 percent (Immergluck and Smith 2005). In Connecticut alone, that figure increased by over 42 percent; notably, the increase was by more than 85 percent in neighborhoods where more than half the population was people of color (Collins 2000). Case studies in major metropolitan areas around the country indicate similar patterns in their findings. For example, one study in Philadelphia found that while conventional lending increased by 61 percent between 1992 and 1998, subprime lending exploded by 4800 percent in two particularly economically poor census tracts. A measure of the damaging effects of these loans can be seen in the fact that foreclosures in these two tracts jumped by 93 percent since 1990 (ACORN 2000).

Subprime lending appears to target poor communities and people of color. In Atlanta for example, subprime lending in 1997 in low-income neighborhoods was 30 percent higher than elsewhere in the city, and communities of color received 250 percent more subprime loans than all of Atlanta (Gruenstein and Herbert 2000). In Ohio, subprime lenders provided more than two-thirds of the refinance loans in census tracts largely populated by people of color (National Community Reinvestment Coalition 2007). In North Carolina, the most recent data from the Housing Mortgage Disclosure Act indicated that subprime lending was concentrated in counties with high populations of African Americans. African Americans received 10 percent of conventional loans, but 20 percent of subprime loans (Bradley 2000). Noted McNally (2010, 1124), "by 1998, . . . subprime mortgages comprised one-third of all home loans made to African Americans and a fifth to those made to Latinos [sic]," and those figures continued to rise steadily into the next century. Krivo and Kaufman (2004) found that both groups were given mortgage loans with significantly higher interest rates than those given to whites, and are 1.5 to 2.5 times more likely to pay interest of 9 percent or more. Most notably, these borrowers were not steered into subprime mortgages because they represented a high risk: nearly two-thirds of these borrowers "qualified for traditional mortgages" (McNally 2010, 124).

Why would banks place mortgages that clearly will not be viable at some point in the future? And why target populations that are unlikely to be able to sustain the mortgage payments in the long run or deliberately structure loans with a high probability of future failure? Part of the answer lies in the change in the industry prompted by federal bank deregulation policy from one dominated by conventional mainstream lenders to an industry with a wide array of financial actors. Some financial service providers are not subject to CRA-regulation because they simply did not exist when CRA legislation was passed and so were not included (Temkin, Johnson, and Levy 2002); many of these providers specialize in offering subprime credit, originating a higher percentage of loans and higher percentage of subprime loans in low-income communities (Courchane, Surette, and Zorn 2004; U.S.

Department of Housing and Urban Development 2000). These new sources of credit, ungoverned by CRA legislation, operate under the radar of CRA protections for the community. And they easily become hand servants to the cynical abuses of those institutions that are subject to CRA challenges: when larger banks aggressively secure unfair mortgages in previously underserved communities, they immediately sell them off to the secondary market of these smaller investment banks; as such, the originating bank now appears to be acting in good faith to serve the community in which it currently does business while avoiding the inevitable foreclosure when the mortgage can no longer be paid. Originating banks have targeted the poor and people of color because these are the citizens who have previously been ignored in the market for homeownership, and are thus far more vulnerable to the aggressive offer of an opportunity to access the previously unattainable American Dream of homeownership, incidentally, also illustrating the crucial need for an analysis that looks at the axis between race and class.

For most of those borrowers targeted by predatory lending, accepting the terms of the mortgage being offered is the only chance to own their own home. For banks, it is the chance to circumvent CRA restrictions imposed by underserving a community. But while this arrangement helped banks avoid the restrictions of CRA, and at least temporarily put previously ignored people into their own homes, the dream of homeownership was short-lived: the predator was at the gate, and the foreclosure crisis soon loomed over the homeowners (particularly homeowners of color, who as a group were just beginning to finally join the American Dream in ever-larger numbers), the communities in which they lived, and the wider economy. By 2010, banks were estimated to repossess more than 800,000 homes (Associated Press 2011); overall, 2.7 million of the 42.2 million Americans who took out mortgages between 2004 and 2008 lost their homes to foreclosure (Berlin 2012). Notably, more than 56 percent of African American homeowners have lost their foothold in the American Dream to foreclosure (McNally 2010, 126; see also Beeman, Glasberg, and Casey 2010). And former Bank of America employees have alleged that the bank "deliberately denied eligible home owners loan modifications . . . to shepherd homeowners into foreclosure . . . [which] yielded the bank more profits than the government-sponsored Home Affordable Modification Package," and offered cash bonuses and gift cards as incentives to employees who hastened foreclosures (Conlin and Rudegeair 2013).

It is important to note that this was not simply a crisis of individuals over-extending themselves into mortgages they could not possibly afford; it was a crisis of a zealously calculated and predatory strategy to circumvent the provisions of CRA that empowered communities in order for banks to continue to amass private profit. It was not simply a crisis created by rogue individual bankers; it was a crisis borne out of the standard practices of the industry in its pursuit of profits and a drive to subvert CRA and the empowered community activist organizations. Sadly, standard operating banking and finance practices designed to subvert state policies and safeguards continue to plague the economy, in the United States and around the world. Witness the 2012 admission by James Dimon, JP Morgan Chase's president and chief executive officer (and member of the Board of Directors of the New York Federal Reserve), that the firm's dubious practice of hedge investments and trading had resulted in an mind-boggling $2 billion loss.

This latest revelation illustrates that the same practices that ignited the Great Recession continue unabated and are being preserved and protected by the same owning class who continue to block (and to fund and support politicians who block) any real regulation and oversight. That is, the balance of political forces has continued to reassert capital accumulation interests, although it occasionally tips away from those interests because of concerted, organized efforts from below, including institutional actors similar to the now-bankrupt and closed nonprofit ACORN, but also a host of extra-institutional social movement actors resisting the period of austerity directly proceeding from the bank bailouts and 2008 financial crisis (Shannon 2014). Indeed, far from hindering private capital accumulation, the Obama administration and the Justice Department have not pursued federal fraud charges and indictments against predatory lenders or hedge fund managers. And despite the creation of the Consumer Financial Protection Bureau and a promise to "clean up Wall Street" and create a "fair playing field," the state has not been particularly anxious to reregulate the banking and finance industry, despite the strategies of resistance put into play contemporarily.

STATE PROJECTS AND THE GREAT RECESSION
OF THE TWENTY-FIRST CENTURY

The foreclosure crisis was not simply a random or unique blip on the economic radar, nor was it restricted to the single industry of banking or housing; it was a severe crisis in a central element of the overall economy and therefore positioned to send more than mere ripples throughout the economy in the United States and abroad. The foreclosure crisis was to become ground zero for the worst, most protracted recession since the Great Depression. All of it was an outgrowth of the process attending the state project of economic intervention and the ebb and flow of the balance of political forces. And the reach of the state project went well beyond the borders of the United States.

By 2008, the Great Recession was clearly in full swing after more than three decades of extended economic growth and unprecedented stock market values. Stock markets in the United States and abroad tumbled in a free fall to depths not seen in decades, and at alarming rates. Millions of people lost their homes; tens of millions of workers, including those with high levels of education and training, lost their jobs; manufacturers shuttered their doors, either because they went bankrupt or because they were relocating to cheaper locations; financial institutions, including some of the biggest household names in banking and investment like Lehman Brothers, ironically faced bankruptcy themselves or became targets for mergers and takeovers.

This was certainly not the first time that the structure of the financial industry had been at the epicenter of economic crises, nor was it the first time that the crisis had a global reach. Even before formal deregulation of the U.S. banking industry began in the 1980s, the unregulated international financial market allowed banks to engage in predatory lending practices with developing countries similar to those used with private homeowners in the United States. Banks sought to place development loans in countries struggling to escape domination by the international aid regimes of the World Bank, the International Bank for Reconstruction and Development, and the International Monetary Fund. These aid regime members all imposed severe restrictions specifying precise projects for which the loans could be used, as well as required structural adjustment programs as strings attached to development capital, thereby essentially taking control of domestic policy making of these countries. Aid regimes thus became external forces affecting the balance of political forces and shaping state projects in developing countries. Private banks placed no such restrictions on their loans. Borrowing nations were free to use the loans in any way they saw fit, and so private bank loans offered an irresistible opportunity to escape from international aid regimes. In their zeal to place these loans, banks aggressively reassured the borrowing countries that they would have no problem servicing the debt. Developing countries' emancipation from the international debt regimes carried a steep price: after 1973, developing countries' combined global debt grew by over 500 percent, to almost half a trillion dollars (McNally 2010, 127), just as the oil crisis of 1973 plunged economies throughout the world into severe recessions. In response to the debt crisis, banks sharply increased the interest rates for these loans, sending developing countries tumbling over into deep recessions and near-bankruptcy. Thus, many former dependent nations in colonial relationships with Western countries entered into *economic* colonial relationships (or "colonization by proxy") with state and private actors from the West taking the reins of policy control away from those colonized countries through development funds.

The International Monetary Fund reappeared to offer rescue from insolvency and bankruptcy. But their life-saving offer demanded the imposition of a standard austerity package that required, among other things, a severe devaluation of the troubled economy's currency; a discontinuation of imports coupled with a substantial increase in exports to generate dollars in income; and sharp cuts if not outright elimination of social welfare expenditures, to support redeployment of gross national product to service the private bank loans. The combination of developing countries' crushing debt burdens and their subsequent acceptance of the draconian austerity package threatened the economies of the wealthier, industrialized and postindustrialized, countries. This is because the wealthier economies could ill-afford the tsunami of cheaper goods sure to be coming from the struggling economies and the loss of exports to them. But although the wealthier countries certainly felt the impact of the austerity packages, the greater economic wallop was felt in developing countries, where significant economic resources were being siphoned out of much-needed domestic programs and sent instead to private banks in the industrialized and postindustrialized West.

In an attempt to avoid accepting the standard austerity packages, many developing countries sought "debt for equity" swaps that ostensibly were designed to help ease developing countries' debt burden; but these essentially gave creditors a claim on valuable resources as the price of "forgiveness" of debt and accelerated the financial resource drain to the Western private banks (McNally 2010). And, because of persistently high interest rates, developing countries were unable to pay off their debts, even when they maintained minimum regular repayments, not unlike individual credit card users who find that minimum monthly payments to the banks mostly pay off interest owed, rather than paying down the principal.

Take the case of Argentina, for example, where debt grew from $40 billion to $132 billion between 1982, at the dawn of the debt crisis, and 2001:

> At IMF request, the government introduced repeated austerity programs. But its debts grew anyway, despite its two-decade effort to repay them. The most recent austerity program, announced in 2001, required the government to cut salaries and pensions for government workers. Teachers have not been paid for months, schools can no longer afford to boil water to make powdered milk for malnourished children, and public health officials no longer vaccinate dogs for rabies, leading to a widespread outbreak of the disease. (Schaeffer 2003, 110)

The austerity program, intended to reorganize Argentina's economy to stimulate recovery, resulted instead in severe social and economic consequences that ironically thwarted any possibility of economic recovery: unpaid workers will not be able to purchase consumer goods; malnourished children and a disease epidemic undermine the development of a strong and healthy workforce that are critical to the growth of a robust economy. Notably, Argentina was hardly alone in its economic struggles. UN reports suggest that what happened in Argentina was widespread, and a result of lopsided or "selective" capitalist development. Where a neocolonial approach to global capital emphasizes state actors managing imperialist systems as the key to the problem, Schaeffer's (2003) concept of "selective globalization" suggests a more structural explanation: capitalism works to centralize privately appropriated capital and wealth at the expense of impoverished populations who are systematically excluded from opportunities for financial independence. The implication here is that the balance of political forces operates on the global level as it does internal to nation-states to significantly affect state projects.

But where the concept of "selective globalization" suggests that crushing debt and economic crises beset impoverished states more profoundly than wealthy and advantaged states, the restructured global "free market" means that powerful states are actually similarly constrained. A notable feature of the global economic system is that this neoliberal, "free market" model binds states, their economies, and their banks in problematic dependent relationships. What started as mortgage and credit crises in the United States has quickly become a global recession. As a result, global populations continue to suffer, including those in more powerful states such as the United States, China, and several members of the European Union (as the struggles among European Union nations over Greece's most recent near-bankruptcy in July, 2015 demonstrate).

The severe economic contraction in the United States that began in 2008 thus was not isolated within its borders. National economies around the world plunged into the depths of economic crisis, including erstwhile prosperous European economies like Greece, Spain, Britain, Italy, Portugal, and Ireland, and oil-rich economies like Dubai. All faced the daunting challenge of balancing budgets plagued by a loss of tax revenues fueled by rising unemployment while facing increased pressures to address rising expenditures and debt to support the huge costs of post-911 military and security programs, corporate welfare, and social welfare. Bond markets, panicked by the constant stream of reports of deepening and widening economic crisis, downgraded the bond ratings of national economies; investors substantially divested their bond holdings, further exacerbating the situation and threatening to plunge some of the biggest economies in the world into default and bankruptcy (Taibbi 2011).

Faced with the horrendous prospect of a global economic meltdown, the world's wealthiest nations' central banks embarked on new incarnations of the state project of economic intervention. In the biggest bank bailout in history, spearheaded by the U.S. Federal Reserve, a transfusion of trillions of dollars was pumped directly into banks and into stimulus packages to encourage consumer spending. "All told, governments in the world's largest economies anteed up something in the order of $20 trillion—an amount equivalent to one and half times the U.S. gross domestic product—via a massive intervention without historical precedent" (McNally 2011, 2–3).

Here, the balance of political forces tilted once again toward the banks as state after state hesitated to antagonize the financial institutions whose decisions about allocating finance capital could negatively affect them: none of these governments demanded changes in how financial institutions do business as a quid pro quo for bailing them out. The very institutions whose high-risk and predatory practices plunged that state and the globe into the closest encounter with a Great Depression since the 1930s was going to be bailed out at no cost to itself and no changes in how they functioned. Unlike the banks in 1978, the state in 2008 missed an opportune moment to reassert banking regulations to rein in the behaviors that created the problem. And worse, at least in the United States, the same financial institutions that benefited from the federal bailout within months announced staggering bonuses for the executives who led these institutions, and the national economy, to disaster (Taibbi 2011; Ferguson 2012). The Great Bank Bailout did seem to avert an unthinkable national and global Great Depression, but did not erase the problem: "the bank debt that triggered the crisis in 2008 never went away—it was simply shifted on to governments . . . the bank crisis morphed into a sovereign debt crisis . . . it *mutated* [emphasis in original]" (McNally 2011, 4). And now, with all the risks and costs of the bailout firmly on the shoulders of the state, the burden and the costs ensuring private largess shifted to those who never benefited from that largess or worse, were unimaginably harmed by the institutional arrangements that enriched the few at the vast expense of the many.

CONCLUSION

This history of the state project of economic intervention illustrates some key elements of our MSP approach to state theory. The state project of economic intervention is a process whereby seemingly isolated and unrelated individual policies and practices are woven together over time, each influencing and shaping the other. That process is informed by the balance of political forces, which are animated and affected by factors such as the resources various participants can mobilize and apply in political opportunities to their advantage; the extent of unity within each of these interests and between these interests; and the resources and unity within and between state actors and agencies. Note that even the most potent and resource-rich institutional forces are not omnipotent (even when they enjoy collective control of a unique and critical resource, as the financial industry does): they do not get everything they want all the time (e.g.,, the passage of Glass-Steagall and CRA legislation). But they remain powerful forces in reasserting their interests better than many (or most) other actors, or at least in finding ways to subvert state project entries that impinge on their ability to do so, absent of a countervailing, well-organized and resourceful force, including the state itself. Moreover, state projects are not isolated within the borders of nation-states, but are instead permeated by external influences well beyond these boundaries.

Further, this history illustrates the necessity of an approach to state theory that attends to class divisions, but is not economistic, nor limited to class. The lending practices of big banks *and* global financial institutions demonstrate a tendency for working class and poor people of color to be targeted, while they bear the major costs of financial malfeasance; and global patterns of colonialism and neoliberal development lending tend to target poorer nations, while they bear the major costs of *global* financial malfeasance. One cannot isolate relations of inequality in the context of race, class, and nation of origin when examining state economic projects and the balance of political forces affecting those projects. Rather, clear lines can be drawn between these state projects and the complex intersections of imperialism, capitalism, and white supremacy.

What this discussion has not foregrounded here is the role of selectivity filters and framing. We now turn to those elements in the MSP approach by investigating state projects around sexuality and kinship, reinforcing heteronormativity.

Chapter 4

State Projects and Heteronormativity
Framing and Selectivity Filters

In addition to the process of balancing political forces discussed in the previous chapter, selectivity filters also function to frame and influence larger state projects. In this chapter, we will concentrate on the concept of identity to elucidate the ways in which selectivity filters function, maintain, and challenge heteronormativity within the heteronormative state project in the United States. Selectivity filters frame and shape meaning-making processes that affect, inform, and buttress the state project. They are created, maintained, challenged, and transformed through various forces from above (e.g., the state) and below (e.g., social movements focusing on policy change, cultural change, and altering daily life). The power to frame issues and affect selectivity filters raises questions such as: How are selectivity filters controlled, influenced, or affected? What factors allow selectivity filters to transform? What is the relationship between selectivity filters, framing, and the state? In this chapter, we will largely focus on heteronormative framing by using the lens of identity in order to demonstrate the power that accompanies access to frame concepts through selectivity filters within state projects. As noted previously, access to the power to shape and inform selectivity filters are held by both the state from above and subordinates from below in an ongoing process and struggle of meaning-making (oftentimes located within social movements).

Within the literature on critical theories of the state, a particularly useful concept emerged to show how the state has the ability to legislate around given issues precisely because they have cultural visibility—that is, the issues are socially legible. That concept, selectivity filters (Jessop 1990), outlines how our political economic organization is heavily influenced by the available language, framing, and social lenses which filter some things in for state policy while simultaneously filtering others out because they are not socially legible. In this chapter, we argue that the concepts of both 1) "sexual orientation" (and its concomitant rise as an identity that began to emerge in the mid-1800s and solidified in the twentieth century); and 2) binary gender act as selectivity filters for how the state legislates and recognizes some gender and sexual practices in policy making, but ignores or disciplines others. For example, because sexual orientation is a gendered (and binary) understanding of *sexual* practice and desire (meaning, as a concept and term, it describes sexual attraction in terms of binary gendered attraction, e.g., heterosexual/straight or homosexual/gay), it acts as a selectivity filter by filtering out sexual practices not primarily defined by their relationship to binary gender—this omission, for example, includes practices of having multiple lovers and romantic partners and a range of (consensual) non-monogamous relations, as well as nonnormative familial configurations. Likewise, the concept of binary gender acts as a selectivity filter for how the state heavily legislates around gender, as is demonstrated in the struggle for access to public bathrooms by transgender, nonbinary, and other gender nonconforming people.

Selectivity filters function alongside the process of balancing political forces discussed in the previous chapter to inform and shape larger state projects. We focus here on how selectivity filters frame policy with regard to sex, gender, and sexuality through the lens of identity, and how some social movement actors are attempting to access and transform these selectivity filters. We will trace the role of framing in the development and dispatch of selectivity filters by examining heteronormativity as a strong organizing and governing principle in the gendered and sexualized system of oppression and inequality by first defining heteronormativity and then examining the role of the state in defining gender and sexuality and upholding normative gender and sexual relations, as well as demonstrating the importance of incorporating gender and sexualities into state theory.

DEFINING SELECTIVITY FILTERS

The study of state projects falls within a wider discussion and debate around state theory. Within the field, debates surround different theories of the state including but not limited to: pluralism, instrumentalism, business dominance, capitalist state structuralism, state-centered structuralism, and class dialectic perspectives. These theories differ, as well as coincide, on issues of state autonomy, bases of political power, forms of conflict, the "nature" of the state, and what can be considered the agents of social change.

Jessop's (1990) concepts of state projects, selectivity filters, and the balance of class forces help to explain not only the relationship of state to society, but also the relationship among state, society, and oppression. One of

Jessop's contributions is to suggest that the relationship between state and society is not unidirectional (Glasberg and Shannon 2011, 173). Thus, the state does not lay claim as the only force able to affect change in the state-society relationship, but rather that society can, and also does, affect the state.

In simple definition, Jessop's (1990) "state project" is a set of state policies and agencies that are unified around a particular issue or goal. The balance of class forces is an ongoing process by which the social and political factors that affect class relations redefine these relations at particular points in time. Structural selectivity filters are the social, political, and perceptual filtering mechanisms that "offer unequal chances to different forces within and outside the state to act for different political purposes" (Jessop 1990, 367). Jessop (1990) claims that the way to understand the development of state strategies is by evaluating previous political strategies which have been debated and instituted. Political strategies build upon one another and outlast the actual people within the state—they become part of state projects. A state project includes a series of policies and the institutions that create them, the processes by which policies are implemented and changed, and how effective they are when implemented. The state project as a whole represents a relatively unified state strategy. Jessop (1990) does not focus on the power of the state as an *actor*, but as different dimensions of the state in the process of acting, reacting, and interacting.

In this concept, the state is both an "arena of struggle and an actor that above all other actors has the unique authority to codify social constructions into legalized norms and to enforce these in ways that shape cultural repertoires and social behaviors" (Glasberg and Shannon 2011, 176). At times, the state, and the struggle between the state and political forces, may result in policies that, for example, contradict heteronormativity. To understand what shapes these struggles it is necessary to understand the role of selectivity filters.

Selectivity filters are mechanisms through which policies (and the concomitant struggles against) are shaped and framed (Glasberg and Shannon 2011, 176). These can include cultural and ideological frames such as "anatomy is destiny" in the case of gendering, or "monogamy is morally superior to any other form of romantic relationship" in the case of understanding how monogamy as a part of state projects surrounding family, sexuality, and kinship are informed and framed. Both of these ideological frames are also constructed on embedded assumptions of sexuality and gender identity as binary and sexuality as occurring between only two people. These ideological frames shape policy makers' collective perceptions and the possibility of consideration given to alternative policies (Glasberg and Shannon 2011, 177). To be clear, this is not suggesting the state is neutral, but that "some interests or points of view become part of the process while others are ignored, silenced, or never considered," and thus, over time, "selectivity perpetuates biases in the state-society relationship" (Glasberg and Shannon 2011, 177). Part of this work is reminiscent of Armstrong and Bernstein's (2008, 85) work on the multi-institutional politics approach to social movements in which they write, "The state is as important for its role in establishing and supporting systems of meaning and classification as it is for its role in the allocation of resources." But what affects these selectivity filters?

Glasberg and Shannon (2011, 181) explain the process and relationship between state projects, selectivity filters, and the balance of political and institutional forces as such: 1) state projects as selectivity filters framing issues, 2) policy initiative, 3) passage of policy, 4) implementation of policy, and 5) entry of policy into larger state projects. Selectivity filters affect each one of these steps, as do the balance of political and institutional forces, making for a complex relationship among all three concepts. For example, these concepts can be used to examine the ways that the state legislates *against* non-monogamy (by passing and implementing laws, as well as framing political and cultural issues, which support and uphold monogamy as the "correct," and many times, *only available*, recognized romantic relationship formation, see, e.g., Heckert 2010).

What role do selectivity filters play in the state project of heteronormativity? To investigate this question, we must first understand the concept of heteronormativity.

DEFINING HETERONORMATIVITY

There is currently a substantial amount of theory and research centered on analyzing and investigating heteronormativity (see, e.g., Rubin 1984; Weeks 1985; Elman 2000; Stychin 2000; Seidman 2001; Schilt and Westbrook 2009; Andersen 2011). The term *heteronormativity* is often used to, perhaps primarily, describe the normative and expected *gender* configuration of romantic/sexual relationships, but the term is also a concept that refers to other normative expectations that, combined, make up heteronormativity: binary gender; dyadic, monogamous couples; marriage; procreation; cohabitation. Heteronormativity shapes and informs legal frameworks, legislation, and social and cultural expectations and assumptions. But before we move on, it is important to distinguish among the terms we are using.

We will be complicating these terms throughout this chapter, but the following definitions are the mainstream understandings which serve to reinforce heteronormativity. Heteronormative logic employs the following definitions: *sex* refers to physical anatomy (male, female, intersex); *gender* refers to the symbolism and social and cultural meaning attached to femininity and masculinity, as well as our legal status as women and men; *sexuality* refers to the capacity for erotic experience and response; and *sexual orientation* (often conflated with sexuality) refers to sexual identity in regards to one's gender and the gender they are attracted to (heterosexual, homosexual, bisexual). We complicate these definitions in this chapter; we argue that "sex" is likewise socially constructed and not solely "biological," that gender identity does not need to "match" one's sex, but can be an autonomous choice rather than a compulsory assignation, that gender identity and expression can refer to more than solely femininity and masculinity (e.g., gender nonconforming, nonbinary, gender-fluid, genderqueer, etc.), and that sexual orientation need not be solely understood through the prism of binary gender and that it is likewise not compulsory (not all people identify by their sexual desire). The heteronormative state project, as argued in this chapter, is predicated upon and maintains heteronormative conceptions of sex, gender, sexuality, and sexual orientation—a dynamic that cannot be explained by solely class-based models of the state and society relationship or class-based policy arenas.

Heteronormativity also describes the assumption of a linear and naturalized assumptive equation that aligns "biological sex," gender (identity and expression), and sexuality ("sexual orientation" and desire, broadly defined), as well as configuration of romantic and familial relationships. Several examples of legislation in the United States demonstrate a heteronormative logic or equation that frames policy-making activities: particular chromosomes lead to particular gonads, which lead to particular secondary sex characteristics, which lead to a particular gender, which leads to a particular gender identity and expression, which leads to particular gendered sexual orientation/desire, which ultimately leads to a desire to form a particular familial configuration. In this heteronormative logic, each one of these steps is assumed to lead toward, and be aligned with, the next step. Included in this logic is that assumptions can move backward along the same line: if a person's gender expression is known, then their gender identity and sex (and by extension, their X and Y chromosomal make up and their gonads, as well as the appearance of their secondary sexual characteristics) can likewise be deduced. It is this heteronormative logic that acts as a selectivity filter in numerous state and federal policies in the United States such as the recent moral panics around public bathroom usage as well as marriage policy remaining between two and only two people after the passage of legislation affirming same-sex marriage. Heteronormativity functions as a frame that social institutions and policies use as a filter when writing and enforcing policies that ultimately reinforce the presumption that heterosexuality is the norm and that gender and sex are natural and aligned binaries. This process within the heteronormative state project cannot be reduced to class-based explanations of relationships of domination, likewise demonstrating the need for a multi-sites of power approach to state theory.

Binary gender buttresses heteronormative logic which then serves as a selectivity filter. Binary gender refers to the assumption that there are two and only two genders, that these two genders are mutually exclusive (such as they can be viewed as different or "opposite" entities) and exhaustive (meaning that they, together, are able to describe and account for all existing human gendered expression and identity). Binary gender also informs what we know as "sexual orientation": an identity that describes a particularly gendered sexuality. Under heteronormative logic, there exists two sexual orientations: heterosexuality and homosexuality. Other forms of sexual identity or desire that have not manifested as sexual orientation are thus invisibilized (such as polyamory). Sexual orientations that may defy binary gender logic, such as bisexuality, are also invisibilized in larger mainstream culture and in legislative activity. Because configurations of desire have not (yet, perhaps) formed into a recognized "sexual identity," they are off the radar of many policy-making activities because they are not included in the selectivity filter of the state (Emens 2004; Tweedy 2011; Robinson 2013).

Given that part of the behavioral norms that make up heteronormativity can also be applied to same-sex relationships, *homonormativity* has been introduced as a term to describe otherwise normative relationships (binary gender, dyadic couples, monogamy, marriage or something "similar," cohabitation, etc.) that happen to be between two people of the same gender, or often normative expectations about relationships within queer communities (see, e.g., Elman 2000; Stychin 2000; Seidman 2001; Emens 2004; Jeppesen 2010; Mepschen et al. 2010; Andersen 2011). In the next section, we focus on particular policy-making activities to demonstrate the need for a multi-sites of power approach to state theory and state projects.

HETERONORMATIVITY, SELECTIVITY FILTERS, AND MULTIPLE SITES OF POWER

Legislation around sex, gender, sexuality, and kinship are informed by particular ideologies that then inform the selectivity filters that shape and frame policy initiatives and implementation. For example, anti-miscegenation laws in the United States were in effect from the late seventeenth century until 1967 when they were ruled unconstitutional under Loving v. Virginia. Anti-miscegenation laws enforced racial segregation by criminalizing inter-racial marriage (as well as sex and cohabitation between members of different "races"). One reason a multi-sites of power approach to state theory is needed is we can utilize an intersectional lens when looking at the case of, for example, anti-miscegenation laws. Using an intersectional lens, we can investigate both a racialized *and* heteronormative state project. In the United States, marriage and intimate relationships are controlled through state legislation that is influenced by not only normative expectations of gender and sexuality, but *racialized* normative expectations of gender and sexuality. That means we need a way to investigate how state projects of oppression intersect, such as the racialized state project and the heteronormative state project. That is, we are better equipped to understand the creation, implementation, and resistance to anti-miscegenation laws if we understand oppressions to be linked and interconnected.

Similarly, trans-discriminatory legislation also requires an intersectional lens to understand the selectivity filters that shape and frame this debate in the United States. It is difficult to grasp the complexity of these legislative debates unless we view gender and sexuality as overlapping, intersectional forms of oppression (and perhaps, the forms of liberation tied up in them). The same can be said about same-sex marriage. We cannot understand the terms homosexuality or heterosexuality without viewing gender as binary. Both homosexuality and heterosexuality rest on the assumption that there are two and only two genders.

For example, North Carolina's *House Bill 2* demonstrates how particular ideologies around sex and gender inform the selectivity filters that frame the policy initiatives, debates, passage, and effects of its implementation. Formally titled, *An Act to Provide for Single-sex Multiple Occupancy Bathroom and Changing Facilities in Schools and Public Agencies and to Create Statewide Consistency in Regulation of Employment and Public Accommodations*, this bill is considered to be the height of anti-LGBT legislation in the United States.[1] In the formal text, reference is made to both "biological sex" and "opposite sex," which are two terms that contain meaning beyond mere description. Biological sex is a term used to signify that sex is immutable, unchangeable, and merely physical biology with no concomitant infused social meanings. In the social sciences, that concept of sex has been interrogated and mostly replaced with more nuanced understandings of how categories of "biological sex" are always-already gendered (see, e.g., Fausto-Sterling 1987; 2000; Kessler 1990). To further expose the ideology that informs this legislation, the proponents refer to the bill as the "common sense bill."[2]

Ultimately, this legislation requires that people can only use restrooms and changing facilities in government buildings (which includes public schools) that match the sex indicated on their birth certificates. The ideology here is that of binary gender, which is part of heteronormative logic that "aligns" sex with gender. Thus, if one is claimed as female on their birth certificate they must use the "women's" restroom. It is clear, then, that sex (female) is

assumed to be aligned with gender (e.g., woman). One of the most discriminatory effects of the passage and implementation of this bill is that people
whose gender does not "align" with their sex according to heteronormative
logic are in effect forced to use the "opposite" bathroom. The concept of
"opposite" sex and/or gender further entrenches heteronormative ideology
that there are only two sexes and genders ("opposite" implies binary). Even
further, for most trans and gender nonconforming people to use the bathroom
that best represents their gender identity, they are required to change the sex
on their birth certificate, which further entrenches the idea that one must have
specified body parts to claim "woman" or "man." Currently, the only way to
change the sex on one's birth certificate is to have the required surgery, which
not all trans people can access and not all trans people desire. The legislation
defines "biological sex" as: "The physical condition of being male or female,
which is stated on a person's birth certificate."[3]

The implementation and resistance to this policy expose the selectivity
filters being used and contested, as well as the struggle to offer different
selectivity filters. Mostly, the opponents of this bill argue that it specifically
discriminates against trans people and that everyone should use the bathroom
that matches their gender identity rather than the sex indicated on their birth
certificates. To pass a bill that allows people to use the bathroom of their
choice that represents their gender identity transforms the heteronormative
logic that undergirds the current legislation and replaces it with new framing
that rests on the concept that gender is not necessarily aligned with "biological sex" and is, rather, up to the person to decide for themselves which bathroom to use (gender, then, becomes a more autonomous choice rather than an
assigned category). There have been numerous "selfie protests" which show
trans women in men's restrooms and trans men in women's restrooms in an
attempt to demonstrate how "out of place" they look in the restrooms they
are being forced to use under North Carolina's HB2.[4] However, this opposi-
tional framing might also uphold binary gender at times in a couple of ways:
1) the framing suggests that there should still only be men's and women's
bathrooms, and 2) the framing suggests that masculine-appearing people
don't belong in women's restrooms and vice versa. But what does this framing mean for gender nonconforming, gender-fluid, and nonbinary people—in
other words, what does this mean for people who may not claim either "man"
or "woman" as their gender or for people whose appearance doesn't conform
to normative gender standards, regardless of self-identification?

When civilians and law-enforcers attempt to both de facto and de jure
implement this law, they often become confused, and there are many vid-
eos on YouTube[5] which show masculine-appearing self-identified women
being forcibly removed from women's restrooms for not appearing feminine *enough*. This further demonstrates the heteronormative logic that sets

boundaries for the correct gender one may *claim*, but also the correct way to *communicate* that gender to the public. Fringes of the opposition are struggling for nongender/universal restrooms, which would remove gender as a component of public restrooms.

The struggle over access to public bathrooms highlights the confusion created by the use of language in shaping selectivity filters. It conflates the concepts of sexuality and gender identity, and casually interchanges these concepts incorrectly. We have already identified the important distinction between these concepts: sexuality refers to sexual desire, behavior, or practice; gender identity refers to our personal experience and interpretation of our own gender. Moreover, the struggle over bathroom access highlights the insistence on framing both as binary, a key selectivity filter in the heteronormative state project. A similar set of selectivity filter issues can be seen in the processes defining relationships, both formally state sanctioned (marriage) and informal (practices that are not state sanctioned, such as cohabitation and polyamory). For the remainder of this section, we will focus on same-sex marriage legislation and multi-partnered relationships, as well as normative expectations of kinship patterns, to highlight the role of selectivity filters in the heteronormative state project. Sexual orientation, *as identity*, has served as a selectivity filter in the larger state project around heteronormativity. Sexual identity, then, becomes a selectivity filter with a particular effect on both state projects around sexuality as well as the balance of political and institutional forces around sexuality (favoring identity-based legislative initiatives over more holistic and inclusive initiatives).

Legislation, (same-sex marriage, for example), politicians (Obama saying he supports monogamous gay couples getting married[6]), and media have the power to shape understandings of one's sexual self through selectivity filters. For example, Aviram and Leachman (2014, 1) write, "Same-sex marriage litigation has simultaneously reinforced cultural stigmas against polyamorous relationships—stigmas which constrain the practical utility of those legal tools (especially as means for implementing broader social change beyond the letter of the law)." We can see here how certain forms of legislation work against non-monogamy, for example.

In another, and perhaps broader, example of how legislation frames our understanding of our sexual selves, Zylan (2009, 2) writes, "The interrogation of anti-gay hate crime discourse helps illustrate a fundamental quality of law; namely, its power to constitute social reality. More specifically, I contend that law helps to constitute a predictive matrix of sex, gender, and the body that limits and constrains social expressions of sexual desire and experience." Bourdieu (1992) similarly writes that the role of the nation state is the "holder of the monopoly of legitimate symbolic power" which simultaneously enables certain (sexual) identities while preventing others (and we would argue, wholly excluding sexualities that have not become a "sexual orientation").

Actors like the president of the United States frequently use the "bully pulpit" of the office to declare and enforce selectivity filters. It was 2012 when Obama claimed on an *ABC News Special Report* with Diane Sawyer, "When I think about members of my own staff who are in incredibly committed monogamous relationships, same-sex relationships, who are raising kids together . . . at a certain point, I've just concluded that for me personally, it is important for me to go ahead and affirm that I think same-sex couples should be able to get married."[7] This is notable because this was well before the 2015 passage of same-sex marriage in the United States; Diane Sawyer was correct when she prefaced the report with, "This is a historic political and cultural moment in this country."[8] It was an enormous move for the president of the United States to make this claim on a popular national news outlet, but his utterance of supporting "monogamous couples" was more than merely description, it was actively delegitimizing non-monogamous and polyamorous romantic relationships (see, e.g., Sheff 2011). The relationship between these types of laws which hold significant symbolic power in society is interesting when we begin to examine the ways in which the reverse can be true—how might alternative cultural understandings of our sexual selves be able to (re)shape legislation (which, in turn, reshapes cultural understandings, and so on)? Tweedy (2011), for example, suggests strategically arguing for and recognizing polyamory as a sexual orientation with the purpose of gaining inclusion into the grouping of sexual minority with the intention of that allowing for inclusion within antidiscrimination statutes.

In part, the concept of non-monogamy is not found on our normative political registers because it has not passed through the selectivity filters of the state. One of the reasons for this is that state projects around sexuality are often based on sexual and gender practices which have, through historical processes, crystallized into identities (Jessop 1990; Glasberg and Shannon 2011). Since non-monogamy has not been accepted as a sexual *identity* in the same way identities such as gay, lesbian (and, to an extent, bisexual) have, it makes it very difficult to rally people and organizations around the issue of non-monogamy (see, e.g., Klesse 2006; 2007; 2014; Tweedy 2011). Again, state projects around gender and sexuality cannot be fully understood if we only deploy class-based analyses of the state-society relationship.

Queer theoretical contributions to the study of sexuality offer a space for thinking about sexualities that for various reasons have not formed into identities such as gay or lesbian. Broadly, queer theory interrupts and disturbs the assumptions of linearity and oftentimes the causality attributed to the anatomical sex, gender, and sexual desire "equation." Rather than assume a stable relationship among these three things, queer theory offers a critique of the assumed causality of and among them. Queer theory also offers a critique to what became known as ethnic-based (or "minoritarian") conceptions of sexuality. These ethnic-based understandings of sexuality assumed homosexuality, for example, to be similar to ethnic groups with a shared and traceable history, such as Jews or African Americans (Corber and Valocchi 2003, 2). Such ethnic-based models of sexuality were exemplified by quite a few famous historical works on homosexual histories in the United States (see, e.g., Katz 1975; Weeks 1977; D'Emilio 1983). One of the methodological problems is that while offering a history of homosexuality, these theories also reified many of the assumptions of stable sexual identities and reinforced the binary relationship between hetero- and homosexuality.

Sexuality-as-identity often relies on an ethnic-based model of sexuality. This model did allow for some positive developments such as creating a "gay community" with a shared identity, but some queer theorists argue that, ultimately, the disadvantages that accompanied this line of thinking outnumbered the advantages (Corber and Valocchi 2003). Some noted disadvantages were that a "normal" homosexuality began to develop which cast "abnormal" queers out—the beginnings of a form of homonormativity. This had the result of reinforcing notions of the "good" gay man or lesbian and the "bad" queer. As noted earlier, Obama upheld this concept of the "good gay" by placing committed, monogamous couples who are raising kids together as an example of an approved type of gay person. Again, instead of dissolving binaries and their concomitant unequal distribution of resources (tangible and not), this model reinforced sexual binaries, therefore ultimately upholding the stratification of different forms of sexual desire as well as the hierarchical organization of these different sexual identities which kept some from material and symbolic reward while allowing others to have plenty. Corber and Valocchi (2003, 3) noted that the gay and lesbian movement, then, became one (solely) for gay and lesbian *identity* rather than dissident sexualities—this difference is meaningful when applied to theory and practice. A decade later, this focus in the movement for positive gay and lesbian identities rather than recognition and de-stigmatization of all dissident sexualities (in essence, to abolish the idea of a dissident sexuality) is still quite pertinent. Under these conditions, non-monogamous and polyamorous people (regardless of sexual orientation) are stigmatized in law and culture (Moors et al. 2013).

The "good gay" and the "bad queer" can be explained further by Gayle Rubin's (1984) concepts of the charmed circle and outer limits: the charmed circle represents culturally approved and recognized sexualities while the outer limits represent dissident sexualities. For various reasons, alterations in the state project of heteronormativity allow dissident sexualities to enter the charmed circle (as when same-sex marriage was legalized in the United States in 2015). Rubin argues that by allowing others into the charmed circle, the schism between the "acceptable" families (and humans) and the "unacceptable" families (and humans) is reinforced even while the charmed circle is "widening." Now that we have witnessed the passage of same-sex marriage, we can see how this prediction has unfolded: rather than a multiplicity of romantic relationships being recognized by the state, we are seeing alternative forms of relationship recognition such as civil unions disappearing (see, e.g., Lowder 2015), leaving only state-sanctioned marriage as the sole form that romantic relationships must take to gain state recognition and the plethora of rights and benefits attached. As Rubin (1984) suggested decades ago, the effect of widening the charmed circle by letting other groups in (in this case, same-sex marriage) is that the charmed circle becomes reinforced and the outer limits become even more "abnormal," rather than the distinctions lessening or dissolving.

The dialectical relationships between state, society, oppression, and, perhaps, liberation become visible when we begin investigating the state project of heteronormativity, especially through the lens of identity as selectivity filter. For instance, some have found that there is quite a debate among people who practice non-monogamy as to whether non-monogamy (and/or polyamory) is a practice or an identity (see, e.g., Willis 2013). What's at stake when society views it one way or another and when the state views it one way or another? What's the relationship between the two entities and how can we struggle against the reproduction of any (consensually engaged) sexuality being considered deviant, abnormal, or dissident (Rubin 1984)?

Glasberg and Shannon (2011, 197) write, "the discursive frames that have been historically created in the history of sexuality can also serve as selectivity filters for what gets discussed and what gets ignored in state policy." This is largely because "sexual orientation" has come to only define *gender-specific* sexualities, namely, heterosexuality and homosexuality (and bisexuality, to an extent that it is recognized). This has had the effect of only legitimating and accepting *gendered* sexual orientations, recognized as identities, which then serve largely as a prerequisite for people of a certain sexual practice to be recognized as sexual minorities in the first place (which is then required for inclusion in antidiscrimination statutes).

Using the lens of identity as a selectivity filter in the larger state project of monogamy, for example, allows us to ask questions about how the framing of sexuality-as-identity trickles down into communities' and individuals' processes of meaning-making and vice versa—how these meanings also shape how sexuality is framed in state policies and their implementation. When Obama supports same-sex marriage for "*monogamous couples*," what type of meaning can be taken from this and used to form our understandings of "appropriate" sexual/romantic configurations? How might cultural meanings "trickle up" to oppose Obama's claim that to be "committed" equates to being in a monogamous dyadic relationship? How does this meaning get reproduced and resisted within communities? How can we challenge the idea that to be responsible in romantic configurations necessarily means being monogamous, being committed for life, and other numerous normative expectations of romantic partnerships (e.g., "raising kids together" and so on)? How can supporting or challenging the meaning of identity, in regard to non/monogamy, serve as a selectivity filter for the ways monogamy is framed within state projects—(how) can this be used as a tool for change?

TRANSFORMING SELECTIVITY FILTERS

When looking at state projects and how non-state actors can effect change, challenging the content of selectivity filters around particular issues and legislation is a fruitful endeavor. Selectivity filters frame issues in particular ways which then affect policy initiatives that lead to the passage of particular policies, implementation of these policies, and their entry into larger state projects. This is precisely why social movements often challenge language usage, conceptualizations and symbols, as well as state policy and everyday practice as they struggle through the balance of political forces. As such, selectivity filters, as well as the balance of political forces, as we demonstrated in the previous chapter, affect each and every step of state projects. The power to frame issues through selectivity filters is not solely held by the state. How do social movements vie for access to shaping, reframing, or transforming selectivity filters? Selectivity filters are social, political, and perceptual filtering mechanisms that "offer unequal chances of different forces within *and outside the state* to act for different political purposes" (Jessop 1990, 367, emphasis added). Given that the state is both an arena of struggle *and* an actor, who are the other actors outside of the state that are able to influence selectivity filters? Social movements, as we explore in the next chapter, often strategize to challenge the ideology informing the filters through which policy is made. In our next chapter, we focus on the racial state project and racial formation theory to examine the role of social movements in state projects.

CONCLUSION

Unpacking the heteronormative state project offers some insight to our MSP approach to state theory. The state project of heteronormativity is informed by selectivity filters, which are shaped and framed by both prior legislation, current legislative debates, current implementation of passed legislation, as well as how various participants and social movements can mobilize and influence and change the frames and selectivity filters to their advantage. Although Bourdieu (1992) said that the state is the "holder of the monopoly of legitimate symbolic power," the state is not omnipotent and must contest for the power to shape and frame selectivity filters, along with social movement actors. Moreover, and importantly, the state does not always win: sometimes there is passage of legislation that does not support the heteronormative state project (e.g., it could be argued that the passage of same-sex marriage is a legislative move against heteronormativity, though we argue that parts of the law also actually reinforce it). However, the state remains a powerful force in influencing selectivity filters and appropriating social movements' attempts to offer new and improved framing.

Investigating the heteronormative state projects illustrates that a state theory is needed that can explain state projects which are not reducible to class. Understanding heteronormativity as a state project requires recognizing the complex interplay among patriarchy, heteronormativity, white supremacy, and capitalism. Questions about the state's role in the re/production of gender and sexuality formations, and how the state's relationship to society affects these formations and processes are able to offer a more holistic theory of the state—one that includes, for example, the ability to explain the dominance of heteronormative policy making and its effects (Glasberg and Shannon 2011, 172–3). But it is not sufficient to simply replace existing concepts of class-based domination within debates around state theory with concepts attending to gendered, racialized, or heterosexist domination. Instead, "What is needed is a model of the relationship between the state and society that allows for an analysis of multiple oppressions and how they intersect and overlap in policy and everyday life" (Glasberg and Shannon 2015) and this is what the multi-sites of power approach to state theory can offer: an intersectional lens through which to theorize state projects.

This chapter demonstrates that the state legislates around existing selectivity filters including, but not limited to, class-based forms of inequality, although the state is, at times, challenged. What power can social movements harness when attempting to intervene in state projects? The next chapter looks at state projects and social movements though the lens of racial formation.

NOTES

1. See http://www.pbs.org/newshour/bb/how-north-carolina-signed-a-bill-dubbed-the-most-anti-lgbt-law-in-the-u-s/

2. See http://thefederalist.com/2016/05/09/the-truth-about-north-carolinas-bathroom-bill/

3. See http://www.ncleg.net/Sessions/2015E2/Bills/House/PDF/H2v4.pdf

4. See http://www.upworthy.com/heres-what-itll-look-like-if-trans-peo-ple-arent-allowed-to-use-the-right-bathroom and https://www.youtube.com/watch?v=5smx1W3wv2c

5. See https://www.youtube.com/watch?v=WYXtUvTl32c

6. See https://www.youtube.com/watch?v=kQGMTPab9GQ

7. See https://www.youtube.com/watch?v=kQGMTPab9GQ

8. See https://www.youtube.com/watch?v=kQGMTPab9GQ

Chapter 5

State Projects and Social Movements

Racial Formation and the State

The ebb and flow of the social construction of race and the racial formation process can be seen to emerge from the dynamics of cultural frames as selectivity filters and the balance of raced forces in social movements. This suggests the usefulness of an expanded use of Peattie and Rein's (1983) notion of the claims process (see also Koopmans and Statham 1999) and social movements as part of a multi-sites paradigm. Insofar as race is culturally conceptualized around assumptions regarding the biological bases of human differences, there is a claims process marked by struggles over shifting the line between the natural (biological) and the artificial (socially constructed) meaning of race. The state is hardly an innocent bystander in that process. Rather, the state is an active participant in the shaping and framing of the concept of "race," through policy and practice in the racial state project. Social movements, then, become an important element in the balance of political forces by galvanizing actors into the claims process and applying organized pressure to the process of the state project.

The concept of social movements is crucial to the notion of the balance of political forces, since it is a key factor stimulating the dynamics of that balance. In this chapter we will foreground the concept of social movements to examine how social movements animate and affect the balance of political forces in the racialized system of oppression in the United States and the racial state project. While the power of the state and of economic dominants in society is formidable in advantaging and privileging them and oppressing others, their power is not absolute. Indeed, throughout the process of state projects, nonelites may pose a significant countervailing force and alter the direction of the state project by resisting, challenging, subverting, and otherwise confronting institutional power relationships and the policies that emerge in the state project. By doing so, they are instigating change from the bottom up, primarily through the mechanism of social movements. The notion of resistance from the bottom raises several questions: When and how do social movements emerge? What factors may affect the effectiveness of social movements? What is the relationship between social movements and the state? Here, we will focus on the civil rights movement in general, and the Black Lives Matter movement in particular, to foreground the impact of social movements on the balance of political forces and state projects.

RACIAL STATE PROJECTS AND THE DEFINITION OF "RACE"

Research in race theory suggests a challenge to state theory that focuses exclusively on economic and class relations and oppression. For example, analysts using racial formation theory (Omi and Winant 1990; Ignatiev 1995; Haney Lopez 1996; Winant 1994; 2000) emphasize that conceptualizations of race as a matter of biology have no meaning. Instead, they argue, "race" is *socially* constructed, the product of ongoing political struggles over its very meaning and its implications for people's political, social, and economic rights (Stevens 1999; Yanow 2003). This analysis implies a role of the state in the process of socially constructing race, since the state is involved in much policy making and political maneuvering relative to racialized issues. As such, the state is a racial state (Goldberg 2002; Calavita 2005). Other observers are more explicit: rather than a racial state in society, the state is a racist state, in which racialized inequalities are embedded in the very structure of the state (Feagin 2001; Cazenave 2011).

At the very least, the state has clearly been an arena for battles over rights, sparked by a claims process challenge posed by civil rights movements. Much like the gendering claims process described by Peattie and Rein (1983), the racial formation claims process involves a struggle over shifting the line between the "natural" or biological and the artificial or political. How much of racialized inequality and oppression is simply a matter of biology, wherein one race (whites) is inherently genetically superior and all others genetically inferior (see, e.g., Herrnstein and Murray 1994), and therefore immutable and nonresponsive to reform policy? How much of racialized inequality and oppression is more a matter of social constructions that therefore can be challenged and altered with political struggle and legislation? Historically, civil rights movements around the world have set such claims processes in motion and challenged the racial regimes that are "steeped in discriminatory or exclusionist traditions" (Winant 2000, 177–8), much like feminist claims processes have challenged gender regimes.

Contemporary racial theory has had difficulty explaining persistent racial inequality and oppression that legislative reform by the state should have been expected to eliminate. For example, ethnicity-based theories (see Smith 2001) of race, which view race as a culturally rooted notion of identity, expect integration, equal opportunity, and assimilation to be the antidotes to prejudice and discrimination: the more contact we all have with one another, the more we will understand, appreciate, and accept one another as equals. However, ethnicity-based theories of race are limited by the fact that despite civil rights legislation, serious structural obstacles persist to limit the success of legislation which may have mandated the social and political rights of individuals to be included but did not mandate the substantive economic resources necessary for accessing those rights (Massey and Denton 1993; Lipsitz 1998). Furthermore, the notion of assimilation was predicated on people of color willingly assimilating to white dominant cultural norms, a prospect that was less than appealing to many. The result of this limitation of ethnicity-based theory is the production of analyses that blame people of color themselves for adhering to a race-consciousness that harms their ability to assimilate (Thernstrom and Thernstrom 1997), or that reasserts the importance of defending a "national culture" threatened by immigration and integration (Balibar and Wallerstein 1991; Taguieff 2001).

Class-based analyses of race saw racial conflict as an arena in which class-based struggles were played out: limited resources and opportunities drove a wedge between members of the same class who were differentiated by their membership in different racial groups and pit them one against the other (Bonacich 1972; 1976; Reich 1981; Gordon et al. 1982; Wilson 1996a; Frymer 2008). These analysts expected class consciousness to override the racial divide, and legislation like affirmative action to correct the effects of prior discrimination. However, class consciousness has not evolved to transplant race-consciousness; indeed, as gainful employment opportunities become scarcer, growing competition causes whites to increasingly seek to protect the invisible privileges of whiteness (McIntosh 1992) and to resist affirmative action programs, making it more difficult to recognize their common class position with people of color. And many observers have noted that while Donald Trump's presidency has not embraced the interests of the working class (beyond the promises and rhetoric of "American jobs" for "American workers"), it has inflamed and capitalized on long-simmering racial divides that obscure the commonalities of workers across that divide.

Where ethnicity-based and class-based analyses of race and racial inequality focus on individuals in racial groups or the groups themselves, racial formation theory focuses on the state and political processes that socially construct the meaning of race. Rather than being an immutable, stable construct of clearly defined categories and dimensions, race becomes an ongoing, shifting process in which meanings, identities, dimensions, rights, and oppression are constantly contested and reformulated politically. Racial formation processes are subject to the discursive and interpretational perspectives and actions of a wide range of actors, from individuals to groups and social movements, as well as to structures and institutions, history and politics, both national and international. Here, the state is both an arena and an actor, engaged in these struggles over legislation and meaning.

The literature of race and the state tends to de-emphasize the state's use and sanction of violence in the reproduction of systems of racial inequality and oppression in the racial state (see, e.g., James 1996; 2000). The state frequently uses racial profiling against people of color in policing (see www. aclu.org for constant updates and press releases of racial profiling), for example, and has historically tolerated lynching of African Americans at the hands of white vigilantes, allowing acquittals of lynchers by all-white juries (Kato 2015). Jury-selection processes that routinely reject the seating of jurists of color have been challenged in many states as racist and therefore unconstitutional in denying people of color the right to due process and a trial by a jury of peers. This practice of jury selection continues today, contributing in no small way to the overrepresentation of African Americans and Latinx in jail and on death row. In essence, when the state sanctions racism in court proceedings and in policing, it is in fact participating in an institutionalized lynching. And when state policy denies convicted felons the right to vote for life, it is compounding the violence by disenfranchising a substantial segment of the population of color, ensuring a hardening of systems of racial inequality that reinforces white privilege (Uggen and Manza 2002).

Yet, as powerful as the racial state is, it is nonetheless not inexorable. It is subject to pressures from below to alter and change the form and content of racial formation processes. This becomes evident in the ebb and flow of racial formation state projects.

RACIAL FORMATION STATE PROJECTS

State projects of racial formation contribute to the social construction of race through legislation, policy implementation, and judicial determinations governing such issues as slavery, segregation and integration, civil rights (including enfranchisement of African Americans in the political process), affirmative action, multilingualism, immigration, and census definitions and redefinitions of racialized categories. These policies, as entries into the state project of racial formation, affect the social construction of race insofar as they participate in redefining the meaning and social significance of race, thereby affecting the life chances of both whites and people of color.

Much of the racial formation state project has served to create and reinforce a social construction of race in a society based on white superiority, such that people of color remain oppressed and subordinate to whites politically, socially, and economically (Marable 1983; Brown 1995; Quadagno 2000; Neubeck and Cazenave 2001; Reese 2005). However, there clearly are policies enacted and implemented by the state that alter the social constructions of race such that the social, political, and economic positions of people of color in a racialized society, and thus their life chances, may be improved (see Fording 2001; King 2017). What, then, are the dynamics of oppression and resistance? How do these affect the state policies that both perpetuate racial formation state projects enhancing racism and white supremacy and expand the empowerment of people of color, thus challenging and mitigating white dominance?

Several researchers have pointed to the role of the state in reinforcing racist stereotypes that reproduce racial inequality. For example, Marable (1983) has forcefully argued that the racist state has served to underdevelop African Americans in the United States through a combination of constitutional amendments, Supreme Court decisions, and institutionalized cultural practices. These include Article I Section 9 of the Constitution defining slaves as three-fifths of a human being, voting restrictions based on race, chattel slavery , sharecropping, segregated educational institutions, etc. (See also Omi and Winant 1986; Wilson 1996a). More recently, welfare reform, with its provisions concerning workfare, has reproduced racist social constructions in that its implementation has primarily harmed women and children of color. This is because women of color face far more limited opportunities than white women in the labor market as a result of institutionalized racist assumptions about work ethic, intelligence, and ability. The state refused to acknowledge racism in the economic institutions as it aggressively enacted and implemented a Draconian welfare system of benefit denial and short eligibility definitions. The state thus contributed to and reinforced racially constructed (and gendered) inequality and oppression (Leiberman 1998; Quadagno 2000; Neubeck and Cazenave 2001). And most recently, predatory lending practices among banks as standard operating procedures have been found to routinely target populations of color such that home ownership, a central element of the American Dream, is denied to people of color through foreclosure, and thus racialized wealth inequality is reinforced (Beeman, Glasberg, and Casey 2009).

Taken together, these policy implementations and interpretations serve to reiterate a social construction of race in a society based on white superiority, such that people of color generally remain subordinate to Euro-Americans politically, economically, and socially. Yet, as we saw in the gendering state project, there are obviously policies enacted and Supreme Court determinations handed down that alter the content of the social construction of race intended to improve the life chances of people of color. The question, then, is: what are the dynamics and the conditions under which the racial state participates in the perpetuation of racial formation state projects that enhance white privilege and racism, but that may also produce policies expanding the empowerment of people of color to successfully challenge that privilege?

Cultural and ideological frames form institutional selectivity filters biasing and shaping the racial formation state project. For example, language functions to reinforce white superiority by privileging whiteness as the standard of normal. The very word "race" is defined as a biological category defining human differences, such that physical attributes such as color of skin, texture of hair, or shape of lips or eyes, or socially constructed attributes such as language (i.e., Spanish) or geographical location (particularly Asia, Africa, and Latin America) are presumed to indicate different subspecies of humans. These subspecies are then hierarchically arranged, with whites at the top of the hierarchy and all others arranged below (see, e.g., Herrnstein and Murray 1994). Repeated themes of white saviors in film and television fare reiterate the notion that people of color are inferior people in need of being saved by well-meaning superior whites (Hughey 2014). Pejorative racial epithets, stereotypes, and cultural tropes used to describe people of color thus underscore assumptions of biological inferiority. While such pejoratives and stereotypes describing white ethnics clearly exist, these are not based on immutable biological characteristics but rather on perceptions of ethnicity as changeable cultural choices (Bonilla-Silva 2013; Moore 1995; Wilson 1996a).

Racist stereotypes describing people of color as less intelligent, less educated, more violence-prone, and less hard-working than whites become institutionalized in the labor market, where people of color are far more likely than whites to be unemployed and poverty-stricken (Wilson 1987; 1996b). Most pointedly, a recent study compared white with African American and Latinx job applicants and found that applicants of color were half as likely as white applicants to be called back for another interview or a job offer, even when white applicants had recent criminal records and jail time (Pager, Western, and Bonikowski 2009). In addition, people of color are also more likely to be underemployed in menial, lower-autonomy, lower-paying, dead-end jobs in the service sector or in nonmanagerial blue collar jobs. Even when people of color do find employment in managerial jobs, they face a glass ceiling beyond which it is extremely difficult to rise (U.S. Department of Labor 1991; Benjamin 1991; Feagin 1991; Turner, Fix and Struyk 1991; Cose 1992; Tomaskovic-Devey 1993; Feagin and Sikes 1994).

Racist cultural stereotypes are reiterated in educational institutions, where children of color are highly likely to be segregated into school systems with inadequate budgets and facilities (Kozol 1991; Clotfelter 2004; Bogira 2011). African American children are disproportionately tracked into classes for the "educable mentally retarded" and white children far more likely to be tracked into programs for the gifted and talented or college-bound (Edelman 1988). Textbooks and other materials tend to be written for a predominantly white Anglo student body, with the historical and cultural contributions of people of color largely ignored or accorded such brief coverage as to imply that these are unimportant, and that only whites have done anything significant and positive (Apple and Christian-Smith 1991; McCarthy and Crichlow 1993), thus symbolically annihilating people of color.

White superiority ideologies and culture together act as selectivity filters reinforcing a framing of racial formation biasing policy formation and implementation. This prism interacts with the balance of raced forces in a dialectical process producing policy creation and implementation. The ability of people of color to gain advantageous policy is shaped by a claims process similar to that in gendering processes in which the line between the biological or natural and the socially constructed notions of race are shifted. This process is conditioned by the balance of raced forces. People of color are more likely to gain passage and implementation of advantageous state policy when there is greater unity of perspective among a large number of people of color (and often with the support of whites, an indication of a lack of unity among whites) who are organized in formal organizations and networks to address racism and racial inequality. They are more likely to become organized when faced with (or when they perceive) an imminent threat to their life chances (King 2017). For example, increased incidents of police brutality and violent hate crimes targeting people of color have elicited organized protests and demands for legal and legislative action, as has mounting evidence of continued segregation and discrimination in schools (Kozol 1991; Bogira 2011; Reardon et al. 2012), labor markets (Wilson 1987; Kirscheman and Neckerman 1991; Cloeman 2011; National Urban League 2014), credit access (Glasberg 1992; Squires 1994), housing (Beeman, Glasberg, and Casey 2009; Iceland, Weinberg, and Steinmetz 2002), and the location of toxic waste sites (Lombardi 2015; Pulido 2000; Westra and Lawson 2001; Bullard 1983; 1993; 2002; Bryant and Mohai 1992).

Such efforts to gain advantageous legislation and implementation of policies and programs are more likely to succeed when whites are less unified in their opposition to challenges to white superiority, when there is disunity between state branches or agencies, or when crises in other institutions increase the legitimacy of the demands of people of color. For example, the Constitution's usage of *freedom from* (as opposed to *freedom to*) supports a notion of negative freedom rather than positive freedom: "Positive freedom involves the creation of conditions conducive to human growth and the development and realization of human potentials. . . . Negative freedom is freedom from restraints and from government intrusion" (Wilson 1996a: 29; see also Myrdal 1948/1975; Dollard 1949).

The emphasis, then, on "freedom from" creates a cultural filter protecting slavery, discrimination, and racism, rather than equality of life chances. This cultural filter remained intact until the Supreme Court altered its patterns of decision-making from an emphasis on equal treatment to one of fair and equitable outcomes, signaling disunity between state branches and agencies. That disunity created an opportunity for an alteration in the balance of racially formed forces, such that an organized civil rights movement could become more empowered to press an agenda of resistance and challenge to racism in the state and society. Civil rights organizations also became highly sophisticated at networking, such that black churches, student organizations such as SNCC, labor unions, and other organizations such as CORE and the NAACP commonly operated together in developing strategies to challenge institutional racialized practices and traditions (Morris 1984). Moreover, the balance of political and institutional forces was further affected by the ability of civil rights groups to create mass disruption through boycotts, sit-ins, marches, and other demonstrations and organized protests (McAdam 1982; Morris 1984; King 2017), as well as riots.

In the 1980s and 1990s, with the civil rights movement in a more quiescent, less militant period of abeyance than in the 1950s–1970s, backlashes and challenges to the shift in the balance of racially formed forces have intensified and redeployed into seemingly nonracial (i.e., class or economic) policy arenas such as welfare reform and attempts to repeal or undermine affirmative action (see Lieberman 1998; Quadagno 1994). The effect of the return to "unbiased" or "neutral" concepts like "freedom from Big Government" in a context of a less-active and vigilant civil rights movement and a more organized, resource-rich, and motivated backlash movement has been a perpetuation of racism (King 2017).

Cultural assumptions that people of color (particularly African Americans and Latinx) are violent and less intelligent than whites are additionally perpetuated by the disproportionate representation of people of color under the control of the criminal justice system, including those on death row (Radelet 1981; Culver 1992; Gottschalk 2006; Garland 2010); police brutality of people of color on the streets, which is frequently condoned by the failure of courts and police review boards to punish such unequal and brutal misapplication of the law (Cashmore and McLaughlin 1991; Harris 2014); differential treatment of people of color relative to whites in bail setting (Houston and Ewing 1992); political disenfranchisement of significant proportions of populations of color through criminal justice policies permanently denying voting rights to convicted felons (Uggen and Manza 2002; Manza and Uggen 2008); underrepresentation of people of color on juries; and the differential treatment of immigrants and the granting of visas based on racist stereotypes (Cose 1992), including the notion of Asians as "model minorities" (Chou and

Feagin 2008) in contrast to immigrants from Latin America and Africa who are largely considered undesirables (Takaki 1982; Zolberg 1990; van Dijk 1993; Haney Lopez 1996; Rose 1997).

Cultural assumptions and everyday practices together act as selectivity filters framing the broader racial state project, and become part of the target in the balance of political forces as social movements coalesce to take issue with their content, meaning, and significance in affecting real lives. What exactly are social movements, and how do they function to affect the balance of political forces?

DEFINING SOCIAL MOVEMENTS

The notion of "race" and the larger racial state project has been, and continues to be, subject to ongoing challenge, resistance, and change. But such change does not just happen randomly or by some haphazard, inexplicable accident. Concerted actions by people shape political and social power structures, whether this occurs at the hands of dominating elites or of oppressed non-elites who resist domination. Importantly, we are not suggesting all elites and oppressed groups enjoy the same ability to affect power structures. Dominating elites and institutions have access to critical resources and opportunities that pose significant obstacles and disadvantages to the oppressed in their quest to redress grievances. But this does not mean that the obstacles or disadvantages are absolute or insurmountable, rendering nonelites completely powerless to resist and affect power structures: social changes clearly do occur, sometimes over and above the strenuous objections of the advantaged and privileged elites.

For example, the social and political position of people of color in the United States relative to whites is quite different, if not equal, today than it was 100 years ago. Supreme Court decisions such as 1954's Brown v. Board of Education, make maintaining segregated schools unconstitutional; and a subsequent series of decisions up to and including the 2016 case of Fisher v. the University of Texas at Austin uphold the constitutionality of affirmative action policies as a way to deliberately interrupt past practices of racist discrimination in higher education admissions policies. Changes in the racial state project such as these raise the question: How do subordinates and oppressed people affect power structures and elicit social change, if so much occurs by and for the already privileged? Specifically, how have people of color challenged and resisted the racial state project to change the social and institutional constructions of race?

Individuals have very limited ability by themselves to effectively resist and challenge the privilege and power of dominant elites and institutions and the power structures that reinforce that advantage. A single, solitary voice alone is unlikely to gain much attention, and indeed may not even get heard. One slave protesting the harsh and inhumane conditions of slavery could easily be ignored if not brutally penalized or even killed for simply raising the question. However, many individuals acting together are more difficult to ignore or silence. An important key, then, to social change from below is collective, organized resistance and action. Organized, collective efforts by many individuals working together, that is, social movements, have historically propelled potent challenges to the powerful. Social movements are large-scale, persistent means of resistance that work beyond the legitimized institutional avenues to redress grievances by engaging in claims making, lobbying and related activity, and direct action that interrupts business as usual. While social movement participants generally share the broad goals of the movements, they are not monolithic: members may disagree about the tactics and strategies the movement adopts, which can affect the efficacy of the movement. And while being well-organized is a necessary element of social movements, that in and of itself is not sufficient for their effectiveness: much depends upon their access to political opportunities to assert their claims as well as the magnitude of institutional response to their efforts (McAdam and Snow 1997). In addition, social movements often involve multiple organizations and networks, and can be "focused on changing one or more elements of the social, political and economic system within which they are located" (Ballard, Habib, and Valodia 2006, 3).

Social movements thus become organized mechanisms to challenge and resist domination. But how exactly do they do so? What facilitates or hinders their effectiveness?

SOCIAL MOVEMENT STRUCTURES, TACTICS, AND STRATEGIES

Social movements focused on resistance against powerful institutional and elite oppression may provide organizational opportunities for producing change from the bottom up within nations. But they may also facilitate the resistance of relatively powerless populations to affect international relations as well. An international resistance movement that included massive organized disinvestment strategies worked in tandem with an internal resistance movement (the ANC) within South Africa to battle against racist apartheid there in the 1980s and 1990s. Civil unrest and protest in South Africa, along with international sanctions, trade embargos, boycotts, and disinvestment of corporations doing business in and with South Africa ultimately led to the dismantling of apartheid and the election of its first black president.

Social movements are commonly networks of many social movement organizations working on issues of common interest. The civil rights movement, for example, has been a broad network of groups such as black churches, the National Association for the Advancement of Colored People (NAACP), Southern Christian Leadership Conference (SCLC), Congress of Racial Equality (CORE), Student Nonviolent Coordinating Committee (SNCC), the Commission for Racial Justice, By Any Means Necessary, and scores of professional organizations such as Black Sociologists' Association, among perhaps hundreds of other local and national groups. While each organization pursues its own specific agenda and set of activities, together they work to apply collective pressure on local, state, and federal governments to adopt and enforce policies protecting and expanding equal civil rights of all regardless of racial identification, and to challenge cultural and ideological perceptions of the significance of "race."

In addition to the loose networking and collective efforts of many social movement organizations, broad social movements may often contain several branches differentiated by their goals and strategies, and these may coexist as part of the larger, more general movement. Within the broader civil rights movement, for example, Dr. Martin Luther King, Jr. and Malcom X each pursued sharply contrasting strategies to press for the eradication of racism. Where Dr. King's tactics involved nonviolence, civil disobedience, and massive demonstrations, Malcom X preferred tactics framed as "by any means necessary," up to and including violence. The two leaders often sparred over the most effective strategy, and followers to be sure pursued actions accordingly while recognizing their common goal (Howard-Pitney 2004; Waldschmidt-Nelson 2012).

Although differences of goals and strategies may splinter social movements into several branches, these divergent branches often share a need to resist and change existing structures of oppression. The question still remains: Why do social movements occur in the first place, and how do individuals' grievances coalesce to become collective efforts in challenging oppression?

EXPLAINING SOCIAL MOVEMENTS

Absolute and Relative Deprivation Theories

Some observers explain the rise of social movements in general and revolutions in particular as ignited by deprivation: when people are deprived of what they need, or what they believe they need, they will rebel. For example, Karl Marx and Friedrich Engels (1967) argued that the capitalist political economy is arranged in such a way as to polarize the working class and the capitalist class: the rich will get richer because of their ownership and control over labor and the means of production, and the poor will get poorer because of their lack of such ownership and control. Eventually, the workers would suffer emiseration, or absolute deprivation: the most basic requirements of survival would be unaffordable for them. In order to survive, workers who are lucky enough to still be employed would have to work longer hours at lower wages; more and more workers would be entirely unemployed as their labor was displaced by machines or their work was exported elsewhere, where labor was exploited at even cheaper wages. Marx and Engels argued that intolerably emiserated workers would eventually collectively revolt to over-throw the social structure that caused their oppression because they would have nothing more to lose.

Popular media analyses of the civil rights movement in the United States often apply a variation of an emiseration thesis in their depiction of the civil rights movement as sparked by a single act of resistance: when Rosa Parks could no longer tolerate chronic racist oppression, she expressed her resis-tance by refusing to give up her seat on a Birmingham, Alabama bus to a white man. The application of emiseration, or absolute-deprivation, theory here points to one of its limitations: not all social movements are prompted entirely by absolute economic deprivation. Rosa Parks may certainly have suffered from deprivation of civil rights, but the fact that she was employed in a cultural context of minimum wage laws suggests that she had at least a minimum, if not middle-class, ability to purchase what she needed for basic survival. And one could argue that slavery imposed a clearer case of abso-lute deprivation in a setting in which mass rebellion in response would have presumably been unsurprising; and yet, apart from episodes of organized rebellion and insurrection, such as the 1739 Stono Rebellion, the 1741 New York City Conspiracy, Gabriel's Conspiracy of 1800 in Virginia, the 1811 German Coast Uprising in Louisiana, and Nat Turner's Rebellion of 1831 (Gates 2013), mass, widespread resistance did not materialize after these episodes were squashed.

Indeed, James Davies (1962; 1969; 1974) took issue with the notion of absolute deprivation as the source of revolutions (and his work sug-gests insights to social movements in general). He found that historically revolutions did not occur when people's material conditions reached a level below basic survival. Rather, he noted, such organized rebellions occurred in response to people's *perceptions* of deprivation, or relative deprivation. Davies argued that people's perception of deprivation is *relative* to conditions around them, conditions they expect, or conditions that previously existed but no longer do. People are more likely to revolt when a gap opens, over time, between the material conditions they expect and the material conditions that actually exist (see also Klandermans, Roefs, and Olivier 2001). Although

Davies's notion of relative deprivation referred primarily to people's material conditions as economic circumstances, his thesis can also be applied to social and political conditions. According to Davies, people can commonly live with that difference between their expected and their real conditions without resistance; revolutions will not occur until real conditions begin to lag further behind expectations. Thus, it is not necessary for real conditions to deteriorate to the point of emiseration, as Marx and Engels believed, or even deteriorate at all; it is sufficient that real conditions simply get worse or stagnate while expectations continue to rise; or for real conditions to continue to improve, but at a slower pace than the improvement of expectations.

As persuasive as the theses of absolute and relative deprivation may be, both explanations imply a spontaneous combustion of social dissatisfaction. They assume that at some point conditions will become absolutely intolerable, or the difference between expectations and real conditions will suddenly become intolerable, and a large group of people will rise together and revolt. But while dissatisfaction may be necessary for social movements and revolutions to erupt, it may not be sufficient. What is missing here is an analysis of what people would need in order to see the situation similarly, notice that others share that vision and a vision of what to do about it, and have the resources to realize that vision and opportunities to apply resources in an effective way.

Resource Mobilization

No matter how intolerable conditions may be, people may not form social movements or revolt unless they have access to resources to help them organize and mobilize a shared definition of their situation and develop a shared vision of strategic responses. They need human resources to articulate their frustration and formulate a strategy for response; leadership to organize and mobilize others; tangible resources, such as financial backing, to disseminate their message, support and legally defend endangered or jailed participants, and communicate widely with other potential supporters; and networks of other groups of people or existing organizations that can contribute their resources in a combined effort (McCarthy and Wolfson 1996; Gamson 1996). More recent researchers have begun to explore the powerful resource of social media and the internet in quickly and widely disseminating information of resistance and in organizing resistance actions (Pudrovska and Ferree 2004; Narayan, Purkayastha, and Banerji 2011).

For example, social media such as Twitter facilitated the quick mobilization and maintenance of resistance movements like the Arab Spring and Occupy Wall Street (Markham 2014; Tremayne 2014; Penney and Dadas 2014; Gerbaudo 2014). More recently, social media became a key factor in quickly disseminating YouTube video footage of excessive and deadly use of police force and violence against people of color on the streets across the United States; a Facebook post by Alicia Garza decried the alarming growth of lethal use of force against people of color, noting that the increase in people's anger was rooted in the insistence that "black lives matter"; and her Facebook post drew widespread attention when Patrisse Cullors hash-tagged that phrase. The use of social media thus sparked the rise and immediate spread of Black Lives Matter, as Garza and Cullors, together with Opal Tometi, created the platform #BlackLivesMatter, generating a nationwide conversation about race, police violence, and racism in the United States (Craven 2015; Edwards and Harris 2015; Lebron 2017). In short, revolutions and other social movements are unlikely to occur in the absence of access to critical supportive resources. Sociologists refer to this explanation of social movements as *resource mobilization theory.*

Morris (1984; 1999) found resource mobilization theory a useful framework to help explain the rise of the civil rights movement in the United States. He found that African Americans everywhere did not suddenly and simultaneously get frustrated enough to rebel against racist oppression. Instead, he found, leaders in several African American organizations mobilized resources and combined their organizational efforts to become a powerful collective force in challenging segregation and other forms of racialized discrimination in the United States.

Morris's analysis reframed popular accounts that personalized the civil rights movement in the defiance of Rosa Parks and the charismatic leadership and civil disobedience of Martin Luther King, Jr. Morris demonstrated that the civil rights movement was much greater than one person. Rev. King was certainly the most visible and stirring speaker articulating the issues, able to galvanize and mobilize great numbers of individuals. But Morris found that the civil rights movement was actually the result of the collective efforts of the National Association for the Advancement of Colored People (NAACP), the Southern Christian Leadership Conference (SCLC), the Student Nonviolent Coordinating Committee (SNCC), and the Congress of Racial Equality (CORE), as well as African American churches, white faith communities, labor unions, student organizations, and local small businesses. Together these organizations combined their efforts and mobilized vast resources in support of the movement. Instead of having to organize individuals one at a time, the leadership was able to capitalize on their existing organizational memberships, communication networks, and monetary resources to quickly and effectively mount boycotts, marches, voter registration drives in hostile southern states, and acts of civil disobedience such as sit-ins at lunch counters.

Morris's research illustrates how social movements rely on the strategic mobilization of resources to empower people who are relatively powerless, disadvantaged, oppressed, and largely disenfranchised from the dominant institutions of society. The civil rights movement managed, against over-whelming odds and historical tradition, to push for reform, if not outright elimination, of oppressive and rigidly racist cultural repertoires, practices, and laws that had denied African Americans basic civil rights. Morris's work also implies the importance of framing and identity as a resource in mobiliz-ing people to participate.

Research on frames and identities explores how people become involved as political actors in and supporters of movements. For example, Snow and Benford (1988, 198) found that social movement organizations and their sup-porters commonly "frame or assign meaning to and interpret relevant events and conditions in ways that are intended to mobilize potential adherents and constituents, to garner bystander support, and demobilize antagonists." Other research has identified frame alignment as the mechanism which social move-ment organizations use to encourage prospective participants to share their interpretations. Tarrow (1983; 1994) and Klandermans (1984; 1988), for example, found that agents within social movements capitalize on existing political culture and coopt symbols to form collective action frames that will galvanize participants. The use of frames in meaning-making is a key ingredi-ent in the emergence and strategic repertoires of social movements (Morris and Mueller 1992; Tarrow 1983).

Frames must resonate powerfully with potential participants in order to effectively contradict dominants' framing of the same issue. For example, when the National Association for the Advancement of Colored People (NAACP) advocated for economic, social, and political and civil human rights in the 1950s, the state and powerful members of U.S. society stig-matized their demands by branding them as anti-American "communism" (Garrow 1981; 2016) To counter this stigmatizing frame the organizers deliberately framed their claims for civil rights as consistent with the cul-tural traditions of the U.S. Constitution (Anderson 2003). More recently, as Black Lives Matter gained widespread attention and galvanized into a movement, some pushback erupted on social media to reframe the con-versation as "ALL lives matter," thereby branding the movement as some-how discriminatory in its implication that "only" black lives matter. That reframing attempt actually helped sharpen the point of Black Lives Matter by opening the door to the clarification that it would be ideal if all lives in fact truly mattered, but that evidence of daily differential experiences on the street, including fatal encounters with police, suggested that somehow black lives did not matter quite as much as white lives do. That is, the point was that "Black Lives Matter, Too." (Gordon, Perkins, Nouw and Durbin 2017). The back-and-forth on social media clearly became a struggle over framing.

While effective framing may link individuals to social movement perspectives, participation in social movements often fosters the development of collective identity or "a shared definition of a group that derives from its members' common interests, experiences, and solidarity" (Taylor and Whittier 1992, 105). Collective identities facilitate a heightened sense of shared awareness of the issues, goals, meanings, actions, and an understanding of the differences between challengers and the opponents (e.g., Melluci 1989; Taylor and Whittier 1992; Touraine 1985). They are often shaped and reinforced through movement organizations (Gamson 1996) that use the shared consciousness and common symbols and strategic repertoires to resist the existing structures of domination. Marx (1967), for example, emphasized the importance of class consciousness as key to anti-capitalist resistance. Similarly, some scholars argue that the development of racial consciousness was key to the struggle for racial justice. They note the swell of "black pride" as a collective identity that emerged through shared struggles and political and cultural aspirations, and a sense of group self-determination and purpose. This collective identity was significant as an inspirational touchstone unifying participants of the various social movement organizations in the civil rights struggle, even as they may have differed on the specifics of tactics, resources, and numbers of constituents who were mobilized (Lawson 1997).

Political Opportunity Structures

Deprivation, perceived or absolute, supportive resources and their mobilization, and a unifying collective identity may be necessary conditions for social movements, but they are not sufficient. There must also be access to dominant political structures, or opportunities for people to apply these resources to disrupt business as usual, or to create their own opportunities for such disruption (McAdam, McCarthy, and Zald 1996; Meyer and Staggenborg 1996; Ballard, Habib, and Valodia 2006). Sociologists refer to this as political process theory, which Goodwin and Jasper (1999, 28) argued "is currently the hegemonic paradigm among social movement analysts." According to this model, social movements emerge when shifting political conditions open opportunities for disruption, and the activities of social movements in turn can alter political policies and structures. These altered political structures then may become a new opportunity for social movements (Tarrow 1998).

Political opportunity structures are "consistent—but not necessarily formal, permanent or national—dimensions of the political environment that provide incentives for people to undertake collective action by affecting their expectations for success or failure" (Tarrow 1994, 85). Political opportunity structures include "openness or closure of the institutionalized political system, stability or instability of elite alignments that typically undergird a polity, presence or absence of elite allies, and the state's propensity and capacity for repression" (McAdam 1996, 27). Thus, institutional actors' engagement or disengagement may affect the development of political opportunities for resistance by framing people's expectations of their own ability to affect oppressive structures and relations.

Researchers using the political process model have variously suggested at least four dimensions of opportunities for social movement emergence: access to political structures and the perception of ability to influence policy affects mobilization; instabilities in political alliances can open opportunities for the creation of new coalitions, primarily in party politics; influential allies among legislators and jurists can enhance the likelihood of affecting policy and practice; and conflicts between elites can create political schisms as opportunities for disruption (Tarrow 1998; McAdam 1994; McAdam, McCarthy, and Zald 1996).

As we previously noted, popular cultural mythology of the civil rights movement often points to Rosa Parks's seemingly spontaneous refusal to give her seat on the Birmingham bus to a white person as the original precipitating event. But Morris's research documents that Parks was, in fact, an active member, and the first secretary, of the local National Association for the Advancement of Colored People. She had been arrested several times before that incident for the same action. Rosa Parks's famous act of defiance was part of an organized, conscious resistance strategy rather than an isolated, spontaneous reaction to racism. She herself insisted, "My resistance to being mistreated on the buses and anywhere else was just a regular thing with me and not just that day" (Morris, 1984, 51; see also Parks 1992; Theoharis 2013). Here, Parks's act of defiance, and many other, similar acts at lunch counters, stores, and public restrooms, as well as mass demonstrations across the bridge to Selma, Alabama and boycotts of public transportation, together created political opportunities to disrupt business as usual, even if temporarily.

McAdam's (1982; 1988) research of the civil rights movement also noted the role of the state as a factor in the rise and fall of social movements as a political process (see also King 2017). For example, elimination of racist barriers to blacks' voting enhanced the likelihood of electing well-placed sympathetic elites such as John F. Kennedy or encouraging politicians such as Lyndon B. Johnson to become more sympathetic. However, McAdam also emphasized that federal support for the goals of the civil rights movement came not so much in response to electoral politics, but in response to insurgency and violent and nonviolent acts that subverted civil order. That is, the state responded to mass disruptions created by strategic actions of civil rights movement organizations. More recently, the Black Lives Matter movement and mass responses to police violence against people of color and to "not guilty" verdicts against police accused of lethal use of force and violence in those cases has caused the state to look more closely at police behavior on the streets (Taylor 2016) and to engage comparative studies of such things as differential stop and frisk practices, traffic stops resulting in violence, arrests, differential use of tasing, and the like (see, e.g., U.S. Department of Justice 2016). And while still not a federal practice, many municipalities now require police to wear body cameras to document their behavior as they encounter people on the streets.

Social movements frequently challenge powerful institutional and social structural arrangements, forcing them to organize outside conventional legitimized avenues to make their claims and therefore develop strategies that will be effective. And they must articulate their perspective and actions so as to persuade people to support their cause. Movement leaders select from an array of "repertoires of contention," according to their perspective of what is likely to work in a given context (Tarrow 1994). The strategies and tactics vary, from civil disobedience and noncompliance as nonviolent confrontation to direct actions and violent confrontation (Chabot 2002; Gamson 1990; Scott 1985). Gamson (1990) found that certain tactics of direct action—such as violence and strikes—have a fair degree of success in moving their agenda forward. On the other hand, Chabot (2002), Brown (1991), Parikh (2001), Hassim (2006), Katzenstein (1995), Scott (1985), and others have demonstrated the salience of nonviolent tactics and direct actions. So how do social movement participants select from the array of tools at their disposal? On the whole, strategies and tactics are often chosen as activists attempt to offset the power of their opponents (McAdam 1983). Some prominent civil rights organizations strategically chose nonviolent marches and boycotts as the strongest "weapon" to publicly challenge violent repression by the state; other groups focused on challenging racial segregation through courts, while still others chose to claim rights on the street, by using direct actions to attempt to desegregate lunch counters, or register people to vote.

That same challenge of selection of tactics ranging from civil disobedience to direct action "by any means necessary" echoed once again in 2015 after a rash of deaths of unarmed African Americans at the hands of police using excessive force; for what it's worth, the violent demonstrations following police excessive use of force in Ferguson, Baltimore and elsewhere in 2014–2015 unmistakably garnered national attention and may arguably have resulted in the subsequent arrest and charge of homicide against a South Carolina officer in the shooting death of an African American man. It most assuredly was acknowledged by the Baltimore City's State attorney Marilyn Mosby in a press conference where she announced that she would criminally prosecute six officers in the death of Freddie Gray, yet *another* unarmed African American man killed by police: "To the people of Baltimore and the

demonstrators across America. I heard your call for 'no justice, no peace.'"
(Capehart 2015). Clearly, the shootings, along with the demonstrations
and increasingly violent clashes between a highly militarized local police
force and increasingly agitated crowds became a contemporary confluence
of resource mobilization and political opportunity to address the long-
simmering problem of continuing institutionalized racism and inequality in
the seemingly "post-racist" society (King 2017). Arguably, it has reignited
the anti-racist movements of decades past, most recently reincarnated in the
Black Lives Matter movement.

Taken together, resource mobilization, organization, and political opportunity appear to be critical. Research thus suggests that social movements can use
political process to affect policy and cultural practices. But observers do cau-
tion that the state is not just an arena for conflicts or a target for social movements; it is also an actor. When social movement actors mobilize resources
to create disruption, the state commonly responds, sometimes with greater
repression and sometimes with an effort to address the challenge with as minimal disruption to the status quo as possible ("baby steps"). Indeed, the state,
as the sole legitimate user of force and violence, may resort to immense means
of repression against insurrection, (Davenport, Johnston, and Mueller 2005;
McAdam 1996). However, although overt and violent repression is a common
state response to insurgency and challenge, researchers note that repression
may take other forms. Ferree (2005) distinguishes between hard repression
(including military action and corporal punishment) and soft repression (such
as the use of public ridicule and stigmatization and silencing insurgents).

Moreover, much of social movement and resistance literature focuses on
the state as the target of such efforts. However, as Armstrong and Bernstein
(2008) note, many social movements actually are multi-institutional in their
targets. Other research shows, as well, that some social movements are less
about organized targeting of institutions to push them to change, but rather
more about taking organized direct action to address grievances. This has
been the central focus of anarchism and its attendant theories.

Anarchist Theory and Direct Action

Anarchist theory, as opposed to Marxist and liberal theories, stresses the
illegitimacy of the state, regardless of the mode of production that a given
society might have. This has important consequences for analyzing social
movements. Indeed, anarchists differ significantly from traditional perspectives on the nature of social movements and their relationship to the state,
apart from some left-wing Marxists (see, e.g., Pannekoek 2003 or Flank
2007), particularly in the state's ostensible liberatory possibilities for human
life.

Marx argued for what he called "the dictatorship of the proletariat," interpreted by some as a state apparatus occupied and run by workers after the workers carried out a successful revolution. According to Marxist theory, particularly as it was developed by Lenin ([1917] 2015), the state exists to manage divergent class interests. According to some interpretations of Marx, after the workers occupied the state (or constructed their own "workers' state") and social classes were eventually abolished, the state would "wither away," along with class society, as there would no longer be any use for the state.

Anarchists, however, argue that the state will never simply wither away and that the assumption that any centralized power structure will gradually allow itself to simply disappear is naive. Rather, anarchists predicted that pursuing socialism through the use of the state would end in tyranny. This idea prompted the anarchist, Mikhail Bakunin (1964, 269), to remark that "freedom without Socialism is privilege and injustice, and . . . . Socialism without freedom is slavery and brutality." Some anarchists have argued that the experiences of the USSR, China, Cuba, and other state-centered experiments in socialism have vindicated this idea. For this reason, anarchists typically prefer direct action to electoral strategies for bringing about social changes, arguing that in the process of acting directly to meet their own needs, people are empowered and learn collective self-management, rather than rule from above (as is the case in statist societies).

Anarchist theories of social movements also bring other questions to the table, such as how to define the term "violence" (the question of whether "violence" can be done toward a building, for example, or if "violence" is a relation between people [Gelderloos 2007]); the question of centralization and leadership within movements (many theories of social movements assume centralization and leaders); a *method* of struggle that is consistent with broad end-goals; as well as the role of in/formal organizations in social movements. As a method, anarchist theory tends toward prefigurative claims that means must be consistent with ends to the largest extent possible. In practice this suggests that if authoritarian methods are used (e.g., a top-down disempowering organizational structure), then authoritarian goals will be achieved (e.g., a top-down result, as anarchists suggest was the case in the Soviet bloc countries or other attempts at anti-capitalist politics rooted in the party form seeking the capture or creation of a state). If a non-hierarchical institutional arrangement is desired as an outcome, then non-hierarchical *methods* must be used to achieve those ends. Anarchist theory also allows room for an analysis of the production of new social relations—rooted in a desire to alter daily life—as part and parcel of any social movement, particularly anarchism that is heavily influenced by the post-1968 global wave of student-worker unrest (Ehrlich 2012).

Although anarchists have no single comprehensive theory of social movements, resistance, or the state (for some interesting comments on state theory, see Harrison 1983 or Price 2007), nearly all advocate for forms of direct action and counterpose it with electoralism and other forms of politics from above (see especially de Cleyre [1912] 2004). While plenty of others have advocated for and engaged in direct action, what anarchists add to this discussion is a theory of the state's role with social movement actors, again, in which they argue that, since the state has interests of its own, the state must be abolished in order to achieve an egalitarian future rather than advocating that seekers of change occupy the state, reform it, or create a so-called "workers' state." In fact, in the anarchist analysis a "workers' state" is an oxymoron, as those who have control of the state apparatus are placed above society, effectively distinguishing them from others without access to state power—therefore, those state actors are no longer workers, but rather those who rule over workers.

While classical anarchist theory was largely framed as a class dialectic, anarchist advocacy of direct action has echoes in the civil rights movement. The history of the Black Panthers in the civil rights movement represents direct action in addressing racism in the United States. While the popular framing of the organization is one of a violent anti-white movement, the organization actually emerged as a community-based direct action organized to protect residents from crime and police violence as well as address issues of hunger and poverty, education, and inequality (Seale and Shames 2016; Bloom and Martin 2016). Where the state either failed to protect its citizens or, worse yet, actively engaged in violence and discrimination against them, the Black Panthers arose to take direct action to ensure the rights of the community. It should be noted, however, that the Black Panthers viewed themselves as a party and *not* as anarchists, showing the utility of direct action methods across ideological currents.

Social Movements, Multi-Sites of Power, and the Racial State Project

Taken together, the material on social movements and resistance suggests that even those who would appear to be among the most oppressed are not victims or passive bystanders in the political process of oppression. While these theories of social movements may disagree about how and why social movements develop and operate, they share the observation that the oppressed often respond collectively to the institutions and cultural repertoires and practices that produce and reinforce their oppression. Some observers note that social movement organizations may not have singular goals, but rather can alternate between policy change and cultural transformation (Bernstein 2003;

Snow 2004; Whittier 2002). But while observers may dispute the meaning of "success" of social movements in attaining their goals, they largely share an understanding that social movements can have an effect on state policies and cultural and political practices writ large (Stetson 2005; Goldstone 2003). However, while formal state policy and practice is often (but not necessarily always) a significant target for institutional change, it is not the only institutional target; nor is institutional change or reform necessarily the only target of social movements and resistance. As anarchist theory and direct action suggests, many times the target is everyday cultural practice and meanings, as well as institutional practice and meanings external to the state.

The material on social movements, direct action and resistance suggests that such activity does not occur within a vacuum. In order to understand the relationships, processes, and structures of such movements they must be placed in the context of their relationship with the wider political and cultural landscape. Social movement literature suggests that the oppressed, and their responses to their circumstances, must be incorporated into a larger vista of the institutions, relationships, processes, policies, and practices that define and shape oppression and people's empowerment in resistance to that oppression. This insight becomes crystalized by incorporating social movements into a multi-sites of power paradigm, wherein they become a key factor animating the balance of political forces in state projects. Here, the racial state project has been propelled by the continually shifting balance of political forces around racial formation processes, policies and practices, framed by racialized selectivity filters. The balance of political forces is galvanized by the ebb and flow of social movement organizations, tactics and strategies of the civil rights movement and organizations like Black Lives Matter and the Black Panthers, and the ongoing institutional challenges, resistance, and responses to these. The salience of social movements to affect this dynamic is dependent upon how well they are organized, the resources they may access, and the political opportunities they either locate or create to disrupt the normal day-to-day functioning of society and the laws and customs that define these, as well as the degree of "push-back" they meet from powerful institutional forces.

Chapter 6

State Projects and the Human Right to Shelter

Balancing Political Forces and Intersecting Relations of Inequality and Domination

In chapter 3 we examined the balance of political forces in the context of bank deregulation (which happened alongside many state projects in the neoliberal period rooted in economic deregulation for industry). The Glass-Steagall Act emerged from the momentous occasion of economic crisis, as the balance of political forces weighed against the interests of financial institutions—particularly those supplying finance capital. From 1933 onward, the leaders of financial institutions collectively leaned on the state to chip away the regulations that came from Glass-Steagall. In the late 1970s, when Chrysler Corporation was in crisis, the financial institutions lobbied for the further erosion of Glass-Steagall as a quid pro quo for providing bailout funds for Chrysler. With the looming loss of Chrysler in the background, the balance of political forces tipped in the banks' favor and they successfully lobbied for the removal of many of Glass-Steagall's regulatory features.

These features were further eroded by the Graham-Leach-Bliley Act (GLBA) in 1999. The GLBA was to serve the ostensible purpose of "modernizing" the banking industry, to adjust for an increasingly globalized capitalism. President Bill Clinton signed the GLBA into law with the effect of formally repealing sections of Glass-Steagall that prevented single financial firms from operating as investment, insurance, and commercial banks. Thus, already-large financial institutions that served different sectors of the economy were allowed to consolidate and integrate, swallowing up both competitors *and* different market sectors without federal regulatory agencies having the power to intervene.

This followed a successful 1998 merger of Citicorp and Travelers Group, a merger prohibited by Glass-Steagall and, thus, a de facto challenge to its already eroded authority. Citicorp was a commercial bank holding company while Travelers Group was an insurance company. Their merger, then, challenged Glass-Steagall's regulations by forming Citigroup, which would function as a company that dealt in securities, insurance, *and* services under the umbrella of a variety of business monikers—combining sectors of the market that Glass-Steagall sought to split. The Federal Reserve met this challenge, not with regulatory control, but with permission in the form of a temporary waiver for Citigroup until, just months later, the GLBA was signed into law allowing these kinds of combinative market mergers to occur legally. Once again, large financial institutions found the balance of political forces tipped in their favor and took advantage of the social moment to push for, and achieve, an economy that increasingly deregulated industry.

THE IDEOLOGY OF DEREGULATION AND THE BALANCE OF POLITICAL FORCES

These patterns of deregulating industry set an important precedent for the housing crisis in 2008 in the United States, the bank bailout that followed, and the global financial meltdown that came in its wake. But before we focus on the housing crisis and the lending practices that led to it, it is necessary to unpack the language of deregulation and clarify how we are operationalizing the "balance of political forces" and how that concept differs from Jessop's "balance of class forces." An analysis of how political economists and sociologists use the term "deregulation" can open up a lens into the MSP approach to state theory and why we argue that we need to widen our critical state theory to account for antagonisms that intersect with, but are not reducible to, social class.

Deregulation is an interesting term that took up steam among the political left *and* right to describe some of the political economic practices associated with neoliberalism. As we outlined in chapter 3, the neoliberal period saw a reconstitution of capital on the basis of laissez-faire capitalist ideology. The goal, accordingly, was to remove state barriers from the market resulting from the neoclassical economic assumption that unfettered markets lead to a natural societal equilibrium. The push and pull of producers, distributors, and buyers on the market, if left without interference, would tend toward a balance due to mechanisms automatically woven into the market, according to this theory of political economy. If one begins with these assumptions, it follows then that removing regulatory controls (such as those imposed by Glass-Steagall) will end in a social benefit—the market will provide a natural equilibrium due to the rational activity of producers, distributors, and consumers working collectively in the market.

What this ideology misses is that private property—indeed, capitalism itself—cannot exist without state interference. That is, society requires the legitimated violence of the state in order for property as we understand it to occur (see, e.g., Shannon 2012). Without the threat of state violence, there is nothing to stop workers from just taking the means of producing wealth rather than producing a profit for the owners of productive property. Similarly, consider the underlying assumptions required for a hungry person to stand outside of a store filled with food begging for money. Why not just go inside and take some food? It is, of course, in part the threat of state violence that demands that hungry people seek the intermediary of money rather than helping themselves to food that is, after all, produced socially.

Therefore, "deregulation" is a bit of a misnomer without the qualifying language "of industry" or perhaps "deregulation from above." Indeed, in the neoliberal period we *did* see decreased state regulation of industry. Sociologists and political economists are right to point this out. But in that same period, we saw fluctuations in terms of regulatory controls directly applied *to workers*. Borders, perhaps, provide one of the best examples here. While capital, commodities, and in some cases even wealthy *people* increasingly had regulations removed from their capacity to flow across borders in the period of neoliberal globalization, workers had an entirely different experience. If a worker wished to cross borders to trade her labor in our so-called "deregulated" and "free" market, borders served a regulatory function, sometimes disallowing migrant labor, criminalizing it, or at the least, heavily regulating it. Thus, deregulation of *industry* from above could often act in concert with heavy regulation of *labor*, mitigating workers' ability to apply pressure from below.

In the United States, in large part as a result of the neoliberal market restructuring embedded in the North American Free Trade Agreement (NAFTA), a large section of the migrant population comes from Mexico, as workers cross the border to sell their labor for relatively higher wages in the United States and use portions of their earnings to send remittances back home to their families. Thus, by "2014, more than 11.7 million Mexican immigrants resided in the United States, accounting for 28 percent of the 42.4 million foreign-born population—by far the largest immigrant origin group in the country" (Zong and Batalova 2016). The deregulation of commodity and capital mobility with the attendant heavy regulation of worker mobility marks a balance of political forces that favors capital at the expense of workers, as this mobile workforce, in large part from Mexico, experiences state policy designed to regulate its movement, even while removing those controls from capital and commodities.

But, in the United States, with its history of white supremacy, the construction of its particular racial state (Goldberg 2002), and white animosity toward people of color in general and Latinx people in particular, it behooves state theorists to also account for racial inequality in the balance of forces at work influencing policy. To be clear, while Jessop's "balance of class forces" can correctly weigh the interests of capital being met at the expense of workers in neoliberal "deregulation," we need a wider net in order to account for the racial divisions that influence state policy in the form of border policy—hence, our reconceptualization of Jessop's concept as the "balance of *political* forces" to attempt to account for multiple, intersecting relations of inequality and domination affecting state selectivity filters, projects, and specific policies.

Amidst a surge in Mexican immigration to the United States, hate crimes against Latinx immigrants in the United States tripled in 2012, according to a Bureau of Justice Statistics report (see reporting by Haglage 2014). While the *number* of hate crimes in that report had remained fairly consistent, the *targets* seemed to be changing—increasingly aimed at Latinx people. This follows white panic about the changing demographics of the country, identified early on by the right-wing pundit and "alt-right" leader, Peter Brimelow[1], as "the browning of America"—one of the more overtly white nationalist monikers for these changing demographics. Part and parcel of this racial fear and resentment has been a reinvigoration (and, at times, alarming normalization) of white nationalism attached to "alt-right" politics, reaching a rhetorical crescendo in Donald Trump's campaign promise to seal the United States from Mexican workers by building a wall across the U.S.-Mexico border and (somehow) forcing the Mexican government to pay for it.

Given these realities, it is necessary to assess state policy along its class lines, which Jessop's "balance of class forces" correctly identifies. But, as we have argued, we might widen that lens to accommodate an analysis of other structured inequalities. In this case, racial inequality and resentment influences state policy just as the interests of capital and workers do. This is why we argue for reconceptualizing Jessop's concept, referring to it as the "balance of *political* forces" to view intersecting relations of domination at work in state activity. The regulatory lens and power of the state, through examining borders and border policy, demonstrates a crucial overlap between the state, capitalism, and white supremacy. This same intersection is central to understanding the housing crisis of 2008 and the global economic crisis that followed from it.

THE HOUSING CRISIS: INTERSECTIONS OF STATE POWER, CLASS, AND RACISM[2]

Housing and food, the central objects of analysis for this chapter and the next, are particularly suited for investigations into state policy. First and foremost, both are needed for humans to live decent and dignified lives (in the case of food, it is needed for humans to live, period). Secondly, both housing and food are rights guaranteed by the Universal Declaration of Human Rights and the International Covenant on Economic, Social, and Cultural Rights, both human rights instruments agreed to by a number of states, including the United States. If we want to see state policy at work, and particularly, if we want to critically evaluate states on the basis of *their own logic, agreements, and protocols*, the rights to food and shelter give us two dramatic examples of state policy failing to meet its own self-defined tasks. Finally, food and shelter, despite being declared social goods through their construction as "rights," are *commodities*—to be bought and sold by those who can afford to enter into those markets regulated (as are all socially legitimated markets) by states. Let us turn to shelter in the context of the housing crisis and its explosion into a global economic crisis in 2008 as an example of state policy and lending activities intersecting with social class and racism. This provides another small window into the utility of the MSP approach to state theory.

Again, as we outlined in chapter 3, financial deregulation from above allowed financial institutions to enter into multiple markets with increasingly esoteric instruments to manage their profit making. Loans (including home loans) could be rolled together by banks and sold, in parts, to speculators. This gave banks some degree of protection from the consequences of lending to people who might not be able to repay their loans—after all, the lender-lendee relationship became redirected through speculation, then speculation upon that speculation, and so on. This was buttressed by ownership concentrations that were previously separated through Glass-Steagall becoming integrated through state processes of deregulation from above. This allowed lending institutions to engage in home loans, along with many other financial activities, that were relatively risk-free (through selling those risks in derivatives to speculators). This set the stage for increasingly *predatory* forms of lending in the housing market—a "human right" guaranteed by the state was transformed into a commodity and then further perverted through state practices of deregulation from above.

Research shows that banks have routinely engaged in predatory practices, particularly in this housing market (both legal and illegal) with a racialized pattern of targets. Subprime lending, in particular, appears to be related at least in part to social characteristics (see Greunstein and Herbert 2000; National Community Reinvestment Coalition 2008; Williams, Nesiba, and McConnell 2005; and Bradley 2000). This relationship is important because in addition to the large number of subprime refinancings, first-time homeownership gains for many borrowers who have historically been excluded from mortgage markets have been fueled by higher-priced, subprime innovations.

In Connecticut, subprime lending increased by over 42 percent overall in the 1990s and into the new century; notably, the increase was by more than 85 percent in neighborhoods where more than half the population were people of color (Collins 2000). Case studies in major metropolitan areas around the country indicate similar patterns in their findings (see, e.g., Bunce, Bruenstein, Herbert, and Schessele 2001; Gincotta 2000). One study found compelling evidence of broader correlation between subprime lending and race (beyond individual metropolitan areas in case studies) (Ross and Yinger 2002). Beeman, Glasberg, and Casey's (2010) research using data for low-income communities in Chicago, Indianapolis, St. Louis, Cleveland, and Hartford echoes these results. They found a strong association between the racial categorization of the borrower or the borrower's neighborhood and the likelihood of becoming a target of predatory lending: in essence, as the borrower becomes "less white" the odds of an equitable loan origination decreases, and that is the case not only for low-income but also for moderate-income African American borrowers alike, suggesting a relative independence of racism operating in these practices. In stark terms, for example, African American borrowers in Hartford are almost three times more likely than white borrowers to receive high-cost mortgages, *regardless of their income*. Similarly, the higher the proportion of people of color in a community as a whole, the lower the odds of an equitable loan origination. As the National Community Reinvestment Coalition (2008) noted, "income is no shield against racial differences in lending." In particular, subprime lending has been found to be concentrated among borrowers of color and in neighborhoods with high proportions of people of color, borrowers who decades earlier had been redlined and denied mortgages.

A number of studies point to the association between higher levels of subprime credit and specific racial and social characteristics of the borrowers and their neighborhoods. For example, the assessed subprime lending in five cities (Atlanta, Baltimore, Chicago, Los Angeles, and New York) found subprime loans were over three times more likely in low-income neighborhoods than in high-income neighborhoods, and five times more likely in black neighborhoods than in white neighborhoods (U.S. Department of Housing and Urban Development—U.S. Treasury National Predatory Lending Task Force 2000). Another study found that as the percentage of African American population increased, the amount of subprime lending increased in Cleveland, Milwaukee, and Detroit, cities with extensive histories of racialized residential segregation (Taylor, Silver, and Berenbaum 2004). In another study, Williams, Nesiba and McConnell (2005) found that between 1993 and 2000, at least half of the gains in homeownership in underserved markets, minority or low-income, were the result of subprime loans rather than prime loans. These disparities are not limited to the neighborhood level, but exist at the individual borrower level as well. Based on individual borrower racial/ethnic characteristics, black and Latinx mortgage holders pay more for mortgages.

For example, one study found that both groups have home loans with higher interest rates when compared to whites and are 1.5 to 2.5 times more likely to pay interest of 9 percent or more (Krivo and Kaufman 2004).

Other research shows that an applicant's race has a significant relationship with the type of lender. Applicants reporting African American, Hispanic, American Indian or Alaskan Native, or American and Pacific Islander as their racial identities were found to have a significant, positive effect on the likelihood that they applied to a nonregulated lender—lenders who are far more likely to offer subprime, high-risk creative mortgage instruments, such as adjustable rate mortgages, or ARMs (Casey, Glasberg, and Beeman 2011). That means that borrowers of color are especially exposed to the vulnerability of losing their homes, particularly in an economy caught in the grips of an economic tailspin such as that in 2008–2009. And that, in turn, fuels and exacerbates racialized economic inequality. Part of this growing inequality can be seen in the widening racialized wealth gap in the United States: since home ownership is the most significant element of most people's share of wealth, access to that piece of the American Dream becomes critical to wealth acquisition. Since people of color are routinely denied access to mortgage credit or are far more likely to lose their homes because of predatory lending, it becomes clear what the culprit is in generating and accelerating that widening racialized wealth gap. Access to finance capital then becomes a key element in the de facto continuation of racialized segregation and inequality that was once an overt, blatant, and clear violation of the Universal Declaration of Human Rights as well as the U.S. Constitution and Civil Rights Legislation (though, of course, business-as-usual under U.S. capitalism). Again, state policy, along multiple sites of power, including but not limited to class, operates in direct contradistinction with its stated aims.

The logic of capitalism dictates that financial institutions must turn quarterly and annual profits in order to remain robust in the eyes of shareholders who are hungry for profits. Placing mortgages, even high-risk ones, can provide at least the short-term appearance of profit making, particularly if the originating institutions immediately sell the mortgage to a secondary bank. That quick sell to the secondary market gets the mortgage off the books of the originating banks, which collect a profit in the sale. Moreover, these mortgages, while certainly high risk, help the originating bank establish the appearance of compliance with the Community Reinvestment Act directive to provide mortgages to underserved or redlined communities (hence, so many adjustable rate mortgages and consequent foreclosures appeared first and most forcefully in communities of color). Predatory lending, as a direct result of state deregulation from above operating within the logic of capital, reproduces and institutionalizes *racialized* economic inequality as an aggressive strategy for banking institutions to survive the pressures of contemporary markets. This is because one important element of wealth is access to mortgage lending and the acquisition of property. And while these predatory practices may help financial institutions navigate the vagaries of capitalism, they do so on the backs of the poor, the working classes, and people of color.

Taken together, this body of research suggests that banking practices, and the state projects of regulation and deregulation embedded within those practices, are promoting and reinforcing *racialized* economic inequality, robbing people of color of an equal opportunity to build equity and wealth. This is significant because it is a contemporary element of a history of practices and policies that together institutionalize racialized inequality insofar as individual prejudice is no longer necessary for the continuation of racialized inequality. It also demonstrates the need for the MSP approach to state theory that can navigate multiple and intersecting relations of domination.

But bundling mortgages, credit, loans, etc. into complex financial instruments could only redirect the risk of these home loans for so long. While the sales of loans and derivatives allowed for a prosperous couple of decades for financial institutions, the balloon of investment eventually bloated and popped, resulting in the financial crisis of 2008. Amazingly, the balance of political forces at this historical juncture still leaned toward those financial institutions responsible for the economic crisis, as evidenced by the bailouts of these banks that had become "too big to fail." Rather than bailing out the families being removed from their homes, the state supplied capital to the banks to help them absorb the costs of their risky lending activities.

It is in social moments such as these, where the consequences of capitalism and other inequalities are not mitigated by the state, when social actors, by necessity, begin addressing these kinds of large-scale problems themselves. After all, if the state cannot be relied on to protect families from losing their homes in eviction proceedings led by predatory banks, who will fill that role? In the wake of the housing crisis, groups like Occupy Our Homes (an offshoot of the Occupy Wall Street movement) began organizing eviction defenses. Take Back the Land organized eviction defenses, but also organized direct action activities, moving un-housed families into foreclosed homes, challenging the state to try to evict them. These kinds of activities show how social movements often respond to state policy (or a lack thereof) to secure basic rights and dignities where the state either cannot or will not. These undertakings spur questions such as: How do people get human rights addressed left unattended to by the state? How do these challenges affect state policy? And what alternatives to the state do direct action movements provide? We address these questions and more in our next chapter on the human right to food.

NOTES

1. Rather than cite or provide a link to the work of a racist demagogue, we refer readers to this 2013 report on Brimelow's work by Right Wing Watch: http://www.rightwingwatch.org/post/peter-brimelow-too-extreme-for-wnd/

2. We owe much of this analysis to prior work Davita Silfen Glasberg produced with Angie Beeman and Colleen Casey, specifically in Glasberg, Davita Silfen, Angie Beeman, and Colleen Casey. 2014. "Predatory Lending and the Twenty-First Century Recession: Preying on the American Dream and Reasserting Racialized Inequality." In *The End of the World as We Know It? Crisis, Resistance, and the Age of Austerity*, edited by Deric Shannon, 55–69. Oakland, CA: AK Press.

Chapter 7

State Projects and the Human Right to Food

Direct Action and Balancing Political Forces

As we stated in chapter 6, food provides an interesting object of study in relation to state projects for some interrelated reasons. First and foremost, while food is needed for humans to live (putting aside the question of what we might need to live decently), it is treated as a commodity, a grouping of items for sale on the market for those with the capital to purchase them. Secondly, and relatedly, the United States (and many other nations) agreed that there should be a human right to food. That is, in the Universal Declaration of Human Rights (UDHR) and the International Covenant on Economic, Social, and Cultural Rights (ICESCR), groups of states, the United States included, agreed to a positive and affirmative freedom *to* food. That is, the framing of food as a commodity to be distributed through market allocation is a competing selectivity filter with food as a fundamental right—a public good, such as education, that everyone should theoretically have access to.

This agreement among states, then, allows us a chance to analyze the state on its own terms—set by itself in its own agreements. Here, we have the capacity to analyze state projects around both food and, since it is a commodity, poverty. Since the United States has affirmed people's right to food in multiple human rights instruments, it is fair to assess how seriously it holds to that international commitment. And if states fail to meet the obligations they promise to their citizens (and others) that they use the language of "rights" to define, we might look to social actors other than states who step in to attempt to fulfill those obligations. As we have pointed out previously, there exists a balance of political forces that affects, and is affected by, state policy and, as examined in this particular chapter, social movement forces are galvanized as a result of the state's *inaction*, tipping the balance of political forces in interesting ways.

We begin this chapter by describing some of the relations of inequality embedded in state projects surrounding food and agriculture in the form of food insecurity. We establish that in the United States, despite the formal and legal commitment of the state guaranteeing the right to adequate food to its people, there are still significant amounts of hunger and food insecurity. Next, we will investigate social movements that attempt to provide food to hungry people, in direct antagonism to the state and as an alternative to it as a form of social organization. Finally, we link direct action from social movements as both a form of social movement practice to guarantee rights and as a possible statement on the future of the state.

A PLACE AT THE BANQUET TABLE? RACE, CLASS, GENDER, AND FOOD (IN)SECURITY

The U.S. Department of Agriculture (USDA 2015) defines "food-insecure" households as "[a]t times during the year, these households were uncertain of having, or unable to acquire, enough food to meet the needs of all their members because they had insufficient money or other resources for food. Food-insecure households include those with *low food security* and *very low food security*." In 2015, according to the USDA, "12.7 percent (15.8 million) of U.S. households were food insecure at some time." Further, "5.0 percent (6.3 million) of U.S. households had *very low food security* at some time during 2015" (emphasis added).

Among those food-insecure households, the USDA (2015) reports that black non-Hispanic households accounted for 21.5 percent. Hispanic households were 19.1 percent. The combined percentage of black non-Hispanic and Hispanic households accounted for around 40 percent of those who are food insecure, despite the most recent U.S. Census (2015) showing that only 13.3 percent of Americans identify as "black or African American alone" with 17.6 percent identifying as "Hispanic or Latino." Households with children headed by a single woman were 30.3 percent of food-insecure households while households with children headed by a single man were 22.4 percent.

These data are instructive. In a society where food is a commodity and thus subject to market allocation and the capacity to pay for it with capital, it stands to reason that households from lower socioeconomic backgrounds are more likely to suffer from food insecurity (and the data seem to bear that out, with "[l]ow-income households with incomes below 185 percent of the poverty threshold" accounting for 32.8 percent of food-insecure households). Black non-Hispanics are grossly overrepresented among food-insecure households, Hispanics are overrepresented as well, as are single women with children vis-à-vis their male counterparts.

Here we begin to see where a variety of relations of inequality affect the capacity for households to achieve food security. Therefore, as people exist in more and more of the demographic intersections that are overrepresented among food-insecure households, the greater the chances there are of being food insecure. Gender, class, and race have an intersecting effect on the capacity for people to provide food for themselves and their families.

The U.S. state, then, calls for the human right to food and adheres to the international covenants of states (the UDHR and ICESCR) that guarantee adequate food to people. Yet, in the United States, we have a food supply chain that is commodified and the state does *not* provide adequate resources to ensure food security for every household. Households are affected differentially by class, race, and gender (among households with children), compounding the issue of food security for those people who live within the intersections of multiple relations of oppression and inequality.

To be clear here—class matters. Food, as a commodity, governed as it is in large part by people's access to capital, is distributed in a way that is highly stratified by class. But the overrepresentation of racial and ethnic minority households and female-headed households of children among food-insecure households demonstrates the utility of the recognition of multiple sites of power embedded in state policy—the U.S. state has agreed to be the guarantor of the right to food, yet that very right is differentiated and stratified by class, race, and gender.

It should be stated, this is not because there is not enough calorically dense foods to go around. As Sen (1981) notes, the crises that arise around hunger have less to do with the availability of food than they do with a lack of access to capital—again, something that should not be a surprise since food is a commodity. And beyond famines and other crises of hunger, as Carolan (2012, 71) notes, "[t]he global trade liberalization policies of the last half a century have been instrumental in transferring responsibility for food security from the state to the market." This is a bitter irony—states have agreed through their human rights instruments to be the guarantors of the right to food and yet they have agreed, at the same time, to shift the responsibility from the state *to the market* to be the provider of food. Given this legislative doublespeak, it is fair to ask the questions: Do states really care to provide food as a right? If they do not, who will? Indeed, in the words of Armaline and Glasberg (2009), "What will states really do for us?"

THE STATE, THE HUMAN RIGHT TO FOOD, AND FOOD NOT BOMBS

The question of the human right to food and its relationship to the movements that have sprung up to guarantee that right is central to questions raised by the "human rights enterprise" (Armaline and Glasberg 2009; Armaline, Glasberg, and Purkayastha 2011; Armaline, Glasberg, and Purkayastha 2015). This approach to human rights discourse notes that the values that undergird human rights are often addressed through extra-institutional actors, including social movements from below. This is despite the fact that human rights "instruments were designed to work from a liberal social-contract model in which states act to preserve and protect their citizens on the assumption that states respect the human rights of domestic populations" (Armaline and Glasberg, 2009, 432). But the state is, quite often, the violator of human rights or, as seems to be the case with food, neither interested in, nor capable of, guaranteeing basic rights. This creates an untenable situation for those who wish to see the values embodied in human rights realized, as well as people who are critical of the state as an institution and vehicle for securing rights.

The approach embodied by "the human rights enterprise" has been put forward as a *sociological* method in opposition to "the dominance of law and political science" where "human rights are primarily defined and discussed in relation to human rights instruments, or human rights as they have manifested as international law" (Armaline, Glasberg, and Purkayastha 2011, 2). Human rights instruments are intended to work with states, or groupings of states, as the guarantors of those rights (Donnelly 1999; 2003). In those cases where replacements to formal state systems of justice are sought, such as truth and reconciliation commissions, it is states who empower them—this is true of retributive, transitional, and restorative approaches to justice within the framework of human rights (for an excellent overview, see Carey, Gibney, and Poe 2010, 197–228).

The human rights enterprise is an attempt to address this state-centric approach, since the dominant approach is rooted in statist justice systems. The three systems of justice outlined by Carey, Gibney, and Poe (2010, 212) are the formal justice institutions of affected countries, the formal justice institutions of another country, and/or international justice systems, which again, outlines the traditional approach of human rights scholarship and practice addressed through the coercive arms of the state. This is partly why Teeple (2005) suggests that *all* theories of human rights are problematic, because expressed human desires and fundamental needs are so often forsaken in pursuit of political economic gains woven into the fabric of state projects of capitalist globalization and state processes of military protectionism (for Teeple, particularly in a post-9/11 world). With food as a commodity for profit making distributed through market processes, of course those political economic gains are part and parcel of how food is governed. The state, then, holds a contradictory position here, at the very least, as both violator *and* guarantor of human rights.

Further, in the tradition of critical legal studies, radical scholars have suggested that it is easy for one "to lose faith in the coherence of rights discourse" (Kennedy 2002, 179). Gordon (1998), perhaps, puts this perspective most succinctly when he notes that "[f]ormal rights without practical enforceable content are easily substituted for real benefits. Anyway, the powerful can always assert counterrights (to vested property, to differential treatment according to 'merit,' to association with one's own kind) to the rights of the disadvantaged. 'Rights' conflict—and the conflict cannot be resolved by appeal to rights." That is, rights discourse is enforced and maintained by the powerful, and an appeal to their legal instruments is always and necessarily an appeal to their power *over* us. In their capacity to define and enforce rights, states and their agents can always remove those legal instruments or counter them with new ones. If we begin, then, with the agreement that access to adequate food should be a human right, the state has likewise agreed to this, and yet the obligation has been transferred to the market, who is to see that this human right is fulfilled given the inadequacy of the market to do so? And what does that tell us about the relationship between the state and society?

These are questions taken quite seriously by activists in Food Not Bombs (FNB). FNB began in 1980 in Cambridge, Massachusetts. It was conceived and created by anarchist, Quaker, and Marxist antinuclear activists in the Clamshell Alliance (for a more complete history of FNB, see Butler and McHenry 2000). It is a "decentralized network of autonomous chapters which function internally on a consensus basis" that "has spread to every continent, with affiliated groups in Turkey, South Africa, Australia, Argentina and India, to name just a few" (Day 2005, 40).

The activity of FNB is fairly uncomplicated. They recover food that is wasted and serve vegetarian meals to anyone who is hungry. Most FNB collectives gather this wasted food through "dumpster diving" (reclaiming wasted food from the trash) and through donations. They then take this recovered food, prepare a meal, and serve it either in community spaces (typically in public parks where they can gather populations experiencing poverty) or activist gatherings (such as protests, book fairs, and conferences). But FNB activists see their work as much more than just serving food to hungry people.

Members of FNB take pains to make it clear that what they do is solidarity, not charity. They are freely sharing a meal with anyone who wants to eat, preferring to blur the distinction between the giver(s) and receiver(s) of food as much as possible. Rather than registering with state agencies and working in conjunction with them, members of FNB prefer to "generally ignore the authorities" and "allow them as little contact" with them as possible (Butler and McHenry 2000, xi). FNB collectives also attempt to "operate outside of the dominant economic paradigm," recovering wasted food and serving it for free (Butler and McHenry 2000, xi). This attempt to escape cooptation by institutions such as the state and capitalism also lends itself to a politics focused on prefiguring the society that members wish to create—a society free of structured hierarchical constraints, such as those embodied by state power.

FNB collectives around the world have modified themselves in four major ways from soup kitchens and other charitable groups that distribute food, as Gelderloos (2006, 64–65) notes:

> Meals are vegan, to draw attention to the violence of industrial meat production and its role in exacerbating global poverty and hunger. . . . Meals are served in the open, to resist the shame and obscurity with which poverty is made invisible, to make a visible, political act out of serving free food, and oftentimes to meet homeless people on their own turf, in the urban parks where they congregate. Thirdly, Food Not Bombs sets itself in opposition to charity, ideally avoiding the paternalism of traditional soup kitchens and striving for the ideal of cooking and eating meals together, to blur the distinction between the giver and receiver of charity. Finally, Food Not Bombs is anti-militarist. This orientation manifests itself in the name, in the distribution of literature by many chapters portraying militarism as a drain on social resources and a cause of poverty, and in the location of Food Not Bombs within anti-war, anti-globalization, and other leftwing opposition movements (either through the other affiliations of Food Not Bombs activists or the collaboration between Food Not Bombs and other protest groups, whereby a Food Not Bombs chapter might cook meals for a protest or conference).

FNB activists are attempting to create a template for a coming society without the need for organizations like FNB. They are a social movement, dedicated to radical social alterations that are critical of the state and top-down politics. Interestingly, despite these anti-statist tendencies, FNB collectives still tend to appeal to rights in their slogan, "Food is a right, not a privilege." At first glance, it seems they agree with the groups of states who have legal agreements stating that food is a human right, except that FNB refuses to rely on the market *or the state* to guarantee the human right to food. Instead, they argue for direct action as a method that is both a way of securing human rights, and a method of organizing society without the need for hierarchical institutions like the state.

But, as noted above, statism is embedded in the liberal framework of human rights. For example, Donnelly (2003, 13) writes that "[h]uman rights ground moral claims to strengthen or add to existing legal entitlements." Likewise, Merry (2006, 228) notes that "legal frameworks govern the practice of human rights."

While anti-statism might not seem an obvious fit for human rights discourse (for one critique, see Shannon 2016), various anti-statists have historically fought in short-term struggles for reforms protected and enforced by the state (like the struggle for the eight-hour workday) in a revolutionary *process*. Chomsky (2009, 73) writes that, while his vision of a future decent society is loosely based on anarcho-syndicalist principles, his short-term goals include defending and strengthening "elements of state authority which, though illegitimate in fundamental ways, are critically necessary right now to impede the dedicated efforts to 'roll back' the progress that has been achieved in extending democracy and *human rights*" (emphasis added).

This orientation toward the state is a central feature of anarchism and its influence in the newest social movements (Day 2005; Bray 2013). And some anarchists have used, and currently use, the discourse of human rights to describe their values. Rudolf Rocker ([1938] 2004, 74) carefully crafted his vision of rights *in opposition to* the state in his famous exposition of anarcho-syndicalism:

Political rights do not originate in parliaments; they are, rather, forced upon parliaments from without. And even their enactment into law has for a long time been no guarantee of their security. Just as the employers always try to nullify every concession they had made to labor as soon as opportunity offered, as soon as any signs of weakness were observable in the workers' organizations, so governments also are always inclined to restrict or to abrogate completely rights and freedoms that have been achieved if they imagine that the people will put up no resistance. Even in those countries where such things as freedom of the press, right of assembly, right of combination, and the like have long existed, governments are constantly trying to restrict those rights or to reinterpret them by juridical hair-splitting. Political rights do not exist because they have been legally set down on a piece of paper, but only when they have become the ingrown habit of a people, and when any attempt to impair them will meet with the violent resistance of the populace. Where this is not the case, there is no help in any parliamentary Opposition or any Platonic appeals to the constitution.

Similarly, as Burley (2014, 259) in his work on housing struggles in the age of austerity puts it:

Human rights as a concept typically presumes something bestowed on us by the State. Periods of austerity undercut this logic, so it is important to note that State measures do not guarantee anything. Social movements do. The short-term solutions can be put in place in terms of State concessions, but the long-term solution we can ask for is the inspiration of people to come together and fight for the change we want to see without relying on politicians. This solidarity, the willingness to come together in the interests of the working people of the world, is going to be the real force of permanent change and the only thing that can ensure the permanence of things we consider to be "human rights."

It is this position toward rights, and the role of states, that leads FNB members to their particular *means*—or form of political practice. It should be stressed, however, that for the participants of FNB, the means *are* the ends. This focus leads to a practice of direct action, as FNB is notoriously antagonistic to state power.

Perhaps Voltairine de Cleyre ([1912] 2004, 47–48) explained the concept of direct action best:

> Every person who ever thought he [sic] had a right to assert, and went boldly and asserted it, himself, or jointly with others that shared his convictions, was a direct actionist. Some thirty years ago I recall that the Salvation Army was vigorously practicing direct action in the maintenance of the freedom of its members to speak, assemble, and pray. Over and over they were arrested, fined, and imprisoned; but they kept right on singing, praying, and marching, till they finally compelled their persecutors to let them alone. The Industrial Workers are now conducting the same fight, and have, in a number of cases, compelled the officials to let them alone by the same direct tactics.
>
> Every person who ever had a plan to do anything, and went and did it, or who laid his plan before others, and won their co-operation to do it with him, without going to external authorities to please do the thing for them, was a direct actionist. All co-operative experiments are essentially direct action.

In this formulation, direct action is the strategy used to see to our own needs without having to rely on external authorities such as the state. But direct action is also used because it teaches lessons in self-organization. To work for a stateless future means practicing in the here and now these things and providing a challenge to the hegemonic notions that naturalize fundamentally coercive and dominating institutions such as the state. FNB, and other groups like it that act as social movements from below who use direct action as a tactic to guarantee rights, assert human rights as inalienable and challenge the state's authority to enforce or guarantee human rights when the state itself is often a source of human rights denials or—in the case of food access—seemingly unwilling to fulfill its purported role in securing them.

FNB activists use a process similar to that of the Salvation Army as described by de Cleyre above. Members tend to ignore the state and pursue meeting a need they recognize as disregarded by the state rather than petitioning the state to do it for them (Gelderloos 2006; Butler and McHenry 2000). They also often suffer police repression, continue going about their work despite arrests, and, surprisingly, sometimes win the right to feed hungry people—all the while pointing out what they see as the fundamental absurdity that the state "governs" the right to feed the hungry and will put people in cages for meeting a human need that it has no interest in addressing in a meaningful way itself (see Butler and McHenry 2000, for many examples of FNB collectives suffering arrests and police violence). To FNB activists, the willingness to challenge the state and risk arrest demonstrates the importance of sidelining the state. Direct action and a refusal to cooperate with the state is seen as central to FNB work *as FNB*. FNB activists suggest that state bureaucracy necessarily leads to the management and defanging of radical challenges to the capitalist economic context within which it operates. For these activists, then, FNB provides both a challenge to the state's refusal to live up to its own legally prescribed promises and the very organization of the state itself, as a bureaucratic, hierarchical institution that rules society from above.

While FNB is a large and global social movement, it might be fair to criticize its work as a form of charity or service provision, despite their sloganeering to the contrary. It might also be fair to criticize FNB for being a group of activists—people who often view themselves as specialists in social change, limiting the capacity for non-activists to engage in their activity and, thus, transform society. Indeed, both of these critiques are picked up in Shannon's (2016) engagement with the human rights enterprise.

But we can look at some segments of particular stateless peoples who try to put similar principles to work in their organization of social life. In parts of Kurdistan, people are advocating for and organizing a stateless democracy (for an outline of this idea, see Dirik 2015). Central to their struggle for autonomy from the state is the formation of a cooperative political economy, a communal life, the empowerment of women, and a commitment to a healthy ecology. In the words of Aysel Doğan (TATORT Kurdistan 2013, 165)

> The best way to create an ecological system is to build cooperatives. One of my greatest dreams is to see the construction of youth and women's villages. They could become models for the ecological system that we're aspiring to. They could provide work for hundreds of unemployed youth. Young people are hungry, and I don't mean only for nutrition—they're hungry in spiritual and psychic ways, and they lack future prospects. If young people and women work in a village cooperative, they won't be exploited and will be paid for their work. A communal life among young people can become exemplary for the whole society.
>
> That's not so unrealistic. Cooperatives can be started in existing villages, or people who fled to the cities can return to their destroyed villages and rebuild. There are hundreds of such villages. [. . .]It might seem difficult, but it's not impossible.

That is, through direct action, we have the capacity to see to our human right to food, but we also might have the capacity to build a different kind of future, to transform society and its institutions.

THE FUTURE OF FOOD, THE FUTURE OF THE STATE

We are not offering a prediction for the future, but some questions about where we might go. The state is a powerful institution and globally it is the central governing structure of humanity. But if history is any guide, institutional arrangements are not eternal. Other possibilities exist. And sometimes changes occur that are so deep and fundamental, few people have the capacity to anticipate those changes and the kinds of institutional alterations that they might entail.

Nevertheless, in this chapter we show the challenge provided by the discourse of human rights in the context of state policy and food. While (some) states have affirmed the human right to food in their shared agreements, within those self-same states exists alarming rates of food insecurity. Instead of addressing those fundamental human needs, in the United States the state pushes that responsibility onto market actors, with food as a commodity. To fill the need that the state seems incapable or uninterested in addressing, social movements from below such as FNB engage in direct action to meet those needs, demonstrating the human rights enterprise at work.

But given their anarchist and anti-statist-inspired principles, many of these movements see the seeds of a new form of social organization present in their practice. This is, perhaps, most strikingly illustrated in the Kurdish struggle, where a stateless people quite often fight, not for their own state, but for a stateless democracy. This might lead us to augment sociology's reigning definition of the state, as the institution that wields and legitimates violence over a given territory. Perhaps another necessary condition for *statehood* is that those governing bodies rule above and beyond the direct control of the populations that they rule. These ideas have been ascendant since the anti-globalization movements, the "movements of squares" such as Occupy Wall Street, and the most recent movements against the presidency of Donald Trump and his "alt-right" supporters. As we argued earlier in this book, our MSP approach seeks both to expand the repertoire of critical state theory into multiple operations of inequality and to add current anarchist and anti-statist discourses to our theoretical pastiche—perspectives that are often ignored by sociologists.

Yet, some of these basic questions of rights, and particularly commodification, require a closer engagement with political economy and what the state offers in terms of assistance to people in need. As such, we turn to welfare policy in our next chapter.

Chapter 8

Intersections of State Projects, Multi-Sites of Power, and the Welfare State

Each of the previous chapters have foregrounded one of the elements of our multi-sites of power model in order to explore carefully how that element operates and affects the relationship between the state and society. In this chapter we will explore how the concepts and elements in our multi-sites framework of power work together in a critical analysis of the welfare state as a state project which affects and is affected by other state projects, particularly those concerning gendering, racial formation, and class. Part of the value of looking at the state project of the welfare state is that so much of state theory has focused on individual policy entries into that project, particularly New Deal legislation. One of the central difficulties of state theory over the past fifty years or so has been the widely divergent takes on that legislation, with little means of reconciling those differences: How is it possible for each of them to be correct in its analysis of the welfare state? For the most part, state theorists have simply explained their differences by asserting that one analysis was correct and the others sadly off the mark. We argue that each of them brought something of value to our ability to understand the bigger picture: much like a table full of people working on a huge jigsaw puzzle, each connected the pieces of a small corner of the puzzle and thought that was the whole picture. We believe the issue is more one of how to connect those partially completed areas of the puzzle to help us see the whole more fully, offering our multi-sites of power framework as a conceptual tool to do so.

Moreover, crucial state theorists have tended overwhelmingly to frame their analyses exclusively in terms of class relations, reducing all to that one dynamic and leaving us unable to understand other significant dynamics such as gendering, racial formation, and heteronormativity. We propose to look at the welfare state project, as one of the important subprojects of the larger state project of economic intervention, as not just a class dynamic but as one fueled by the intersecting state projects of gendering and racial formation.

STATE PROJECTS OF ECONOMIC INTERVENTION

The ideal type of the relationship between the state and society in a capitalist society is often understood to be defined as "laissez-faire," in which the state stands apart from the economy and allows the invisible hand of the market to discipline economic actors. Inefficient and unproductive actors would presumably go bankrupt and efficient and productive actors would thrive, a form of economic Darwinism, if you will. In reality, however, the state has a long history of participation in the economy, forming a state project of economic intervention in which the state acts to secure the conditions of capital accumulation as the basis of a strong and healthy economy.

Critics often argue that there is ample evidence in policy processes to suggest that economic intervention state projects go far beyond simply ensuring a strong economy, extending to class oppression. Even when working-class interests appear to prevail, argue class dialectic theorists, the resulting policies are framed so as not to contradict or hinder conditions favoring capital accumulation. Look, for example, at labor laws governing the relationship between capitalists and workers. During the Industrial Revolution, the state essentially worked to maintain a laissez-faire approach to the economy, allowing capitalists the freedom to develop it as they saw fit. The state's "neutrality" meant, however, that capitalists were free to enrich themselves, if not the overall national economy, at the expense of workers. Those who toiled in the earth's deep recesses to mine the coal and oil that fueled industrial production, as well as those who labored in the factories and fields of that production, worked in highly unsafe conditions and under extremely exploitive conditions. Workers, who were often new immigrants desperate for work and unfamiliar with the language and customs of their newly adopted home, were paid starvation wages for long hours, with no control over their livelihood or their lives. Company towns emerged in the geographically isolated hills and hollers of coal towns, where a single employer provided all the jobs as well as owned the houses the workers and their families lived in, the shops where they bought everything they needed to survive, the schools that educated their children, and the churches where they worshiped. Workers were often paid in company scrip rather than dollars, which meant they could not shop anywhere but the company store at any inflated prices that company chose to charge. Consider the power imbalance such a situation created: workers were not free to dissent or to challenge the employer; to do so was to risk one's livelihood and that of one's entire family. So long as workers existed under a system of

competitive individualism, the power remained firmly in the hands of employers who could pay workers as little as they wanted, under any conditions they
wanted, and charge as much as they wanted for their goods and services.

So far, this story suggests that the state was exclusively focused on securing the conditions of capital accumulation, to the detriment of workers, and
workers had no power but to abide. But the concept of the balance of political forces provides the dynamic mechanisms by which the state project shifts
to secure the interests of workers, albeit in ways that remain consistent with
capital-accumulation interests. By the turn of the twentieth century, workers
increasingly resented and resisted the arrangement of company towns and
workers oppression, and struggled to demand that the state guarantee them
the right to collectively bargain with employers for better wages and safer
working conditions. The unionization movement that blossomed throughout
Europe began to spread in the United States with the help of the Industrial
Workers of the World (IWW, or Wobblies). They advocated an international
industrial union of all workers, regardless of industry or type of work. The
struggle for unionization became quite violent, as capitalists clearly recognized that their monopolistic power edge was being threatened, and fought
back with everything they could, including hiring private enforcers and
Pinkertons to assault and sometimes kill striking workers and firing striking
workers (effectively evicting them and their families from company-owned
housing, often during the most brutal cold of winter).

Workers fought back with collective violence as well, often arming themselves to defend against armed hired enforcers, refusing to work the factories
and the mines, and sometimes staging takeovers and sit-ins on the job. Capitalists became increasingly alarmed at workers' organized rebellion and The
Wobblies' growing attraction to highly exploited and impoverished workers,
and capitalists soon appealed to the state for help. But they were hardly unified as a monolithic bloc in their concerns and their interests, betraying a rift
in the balance of their political forces: capitalists were quite divided on how
and why the state should respond, with big business and the National Association of Manufacturers reluctantly favoring trade unions within industries
as the lesser evil to national or international industrial unions, and small
business and local Chambers of Congress favoring no unions at all. But they
all wanted the state to step in and legislate labor and production relations to
quell labor unrest. Ultimately, big business interests prevailed: in the interest
of maintaining a stable, crisis-free economy, Congress stepped in and in 1935
passed the National Labor Relations Act (more commonly referred to as the
Wagner Act) that provided workers with the right to collective bargaining
(Domhoff 1990; Weinstein 1968; Levine 1988).

While this would appear to be a major victory for labor, state governance of
labor relations and its endorsement of the right to collective bargaining came

at a hefty price: the Taylor law prohibits workers in essential services from striking. Among those the state defines as essential services are police, fire fighters, sanitation workers, transportation workers, teachers, air traffic controllers, and other state workers. So are steel, coal and oil workers, shipyard workers, and munitions plant workers, especially during war and other crises. Since labor strikes were the only source of collective power workers had, this anti-strike clause essentially took the teeth out of their resistance against capital. Further, the right to collectively bargain also carried provisions for binding arbitration, in which the state may force workers and employers to accept and be bound by agreements brokered by the state in order to avoid labor strife, production snags, and economic downturns. The Wagner Act thus became part of the state's economic intervention project that was more a state project of labor control: while it provided workers with the right to collectively bargain in trade unions, it institutionalized labor relations around the boardroom table instead of the streets, and legislated the terms and strategies workers could assume in the process. The power imbalance between the working class and the capitalist class remained to advantage capital.

After the Great Depression of the 1930s, Congress again moved to expand the state project of economic intervention to ensure that monopoly capitalists did not greedily threaten the economic well-being of the nation. One of the policies put into effect was anti-trust legislation that forbid corporations from developing and maintaining a monopoly that essentially posed a threat to competition and therefore a healthy economy. The sheer size and power of monopolies posed a "barrier to entry" to the industry, because smaller, newer firms cannot compete with the economy of scale and the market power of much larger firms. Furthermore, monopolies posed a similar noncompetitive edge to workers and consumers, who would be denied alternative options for employment and for goods and services, and thus monopoly corporations could charge whatever the market could bear, and pay as little as they could get away with. Corporations seeking to merge with or buy out their competitors were denied that right by federal legislation. That legislation ultimately led to the breakup of AT&T, the only telephone company prior to 1984, into several smaller competitive firms. Ironically, anti-trust legislation has rarely been invoked against corporations since the 1980s, but instead has often been called up against unions seeking to merge. So while banks, auto manufacturers, and food-processing corporations have been able to merge with little or no interference by the state with its anti-trust legislation, workers seeking to gain a stronger power base by merging into larger unions often face legal restrictions against noncompetition as defined by anti-trust laws.

Most recently, the North American Free Trade Agreement and efforts to expand it to Central and South America are often framed as part of the state project of economic intervention by reducing barriers to trade that hurt the

United States and U.S.-made products and therefore, presumably, jobs for U.S. workers. Yet analyses of the effects of NAFTA indicate that it has erased the political borders that inhibited trade at the expense of workers' jobs in the United States and workers' wages everywhere (Wallach and Sforza 1999). Ironically, the dialectics of class relations are such that the very same state project that is depressing workers' wages, eroding workers' health and safety on the job, and motivating the reduction if not outright elimination of health and retirement benefits, may ultimately help unions organize workers across national borders as well. This is because the structure of the labor market has shifted from the predominantly goods-producing structure of an industrial economy to one of service-sector jobs in a postindustrialized economy. The shift in the structure of the economy thus shifts the balance of political forces here: while goods-producing jobs can easily be automated or redeployed elsewhere, service jobs are less amenable to such strategies. Certainly, some service jobs, like bank tellers, data entry, and tech support, for example, can be automated or shifted abroad; even teachers can similarly be replaced: witness the rise of online education. But many others are point-of-service and cannot be automated or exported, such as delivery truck drivers, janitors, healthcare workers, and the like. This shift, then, alters the balance of political forces and helps explain why striking UPS workers in 1997 were able to revive the power of the strike to elicit better working conditions, better pay, better pensions, and more opportunities for full-time employment instead of involuntary part-time employment. Thus, because of the balance of political forces, the state project of economic intervention, while largely favoring capital-accumulation interests at the expense of workers' interests, has at times tilted in support of workers' interests.

This historical tale of improved worker rights over time (including antipoverty programs) has led many to frame the state project of economic intervention as a state project of the welfare state.

THE MEANING OF "THE WELFARE STATE"

There is no single form of "the" welfare state; Esping-Andersen (1990) identified at least three welfare state regimes: liberal welfare regimes, corporatist (or conservative) regimes, and social democratic regimes. Liberal welfare state regimes are those that provide relatively low levels of means-tested support framed in concerns for their effects on market efficiency, as found in the United States, United Kingdom, and Australia. Corporatist welfare state regimes are conservative systems that provide a greater level of social supports and rights than found in liberal welfare state regimes, with less concern for the preservation of market efficiency, typically found in countries in the

European Union. Social democratic welfare state regimes provide social supports with no regard to means testing; rather, social supports are universal and de-commodify labor from market efficiency. These regimes are more typically found in the Nordic countries of Sweden, Norway, and Finland. The form of welfare state regime present in any given country is largely a historical product of the degree of class coalition formations, suggesting the effect of the balance of political forces. Esping-Anderson's works also implies the significance of framing in his observation that anti-welfare state attitudes are least likely to emerge in welfare state regimes with the strongest welfare spending. However, this observation is limited by its narrow definition of the welfare state, with the attendant implication that it is simply about class.

Esping-Anderson's work, like much scholarship concerning the welfare state, and indeed the popular media, largely refers to the welfare state as those policies and practices that together focus on *social* welfare. These are policies and expenditures by the state to redistribute wealth from the rich to the poor or to alleviate the symptoms of poverty and inequality, including programs such as Temporary Assistance to Needy Families (TANF, formerly Aid to Families with Dependent Children), Food Stamps, WIC (a nutritional program for women, infants, and children), Medicaid, heating and low-income housing assistance, etc. However, social welfare is but one leg of three defining the welfare state. In addition to social welfare is gilded and corporate welfare, which we will discuss shortly. Furthermore, the welfare state project is not just an economic or class project; it affects and is affected by the state projects of gendering and racial formation, to which we now turn.

GENDERING STATE PROJECTS AND THE WELFARE STATE

Feminist theories of the state shift the focus of the analysis from one of class relations to one exploring the role of the state in gendered oppression processes that shape and frame social constructions of gender. In particular, much of the focus here is on how the state created and reinforced women's subordinated status as an inferior gender and how differentiated states participate in a dynamic process to produce gender regimes (Haney 2000; Brush 2003). Let's examine feminist models of the state to see how this shift in focus helps us to see the hand of the state beyond economic and class relations.

Feminist state theorists investigate how the state reproduces patriarchal relations that privilege men and subordinate women, particularly (but not only) through welfare and family policy (MacKinnon 1989). According to these analysts, welfare policy and the concept of the family wage (with the presumption of males as family breadwinners) buttressed the nuclear family and its gendered hierarchy of male dominance and female dependence on individual men to protect them from poverty (Hartmann 1976; Abramovitz 1996; 2000). Patriarchy and class reproduction thus become linked in support of the capitalist economy where, depending on capitalist need, women's roles alternate between keeper of the home and as a low-cost reserve army of labor (McIntosh 1978). These sometimes conflicting roles for women highlight the tensions and conflicts of a capitalist society. But, some argue, class and capitalist reproduction needs, and the accompanying subjugation of women, are not constant at all times in all societies and they therefore need to be viewed in their ideological and historical context (Barrett 1990). This last point suggests the salience of selectivity filters and framing in socially constructing gender and the role of the state is doing so.

There are slight variations on this theme among researchers using a perspective of the state as patriarchal. Some argue that the welfare state extended women's dependence on individual men to a broader dependence on a male-dominated state (Brown 1981; Boris and Bardaglio 1983). Others disagree, noting that the dialectics of patriarchal state processes may in fact produce ample welfare state programs that can serve to actually decrease women's risk of poverty or to provide material resources to help women and children survive when there is no male source of support (Kamerman 1984; Ruggie 1984; Piven 1990; Edin and Lein 1996). But some see the economic protection these programs may offer as evidence of a patriarchal state seeking to protect women from the brutality and devastation of the male preserve of the economy. Social welfare programs operate under the assumption that women are the "natural" caretakers of children, and commonly absolve individual men from any such responsibility. These differing viewpoints on the meaning of the state's patriarchal position do not obliterate what they have in common: the view of the state as a centralized, patriarchal institution that subordinates women.

Gendered state subsystem analysts reject the view of patriarchal state analysts of the state as monolithic and centralized. Instead, they argue that the state is a more complex and dynamic institution, and thus so is the relationship between the state and gendering processes (Orloff 1996). For example, some researchers found that welfare states were actually comprised of layers of institutional subsystems (Gordon 1990; 1994). "Masculine" social insurance programs such as workmen's compensation, unemployment insurance, and Social Security responded to the limitations of the private labor market to provide stable, secure, and gainful employment for breadwinners. These programs were based on the assumption that men were entitled to such support to help them fulfill their "natural" male roles as providers and breadwinners (Nelson 1990; Sapiro 1990). In contrast, need-based, means-tested "feminine" social assistance programs like Aid to Families with Dependent Children (now Temporary Assistance to Needy Families), Mothers' Pensions,

WIC, and Aid to Dependent Children were based on the assumption that women needed a male breadwinner to avoid poverty, and the state would step in only when such a breadwinner was absent (Mink 1994). When the state does take over the role of the male provider, it also assumes the role of male dominator in women's lives. This often happens in the administration of the highly regulated social welfare programs, which typically subject women to a great deal of surveillance/observation, evaluation, and control as the state tries to establish women's eligibility for benefits (Nelson 1990)

While this multilayered structure of the welfare state does indeed offer a more nuanced view than the previous conceptions of a centralized state, it remained focused on income-maintenance programs of the welfare state, particularly in the United States (Gordon 1994; Orloff 1996). In contrast, gendered welfare regime analysts broadened their focus to examine a wider array of the kinds of policies pursued by welfare states. They found that policies dealing with issues such as citizenship, care for family members, women's employment, and reproduction also affected women's material well-being and contributed to gendering processes that shaped and framed gendered oppression. Furthermore, their expanded view, as well as a more cross-national comparison of welfare state types, revealed wide variations of gendered regimes in welfare states (Esping-Andersen 1990; Leira 1992; Lewis 1992; O'Connor 1993; Orloff 1993; Shaver 1993; Borchorst 1994; Gustafsson 1994; Hobson 1994; Sainsbury 1994; 1996; O'Connor, Orloff, and Shaver 1999; Huber and Stephens 2000; Korpi 2000). This research suggests that welfare states are not only not monolithic in structure or single-minded in their patriarchal allegiances; there are wide variations on this theme of gendered welfare states.

Gendered state process analysts focus less on redistributive policy and more on processes and relations of discourse and gendered meaning in welfare states, suggesting selectivity filters as significant features. In these analyses, the welfare state is not only a policy-making institution but also an arena of struggles over the contested terrain of the social construction of gender (Fraser and Gordon 1994; Curran and Abrams 2000; Zylan 2000). Here, claims processes involve shifting the line between the "natural" and the "artificial" or political definitions of gender, which then frames the discourse concerning the identification of needs and appropriate policies to address these (Peattie and Rein 1983; Pringle and Watson 1992). The struggle therefore becomes one of defining what is biological or natural, and therefore immutable and unchangeable with policy, and what is really more a social construction of gender and therefore amenable to policies that redistributed resources, redefined roles and responsibilities, and established rights. These analyses introduced the notion that the welfare state is not just a masculine structural creation imposing patriarchal gendered meanings and oppressions;

it is also an arena galvanized by the balance of gendered political forces in which those social constructions are challenged and resisted, where the very meanings of motherhood and dependency could be fought over, and where these contested terrains could affect not just notions of gendering but also the formation of the welfare state itself (Bock and Thane 1991; Muncy 1991; Skocpol 1992; Koven and Michel 1993; Sklar 1993; Goodwin 1997; Abramovitz 2000).

Together, these perspectives on the gendering state project suggest that the welfare state project is gendered as well as classed. We suggest that it intersects as well with the racial formation state project, as can be seen in the structure and dynamics of the welfare state.

CLASS, GENDER, AND RACIAL STATE PROJECTS AND THE WELFARE STATE

The literatures on class, gendering, and racial formation projects together suggest their intersections in the welfare state project insofar as this project focuses on social welfare as a gendered and racialized project. Why is this selectivity filter of the meaning of the welfare state project significant? The definition of the welfare state as one devoted to social welfare becomes a selectivity filter that obliterates other dimensions of the welfare state, such as gilded and corporate welfare. Before we tackle these other dimensions, it is worthwhile examining the social welfare state project.

Organized struggles shaped by the balance of political forces in the 1950s and 1960s succeeded in gaining many civil rights, women's rights, and anti-poverty, education and job training, and health programs. But since the late 1970s the state has restructured the economy more straightforwardly in favor of business interests and to the disadvantage of labor, the poor, women, children, and people of color (see, e.g., Lieberman 1998). Two key restructuring projects were the New Federalism of the 1980s and welfare reform of the 1990s.

NEW FEDERALISM

What came to be called New Federalism was based on the conservative political philosophy that the federal government should be involved only with taxation and national defense; all else, particularly social welfare programs, should be the responsibility of state and local governments. Under New Federalism battles previously won by disadvantaged groups would have to be fought again in the future.

New Federalism began quietly in the late 1970s under President Jimmy Carter. The state responded to an ailing economy by lowering federal social welfare expenditures, reducing the burden of taxes on the wealthy in the attempt to stimulate increased saving and investment, and relaxing or eliminating federal regulation of corporations. The goal of New Federalism was to regulate the economy to the advantage of businesses, particularly large corporations. The assumption was that firms would reinvest their increased profits to improve productive capacity, thereby creating new jobs. President Ronald Reagan greatly expanded this approach, which came to be called supply-side, or trickle-down, economics. Its supporters argued that benefits to capitalists would trickle down to benefit labor; eventually everyone would benefit from New Federalism: "A rising tide raises all ships" was the supply-siders' motto.

In practice, though, many ships sank. Tax cuts instituted under President Reagan in the 1980s greatly benefited the wealthy and large corporations who did not reinvest their newfound wealth in job creation but instead invested it in stocks and other investment instruments that enriched themselves. Meanwhile, the economy continued to suffer, increasing the ranks of the poor, the hungry, and the homeless. While their needs grew, some social welfare and entitlement programs originally designed to catch economic victims in a federal safety net were slashed; others' eligibility requirements were redefined to reduce the number of people the programs served (Abramovitz 1996).

Critics decried the New Federalism as a "mean season" attack against the welfare state and a massive attempt to dismantle it (Block et al. 1987; Piven and Cloward 1993). The effect of the state's twist on Robin Hood could be seen on the individual level. Overall, the economic distance between the wealthy and poor in the nation widened to a gap unseen since the Great Depression in the 1930s. The average family income of the poorest 20 percent of the U.S. population declined by 10 percent between 1967 and 2000, while the average family income of the wealthiest 20 percent increased during the same period by 13.2 percent. More strikingly, the average family income of the wealthiest 5 percent increased more than 20 percent (U.S. Census Bureau 2001). New Federalism had succeeded in redistributing income from the poorest to the wealthiest.

New Federalism particularly impoverished women. While women's share of jobs in the labor force increased during the 1980s, their share of poverty increased quite dramatically as well. This was because the vast majority of new jobs created were minimum-wage, part-time service-sector jobs with no healthcare or retirement benefits. Even if a mother of three worked full time, year round at the minimum wage, she would not be able to make enough on her own to rise above the federal poverty line. Working part-time guaranteed that both she and her children would be entrenched in poverty, be hungry, and possibly be homeless. If she did not have a wage-earning partner, a mother was likely to face impoverishment. Single-parent families increased from 13 percent of the total number of families in 1970 to 29.7 percent in 1992, and most of these were female headed. While the median family income of married couples increased 9 percent between 1980 and 1993, the median income of female-headed households actually declined by 1.7 percent (U.S. Bureau of the Census 1994). Thus, while the overall rate of poverty in the United States in 1993 was 15.1 percent, the rate of poverty among female-headed families was an astounding 35.6 percent (compared with a rate of 16.8 percent for male-headed families) (U.S. Bureau of the Census 1994).

New Federalism also disproportionately hurt people of color. The poverty rate for whites in 1993 was 12.2 percent, but the rate for African Americans was 33.1 percent and for Latinxs, 30.6 percent (U.S. Bureau of the Census 1994). According to the Bureau of Labor Statistics, African Americans were more than twice as likely as whites to be unemployed in 1992, and Latinxs were almost twice as likely. The gap between African Americans and whites in terms of wealth and median family income widened, regardless of education levels.

Meanwhile, the New Federalism benefited corporations quite well without producing the much-heralded expectation of benefits for the working class. Deregulation of industries, relaxation of anti-trust laws, and huge tax windfalls for corporations were supposed to increase productivity and stimulate the creation of new jobs. Instead, they fueled more than a decade of merger mania. Between 1980 and 1988 the total value of corporate mergers and acquisitions "exceeded two thirds of a trillion dollars" (Phillips 1990, 172). Mergers and acquisitions do not increase productive capacity, nor do they stimulate the production of any new jobs; they simply reshuffle who owns the existing production facilities. In fact, mergers often entail job loss, as the acquiring firm tries to streamline operations to help pay off its debt. While there is little documentation of the number of jobs lost through mergers, AFL-CIO secretary-treasurer Thomas Donahue testified before Congress that an estimated 80,000 union jobs were lost as a direct result of mergers and another 80,000 as an indirect result (*National Journal* 1989). His estimate is conservative, since it does not include the number of nonunion jobs lost through mergers. Corporations were using their increased profits from New Federalism policies to buy one another out, not to create new jobs. The rising economic tide was not raising all ships. Only the largest corporations were rising; smaller businesses were capsizing. Between 1985 and 1992, there were 533,000 small-business failures, a significantly larger number than in previous years (Federal News Service 1993).

These attempts to dismantle the welfare state "as we know it" continued through the 1990s under welfare reform.

WELFARE REFORM

The Personal Responsibility Act of 1996, more familiarly known as "welfare reform," dramatically changed how public assistance is administered and gave individual states far greater flexibility in determining how such programs would be implemented. Key provisions in the national policy included a sharp reduction in benefit amounts as well as reductions in length of time over a lifetime that recipients would be permitted to collect (the Act established a national limit of five years, but twenty-two states have since instituted far more stringent time restrictions). Recipients must find paid employment in order to continue to be eligible for assistance (Beaulieu 1998). These reforms were based on the stereotype of the lazy "welfare queen" who continued to live off the public dole indefinitely, refusing to work, having more children in order to increase her benefits, and acting as a financial drain on public resources (Sidel 2000). Moreover, the selectivity filter that framed the "welfare queen" as an African American single mother further fueled public animosity to social welfare programs, pitting poor and working-class women of color against white middle-class families (Neubeck and Cazenave 2001).

The stereotype of the "welfare queen," however, never matched the reality: relatively few recipients ever actually remained very long on welfare (over 70 percent received welfare assistance for less than two years, and only 8 percent remained on welfare for over eight years); the average family size of welfare recipients, at two children, was no larger than the average middle-class family size and more than 75 percent of welfare recipients had three children or fewer; and most welfare recipients were not lazy people who refused to work, but instead were women who had lost jobs or who worked at low-wage jobs that failed to provide income above the poverty level (Seccombe 1999; U.S. Department of Commerce, Census Bureau 1999), a situation that continues today. These facts did not dissuade those in Congress who were intent on further dismantling social welfare programs.

When welfare reform of the Personal Responsibility Welfare Reform Act was implemented in 1992, the number of people on public assistance or welfare dropped sharply. The assumption has been that this decline indicates the success of the program of weaning those who have grown dependent on the state by forcing them to get jobs. But the question remains: Where did these former welfare recipients go? Are they off the welfare rolls because they are now gainfully employed? Has welfare reform thus served to significantly reduce poverty? The answer to both questions apparently is "no." Many former recipients have simply run out of benefits, but have been without an opportunity to complete education or training programs to secure decent jobs. Others have jobs, but these are minimum-wage or low-paying jobs that often carry few or no benefits (Casey 1998; Abramovitz 2000; Neubeck 2006). The Urban Institute found, for example, that 61 percent of welfare recipients had jobs after leaving welfare, but they were earning a median wage of $6.61 per hour, and fewer than one-fourth of them had medical benefits from their jobs (Gault and Um'rani 2000).

Evidence from individual states confirms the finding that welfare reform is not reducing poverty, even if it is reducing the number of people receiving welfare assistance. The Wisconsin Works (W-2) program reduced welfare rolls by half in three years, but most participants have remained in poverty: one-fourth of those who left welfare returned for cash assistance, and half of those who found jobs are earning so little they remain below the poverty line (www.legis. state.wi.us/lab/reports/01-7full.pdf). A mother of two working full time, year round at a minimum-wage job simply does not have enough income to move her family above the poverty line, and the loss of benefits such as medical care compounds the poverty. Other former recipients have simply disappeared out of the system, perhaps to the streets among the homeless.

Among the hardest hit by welfare reform have been women of color and their children. This is partly because Latinx and African American women "are more vulnerable to poverty than white women," having higher rates of both poverty and unemployment. Researchers attribute this racial disparity to educational disadvantages and both gender and racial discrimination by employers (Gault and Um'rani 2000, 2; see also Neubeck 2006). Many states have compounded the likelihood of continued poverty among former welfare recipients, particularly among women of color and children: in their enthusiasm for welfare reform, they have failed to inform recipients and the working poor who leave welfare that they or their children are still eligible for programs like Food Stamps, Medicaid, housing assistance, and the like (Houppert 1999).

Evidence strongly indicates, then, that welfare reform and the significant cuts in anti-poverty programs under the New Federalism have served to intensify poverty, particularly among women, children, people of color, and people with disabilities (Schram and Beer 1999). Programs such as welfare reform and the New Federalism are based on the assumption that the capitalist economy has the ability to solve social problems like poverty. However, an economy that increasingly offers minimum-wage service work with no benefits as the only real option to the poor, and which does not seriously address discrimination in employment and education opportunities or the need for a living wage, is in no position to reduce structured economic inequality (Blau 1999; Huber and Kosser 1999; Eitzen and Baca Zinn 2000).

DISMANTLING THE WELFARE STATE?

As much as the New Federalism and welfare reform have clearly contributed to a growing gap between rich and poor, between men and women, and between whites and people of color, it is important to note that these policy changes do not necessarily represent a dismantling of the welfare state. This is because these programs together constitute only one part of the welfare state, namely social welfare, which includes state policies and budgetary expenditures that redistribute wealth from the affluent to the poor in order to subsidize the needs of the poor and people with disabilities. There are two other components of the welfare state, however, and these remained largely untouched or even enhanced under the New Federalism. They are *gilded welfare* and *corporate welfare*.

Gilded welfare involves state policies and budgetary expenditures to redistribute wealth from the poor and working class to the middle class and the affluent. These include Social Security, Medicare, federal income tax deductions for homeownership and local property taxes, dependent children tax deductions, and home business tax deductions. While much of media and public attention has embraced the selectivity filter of social welfare expenditures, the fact is that gilded welfare spending far outweighs social welfare spending. For example, in 2011 the federal government spent over $1.3 trillion on gilded welfare programs (not including middle class and affluent tax deductions and allowances), but only $622.7 billion on anti-poverty programs (www.census.gov). That means that social welfare spending represented slightly more than 16 percent of the total federal spending. Despite the media and popular perceptions that social welfare represented a drain on the federal budget, it certainly appears to be a very small slice of that pie.

Even more expensive have been the corporate welfare expenditures. Corporate welfare involves the state policies and expenditures that redistribute wealth to corporations and the affluent by directly or indirectly subsidizing, supporting, rescuing, or otherwise socializing the cost and risk of investment and private profit making. These include subsidies to industries such as agriculture, tax abatements, depreciation allowances for equipment, Department of Defense spending that provides guaranteed markets at noncompetitive prices, and corporate bailouts. Taken together, the corporate welfare programs represent an enormous slice of the federal budget. For example, bailout of the savings and loan industry in the late 1980s represented a massive federal commitment of taxpayers' money to subsidizing the risks of profit making in private savings and loan institutions and rescuing those that had failed as a result of investing in junk bonds and real estate speculation. The bailout itself represented a major increase in corporate welfare: although the federal government has bailed out over four hundred individual corporations since World War II (Lockheed and Chrysler among the largest), it had never before agreed to bail out an entire industry. And while previous bailouts were limited to fixed amounts over a clearly defined and relatively short time period, the savings-and-loan bailout occurred with no discussion of a limited dollar amount and no mention of a specified limited time period. This was, in fact, the first time any corporate entity was bailed out with a "blank check." And what a blank check it has been: the program has not concluded its bailouts and has thus far cost at least $250 billion. Estimates are that the total cost could reach as high as $500 billion before it is over (see Glasberg and Skidmore 1997). Compare this expense of a single corporate welfare program to the entire budget of 1990s anti-poverty expenditures, at a mere $117 billion, and it becomes clearer that the welfare state for the affluent and non-needy is, indeed, alive and well, and growing every day.

What occurred during the 1980s and 1990s was not so much a dismantling of the welfare state but more of a redistribution of resources from social welfare to gilded and corporate welfare. Indeed, when one considers the huge state expenditures devoted to corporate welfare programs, it becomes evident that, far from dismantling the welfare state, the New Federalism had resulted in an expanded welfare state, but one more devoted to corporate and gilded welfare than to social welfare. The state has never been neutral in the struggle between capital-accumulation interests and those of workers, the poor, women, people of color, people with disabilities, and children. New Federalism and the attacks on social welfare it unleashed succeeded in promoting legislation and budgeting practices that unabashedly favored capitalists and redistributed wealth from the poor and workers to the wealthy and corporations. Even conservatives like Kevin Phillips (1990, 1993) could not argue that this was in the common good.

And corporate welfare expanded once again during the recession of 2008–2012, when the federal TARP program bailed out banks' losses from predatory lending practices and subsidized banks' collective profit making with little regard for the fact that their behavior had in fact ignited that severe recession. Worse yet, the bailout occurred without the federal government insisting on the imposition of new regulations to keep track of its investment as a condition of banks receiving TARP money. Incredibly enough, banks blatantly provided huge bonuses to their executives after receiving their share of TARP money, the very same executives who oversaw the bank practices that sent the nation into an economic tailspin. Mean season, indeed. But not against the welfare state; it has been a mean season targeting the social welfare state, disproportionately allocating the misery to the poor, women, children, and people of color while subsidizing the advantages of the affluent and the corporate economy. While the war on poverty sought to redistribute wealth from the affluent, the New Federalism of the current welfare state to emphasize gilded and corporate welfare is redistributing wealth from the poor and working and middle classes to the affluent, largely benefiting whites and men more than people of color and women. The state project of the welfare state is alive and well; it has simply shifted its focus.

ANTI-AUSTERITY SOCIAL MOVEMENTS

While it is clear that the state project of the welfare state has not disappeared, what is equally clear is that its shifting focus has not occurred in a vacuum. Nor has it gone without challenge. The implementation of welfare reform was met with growing resistance among the poor. For example, the Kensington Welfare Rights Union, a grassroots group formed by poor and homeless people in 1991, organized protests and bus tours to gather testimony of the impact of welfare reform on their lives, then staged a march to the United Nations to share the collected testimonies there in a claim of denial of their human rights. They also engaged in direct actions in erecting tent cities and staging squatters' rights takeovers of abandoned housing (Zucchino 1999).

Indeed, much of the increasing convulsions felt around the world since the mid-2000s indicate that the balance of political forces is actively engaged, as are the selectivity filters framing the process. In the United States, for example, there is a growing movement in support of raising the minimum wage to $15 per hour, a claim bolstered in many municipalities by striking workers and large protest demonstrations in support of that wage. Many states and municipalities have already raised their minimum wages to that target, with a goal of raising it further in the coming years. But there is also a growing movement demanding the establishment of a living wage instead of a federally established minimum wage, to allow all workers to rise beyond subsistence and poverty. The oxymoron of the "working poor" should become obsolete, they argue: no one who works should ever be poor or homeless. Their argument is gaining traction as more people begin to recognize the absurdity of poverty among those who work. That significant challenge to the prevailing selectivity filter of the poor as lazy owes much to the efforts of Occupy Wall Street, which called attention to the severe gap between wealth and poverty in the United States as unacceptable (Gitlin 2012). So do growing movements around the country in support of housing for the homeless and food for the hungry. They have had some success in challenging municipal policies and practices that criminalize homelessness with anti-vagrancy laws, "keep moving" policies, spires on benches to prevent sleeping in public, and police actions to tear down tent cities of the homeless. Occupy Wall Street thus ignited an altered balance of political forces in the struggle to reinforce social welfare.

Further, the Occupy protests were a part of a larger global wave of austerity and resistance to its implementation during this time period (Shannon 2014). Occupy Wall Street might have arisen, in part, as a general spread of social revolt that began with the Arab Spring. These led to a larger "movement of squares" as groups like the *indignados* (i.e., indignant ones) arose in Spain, occupying Madrid's Puerta Del Sol; occupiers seized Syntagma Square in

Athens, Greece; protesters in London occupied Trafalgar Square; and social antagonists began occupying public space in cities, big and small, all over the world. In conjunction with these global protests, labor unrest followed in their wake, such as the wildcat strike in South Africa, which led to the "Marikana Massacre," where government forces gunned down disgruntled workers in 2012. Not content with occupying public space, activists began occupying land and buildings throughout parts of Europe and in Latin America. Radical student movements likewise arose, in response to tuition hikes as a result of austerity measures, notably in Canada, Chile, and the United Kingdom.

INTERSECTING SITES OF POWER AND STATE POLICY

Literatures in state theory, feminist state theory, and racial formation theory share some parallel notions of the relationship between the state and society, and the state's role in the production and maintenance of systems of oppression. State projects are dynamic processes of both oppression from above and resistance from below, as illustrated by the case of the welfare state project.

The state is a multidimensional structure that includes not only the legislature but also the judiciary and executive branches of government, and administrative state agencies vested with the power to implement and interpret policy on a day-to-day basis. Moreover, the state is also an actor, subject to the same forces and conditions affecting other groups engaged in policy formation and implementation processes, including unity and disunity between and within agencies and institutional organizations, resource mobilization processes, and access to opportunities to create disruption. Such an approach helps us to explain class-based as well as gender-based and racially based policy arenas by using Jessop's concepts as organizing conceptual tools. These concepts allow us to identify the relationship between the state and class relations as well as that between the state and gendering and the state and racial formation. We can begin then to articulate the conditions under which some policies are more or less likely to develop at particular points in time and some interests are more or less likely to gain power and have their interests addressed.

State projects are not discrete, individual projects that are isolated from each other. Indeed, there are many places where economic state projects intersect with racial formation and gendering state projects, as is the case in welfare "reform" of the 1990s. In the case of welfare reform, what appeared to be an economic issue (work as the antidote to poverty) operates as an entry into gendering state projects where gender is socially constructed relative to class: poor women are socially constructed as good mothers only if they work in the paid labor force and leave the care of their young children to others; middle class and affluent mothers, in contrast, are socially constructed as good mothers only if they remain dependent on their male partners and stay at home to care for their own young children. Moreover, such welfare reforms are also part of the racial formation state project since they largely affect women and children of color more harshly than whites, and imply that the "problems" besetting welfare are somehow a function of a racially framed culture of poverty. Thus, state projects themselves are not isolated one from the other. Rather, they articulate common and intersecting agendas that contribute to intersecting systems of multiple oppressions.

While this chapter shows the utility of an MSP approach to state theory through the lens of welfare state policy, it does leave some questions unanswered. In particular, we might assess the MSP approach we have argued for throughout this book and use that as a general primer into where we might go with state theory. What is the future of the state and political organization? And now that we have outlined the state of state theory, as it were, where might we go? We respond to these questions in our final summative chapter.

Chapter 9

Where Do We Go From Here?

Implications and Steps Forward

With this book, we intend to expand the field of state theory in general and *critical* state theories in particular. It is, in part, a result of large historical forces that Marxism became the dominant model for critical state theory, which explains its tendency toward economism. Marx (1977, preface) is often referenced for suggesting that the economic system of a given society is a major force for producing the culture, politics, and even consciousness of the whole of society:

> In the social production of their existence, men [*sic*] inevitably enter into definite relations, which are independent of their will, namely [the] relations of production appropriate to a given stage in the development of their material forces of production. The totality of these relations of production constitutes the economic structure of society, the real foundation, on which arises a legal and political superstructure, and to which correspond definite forms of consciousness. The mode of production of material life conditions the general process of social, political, and intellectual life.

If one begins with these assumptions, it might be easy to see the class relation as the guiding principle of state theory—after all, the state, accordingly, is but an effect of the organization of production of a society.

Contemporary sociologists tend to reject these economistic assumptions, some arguing that Marx has been misinterpreted, while others argue that we should draw on other perspectives or alter Marx in some way to account for operations of power that are multiple and intersecting (putting aside, for the moment, that there are still sociologists who would argue that we should remain economistic). Among sociologists, it is common for intersectional understandings of relations of inequality and domination to be assumed.

155

Some even argue that intersectionality has gained so much popularity that it has become a buzzword of sorts (see, e.g., Davis 2008).

But despite this popularity and the questioning of readings of Marxism as necessarily economistic, the area of critical state theory has been left largely untouched by these insights. We can, of course, find some pushback in feminist, queer, and critical race theories that deal with the state. These are valuable interventions, but none thus far have attempted to create a coherent and integrated approach that accounts for multiple sites of power and oppression. Our MSP approach is an attempt to do just that.

We propose that many of the ideas and concepts central to critical state theory are important contributions that can be used, expanded, or in some cases altered, in order to give us a clearer picture of the state-society relationship. We might also utilize ideas that have largely been ignored in sociological state theory. Particularly promising are Jessop's (1990; 2008) concepts of state projects, selectivity filters, and balance of class forces (though we alter this last concept to the "balance of political forces" to account for multi-sites of power including, but not limited to, class). Similarly, perspectives that have been left out of critical state theory such as queer theory and anarchism provide fertile ground for expanding our understanding of state and society.

The concept of state projects allows us a view of policies that are not isolated, singular initiatives to be studied divorced from their historical relationship to other policies. Rather, policies are elements of larger state projects, which are sets of state policies and/or agencies (as opposed to singular, unrelated policies and/or agencies) unified around a particular major issue. This concept is used to indicate a process in which the state itself is both an arena of struggle and an actor that, above all other actors, has the unique authority to codify social constructions into legalized norms and to enforce these in ways that shape cultural repertoires and social behaviors, but which is also subject to resistance and modification from below. State projects, then, are not necessarily only produced and reproduced by the state, but are also the production of struggles between the state and political forces over the contested terrain that is state policy.

Selectivity filters function to mobilize bias in that they act as a lens through which actors perceive, understand, and act on issues. Some notions and perspectives are filtered in and others are filtered out of the policy-making process. As such, these filters have a mediating effect that frames and shapes not only perceptions of and discourse about issues, but also the emergence of policy solutions. Selectivity filters go beyond individual policy initiatives and are integral to the dialectic process. The reflexive interplay between selectivity filters and the relations of political forces reverberates through the implementation of that policy and sets the stage for later policy creation, modification, and implementation. These filters include larger state projects, which provide a framework—past policy precedents of state projects influence the viability and content of future policy initiatives, precedents, and discourses that frame debates and perspectives.

Where Jessop talks of the balance of *class* forces, we expand on his notion to one of the balance of *political* forces in our MSP approach to state theory. We do this because gendering, sexuality, and racial formation forces are similarly at work affecting state projects, similar in some ways to class forces. The state engages with a variety of actors, including but not limited to businesses, nonprofits, nongovernmental organizations, and social movements such that the organization of power in society tips, at times, and that directional tip can have effects on state policies (even while state policies and projects can be effected as well).

This framework becomes more rigorous when combined with previously ignored theoretical perspectives, such as queer theory and libertarian forms of socialism, such as anarchism. Queer theory provides a theoretical space for destabilizing notions of identity and for observing patterns of power, particularly those related to gender and sexuality, that might not primarily be rooted in identities. Anarchism and other forms of anti-state socialism have become increasingly popular in social movements and because of their commitment to social transformation from below, they offer interesting examples of resistance to state power as such, particularly in the context of direct action. We outline this approach and put these concepts and bodies of ideas in conversation in chapters 1 and 2.

In chapter 3, we demonstrate how the history of the state project of economic intervention illuminates some of the critical factors of our MSP approach to state theory. First, the analysis makes clear that the state project of economic intervention is not a single policy initiative, but rather a dialectic process in which many ostensibly unrelated individual policies and practices are threaded together over time, each influencing, framing, and shaping subsequent entries. That process is galvanized by the ongoing balance of political forces, which themselves are animated and affected by such factors as the resources various participants can mobilize and apply to take advantage of or create political opportunities to advance their interests; the extent of unity within each of these interests and between these interests; and the resources and unity within and between state actors and agencies, who themselves are participating interests. That is, the state and its agencies are not neutral structures or arenas of conflict objectively adjudicating competing interests in the "common good"; rather, they are active participants in the balance of political forces. It is noteworthy, however, that even the most formidable and resource-rich institutional forces are not absolutely powerful: they do not get everything they want all the time. But they do remain significantly dominant forces in pressing their interests better than many (or even most) other actors, or in finding ways to undermine state project initiatives that may mitigate their ability to do so, unless they are confronted and challenged with well-organized and resourceful opposing forces. And it is noteworthy, as well, that state projects are not secluded within the borders of nation-states, unaffected by factors and forces from other nation-states; rather, as the history of economic state projects illustrates, they are permeated by external influences well beyond these boundaries.

The history of the economic intervention state project further underscores the need of a state theory that pays attention to class divisions, but is not economistic, nor limited exclusively to class as a dimension of individuals within nations. For example, the predatory lending practices of large commercial banks as well as global financial institutions demonstrate a tendency for working class and poor people of color to be targeted, and ultimately to bear the substantial costs of illegal, extralegal, and unscrupulous financial practices. Globally, a long history of colonialism and neoliberal lending policies for economic development tend to target poorer nations, who bear the devastating costs of *global* financial malfeasance. Thus, the analysis of economic intervention state projects evinces that while we might begin the analysis by foregrounding class relations of inequality, we cannot develop a fuller picture without incorporating the context of race, class, and nation of origin. Rather, we can begin to understand how state projects of race, class, and nation of origin resonate in the complex intersections of imperialism, capitalism, and white supremacy.

In chapter 4, we turn to selectivity filters and show how they frame and shape meaning-making processes that affect, inform, and buttress state projects. They are created, maintained, challenged, and transformed through various forces from above (e.g., the state) and below (e.g., social movements focusing on policy change, cultural change, and altering daily life). This chapter focuses on heteronormative framing by using the lens of identity in order to demonstrate the power that accompanies access to frame concepts through selectivity filters within state projects. Access to the power to shape and inform selectivity filters are held by both the state from above and subordinates from below in an ongoing process and struggle (oftentimes located within social movements) of meaning-making.

The concepts of both 1) "sexual orientation" and 2) binary gender act as selectivity filters for how the state legislates and recognizes some gender and sexual practices in policy making, but ignores or disciplines others. For example, because sexual orientation is a gendered (and binary) understanding of *sexual* practice and desire (meaning, as a concept and term, it describes sexual attraction in terms of binary gendered attraction, e.g., heterosexual/straight or homosexual/gay), it acts as a selectivity filter by filtering out sexual practices not primarily defined by their relationship to binary gender—this omission, of course, includes practices of having multiple lovers and romantic partners and a range of (consensual) non-monogamous relations, as well as nonnormative familial configurations. Likewise, the concept of binary gender acts as a selectivity filter for how the state heavily legislates around gender, as is demonstrated in the struggle for access to public bathrooms by transgender, nonbinary, and other gender nonconforming folks.

Heteronormativity relies on a linear and naturalized assumptive equation that aligns "biological sex," gender (identity and expression), and sexuality ("sexual orientation" and desire, broadly defined), as well as configuration of romantic and familial relationships. Several examples of legislation in the United States demonstrate a heteronormative logic or equation that frames policy-making activities: particular chromosomes lead to particular gonads, which lead to particular secondary sex characteristics, which lead to a particular gender, which leads to a particular gender identity and expression, which leads to particular gendered sexual orientation/desire, which ultimately leads to a desire to form a particular familial configuration. In this heteronormative logic, each one of these steps is assumed to lead toward, and be aligned with, the next step. It is this heteronormative logic that acts as a selectivity filter in numerous state and federal policies in the United States such as the recent moral panics around public bathroom usage as well as marriage policy remaining between two and only two people after the passage of legislation affirming same-sex marriage. Heteronormativity functions as a frame that social institutions and policies use as a filter when writing and enforcing policies that ultimately reinforce the presumption that heterosexuality is the norm and that gender and sex are natural and aligned binaries.

Trans-discriminatory legislation requires an intersectional lens to understand the selectivity filters that shape and frame this debate in the United States. It is difficult to grasp the complexity of these legislative debates unless we view gender and sexuality as overlapping, intersectional forms of oppression (and perhaps, the forms of liberation tied up in them). The same can be said about same-sex marriage. We cannot understand the terms homosexuality or heterosexuality without viewing gender as binary. Both homosexuality and heterosexuality rest on the assumption that there are two and only two genders. The MSP approach to state theory allows room for an intersectional lens on state projects that are not reducible to a single identity or relation of inequality.

Investigating the heteronormative state project illustrates that a state theory is needed that can explain state projects which are not reducible to class. Understanding heteronormativity as a state project requires recognizing the complex interplay among patriarchy, heteronormativity, white supremacy, and capitalism. Questions about the state's role in the re/production of gender and sexuality formations, and how the state's relationship to society affects these formations and processes necessitate a more holistic theory of the state—one that includes, for example, the ability to explain the dominance of heteronormative policy making and its effects. But it is not sufficient to simply replace existing concepts of class-based domination within debates around state theory with concepts attending to gendered, racialized, or heterosexist domination. Rather, here we show that sexual identity functions as a selectivity filter guiding state policy.

In chapter 5, we analyze social movements as a significant part of the balance of political forces. Our analysis of the social construction of race and racial formation processes highlights the dynamic relationship of cultural frames as selectivity filters and the balance of raced forces in social movements in a protracted dialectic claims process. That is, race as a cultural concept is predicated on assumptions of the salience of biological bases of human differences; however, this biological assumption is frequently challenged through a claims process of struggles over shifting the cultural boundaries between what is natural (biological) and what is artificial (socially constructed) in conceptualizing the meaning of race. The state is hardly a neutral institution or simply an arena of struggles over this contested terrain: it is, instead, an active participant in the shaping and framing of the concept of "race," through policy and practice in the racial state project. Our analysis of the racial formation state project illustrates how social movements become vital factors affecting the balance of political forces by galvanizing actors into the claims process and harnessing the energy of participants in an application of organized pressure to the process of the state project.

In chapter 6 we used the human right to housing, and particularly the housing crisis in the United States in 2008 (as well as the lead up to the crisis), to show how state policy and legislation demonstrated the intersections of racialized and class power. This was particularly true of predatory lending practices, some legal others not. Throughout this chapter we show how the state projects bound up in housing and the regulation and deregulation of finance capital become intertwined with structured inequalities around race and class and follow patterns that flow from the balance of political forces. Chapter 7 follows a similar trajectory, likewise centered on a human right agreed to by groupings of states, including the United States—the right to adequate food. We show how state projects shift the responsibility of providing adequate food from the state to market actors through commodification and trace its impact along lines of race, class, and gender. Here, because the state refuses to guarantee a fundamental human need (that it has agreed to in legal instruments), we follow in the vein of writers arguing for the "human rights enterprise" (Armaline and Glasberg 2009; Armaline, Glasberg, and Purkayastha 2011; Armaline, Glasberg, and Purkayastha 2015) and note how the balance of political forces can lead to challenges to the state by social movements from below. We briefly draw out the direct action practices of Food Not Bombs (FNB) to show that the state-society relationship is not as simple as the state ruling from above, unchallenged. Indeed, in the case of FNB, activists provide food to needy people in direct challenge to the state, with many of the activists viewing their movement form as a way to move beyond the state, an idea realized to some extent by parts of the stateless Kurdish population (through very different venues than FNB).

Chapter 8 notes how scholarships in state theory, feminist state theory, and racial formation theory echo parallel themes of the relationship between the state and society, and the state's role in the production and maintenance of systems of oppression. However, we emphasize that this relationship is not static, nor is oppression unidirectional and beyond effective challenge: state projects are, instead, dynamic processes of both oppression from above and resistance from below, as illustrated in this chapter by the case of the welfare state project. And state projects do not exist in vacuums, isolated from other state projects; rather, they frequently resonate and intersect in dynamic ways, affecting and framing each other.

In our approach, the state is both a structure and an actor. As structure it is a multidimensional institution comprised of the legislative, judicial, and executive branches of government, as well as a wide range of administrative federal, state, and local agencies assigned the power of day-to-day implementation and interpretation of policy. Beyond simply being a structure, however, the state is also an actor participating in the balance of political forces affecting state projects. As such, the state is susceptible to the same forces and conditions affecting other groups and interests engaged in policy formation and implementation processes and claims challenges. These include unity and disunity between and within agencies and institutional organizations, resource mobilization processes, and access to apply these resources in opportunities to create disruption of business as usual as state projects develop and change.

State projects are not discrete, individual projects that are sealed off from each other. In fact, there are many interstices where economic state projects intersect with racial formation and gendering state projects. Take the case of welfare "reform" of the 1990s. What appeared to be simply an economic issue of work as the antidote to poverty (and its antecedent presumption of laziness and a failure to value hard work and education) actually reflected gendering state projects whereby gender is socially constructed relative to class: poor women are socially constructed as good mothers only if they work in the paid labor force and leave the care of their young children to others; middle class and affluent mothers, in contrast, are socially constructed as good mothers only if they remain economically dependent on their male partners by staying at home full time to care for their own young children. Such welfare reforms also intersect with racial formation projects, in that they are predicated on racially framed assumptions of a "culture of poverty." Policies such as workfare are also part of the racial formation state project in that they more harshly affect women and children of color than whites (in part because of discriminatory patterns in the labor and housing markets). Thus, state projects themselves are not isolated one from the other. Rather, they articulate common and intersecting agendas that contribute to intersecting systems of multiple oppressions.

Our Multi-Sites of Power approach to state theory thus helps us to explain class-based as well as gender-based and racially based policy arenas by using Jessop's concepts as organizing conceptual tools. These concepts allow us to identify the relationship between the state and class relations as well as that between the state and gendering and the state and racial formation processes, and the ways these are dialectically interconnected. Our approach facilitates our ability to begin to untangle and identify the conditions under which some policies are more or less likely to develop at particular points in time and some interests are more or less likely to gain power and have their interests addressed.

THE STATE OF STATE THEORY: WHERE DO WE GO FROM HERE?

As we said in the beginning of the book, there are plenty of reasons for sociologists to reengage with state theory and critical state theory in particular. Through global periods of austerity we have seen the rise of right-wing nationalist and populist movements that put forms of racial politics front and center—particularly in the context of immigration. In the United States, President Donald Trump's reinstitution of the "global gag rule" or the Mexico City Policy cuts federal funds from women's health service providers that offer abortion services, counseling, or advocate for the decriminalization of abortion. This has obvious gendered impacts and, like most right-wing forms of populism, men's control of women's bodies is central to the emerging global wave. In the United States, so-called "religious freedom" bills are currently being challenged in courts that allow people to legally discriminate against same-sex couples and marriages.

These state processes highlight the need for theorists of the state to engage thoughtfully with ideas that it often seems shuttered from and we have taken this task quite seriously. Queer theory, for example, while often applied to gender and sexuality, can be used more broadly as a critique of notions of stable identities. It also implies an operation of power in society that is diffused throughout social life. Thus, discourses of (for example) sexuality that create notions of identity frame state projects around those very identities, at times acting as selectivity filters affecting what can exist within the "gaze" of the state and, as a result, what can be legislated. The practices, understandings, and language we use in our daily lives, then, have impacts on large structural phenomena and vice versa. As we said, the state is not an ossified structure, but interacts with society at the level of daily life. As the Italian anarchist, Errico Malatesta (2015, 178), noted, "[b]etween man [*sic*] and his social environment there is a reciprocal action. Men make society what it is and society makes men what they are, and the result is therefore a kind of vicious circle. To transform society men must be changed, and to transform men, society must be changed." This is true, also, of the state—and queer theory, with its notions of diffused power, gives us a useful lens for describing those social relationships and processes.

Similarly, anarchism and the anti-state wings of Marxism provide us with useful tools for critical state theory, particularly because of the ways they have been ignored by contemporary sociologists and because they are gaining steam among contemporary social movement actors. It is a bit bewildering that critical state theorists often write of the state as if it is an eternal institutional arrangement. And although critical state theory is often rooted in Marxist theory, it rarely talks about the future of the state in the kinds of abolitionist terms that Marx himself used. For Marx, the purpose of the state, as an institution that manages the affairs of the whole bourgeoisie, is to manage class antagonisms. Accordingly, if proletarians were to rise up and abolish class society, the state would no longer be necessary and it would, at the least, be limited to simple administrative functions. While anarchists, of course, have argued that both capital and the state must be abolished in order to liberate humanity from alienated labor and forms of decision-making.

Critical state theorists might use these ideas to describe direct action movements that prefigure forms of social organization without the need for states. This describes movement organizations like Food Not Bombs, that challenge state power, attempting to tip the balance of political forces in their favor through a politics that refuses to wait for the state to address basic issues of human dignity. This can also be applied descriptively in areas of the world where people are attempting to make lines of flight away from state authority and power, such as portions of the Kurdish population who are struggling for what they call "stateless democracy" (Dirik 2015).

This also raises interesting normative questions as well as descriptive and analytical questions. An MSP approach to state theory might evaluate state processes measured against the legitimacy of the institutions that the state governs. While an MSP approach might look at the welfare state, state projects around food, housing, sexuality, and so on, and describe and analyze the state-society relationship, we might also move beyond questions of "What is?" to questions of "What is good?" Thus, future studies might use this particular theory as the foundational basis for normative claims about the operations of power and how it is organized in our daily lives with an eye for how that power *should* be organized to bring about a decent world. As Marx noted many years ago, after all, we need not stop at describing the world—should we collectively have the desire and capacity, we might *change* the world.

Bibliography

Abramovitz, Mimi. 1996. *Regulating the Lives of Women: Social Welfare Policy from Colonial Times to the Present*. Boston: South End Press. Revised edition.

———. 2000. *Under Attack: Fighting Back: Women and Welfare in the United States*. New York: Monthly Review Press. Revised edition.

Ackelsberg, Martha. 2010. *Resisting Citizenship: Feminist Essays on Politics, Community, and Democracy*. New York: Routledge.

ACORN, Pennsylvania. 2000. "Equity Strippers: The Impact of Subprime Lending in Philadelphia." Available until 2010 (when ACORN went bankrupt) from http://www.acorn.org/pressrelease/equity.htm#_ftn1

Akard, Patrick J. 1992. "Corporate Mobilization and Political Power: The Transformation of US Economic Policy in the 1970s." *American Sociological Review* 57:597–615.

Alexander, Michelle. 2010. *The New Jim Crow: Mass Incarceration in the Age of Colorblindness*. New York: The New Press.

Amenta, Edwin, and Drew Halfmann. 2000. "Wage Wars: Institutional Politics, WPA Wages, and the Struggle for U.S. Social Policy." *American Sociological Review* 65(4):506–528.

Amenta, Edwin, and Sunita Parikh. 1991. "Comment: Capitalists Did Not Want the Social Security Act: A Critique of the 'Capitalist Dominance' Thesis." *American Sociological Review* 56:124–129.

Amenta, Edwin, and Theda Skocpol. 1988. "Redefining the New Deal: World War II and the Development of Social Provision in the US." In *The Politics of Social Policy in the United States*, edited by Margaret Weir, Ann S. Orloff, and Theda Skocpol, 81–122. Princeton, NJ: Princeton University Press.

Andersen, Arnfinn J. 2011. "Sexual Citizenship in Norway." *International Journal of Law, Policy and the Family* 25(1):120–134.

Anderson, Carol. 2003. *Eyes Off the Prize: The United Nations and the African American Struggle for Human Rights, 1944–1995*. New York: Cambridge University Press.

Apple, Michael W., and Linda K. Christian-Smith, eds. 1991. *The Politics of the Textbook.* New York: Routledge.

Armaline, William T., and Davita Silfen Glasberg. 2009. "What Will States Really Do for Us? The Human Rights Enterprise and Pressure from Below." *Societies without Borders* 4(3):430–451.

Armaline, William T., Davita Silfen Glasberg, and Bandana Purkayastha, eds. 2011. *Human Rights in Our Own Backyard: Injustice and Resistance in the United States.* Philadelphia: University of Pennsylvania Press.

Armaline, William T., Davita Silfen Glasberg, and Bandana Purkayastha. 2015. *The Human Rights Enterprise: The State, Resistance, and Human Rights.* Boston: Polity Press.

Armstrong, Elizabeth, and Mary Bernstein. 2008. "Culture, Power, and Institutions: A Multi-Institutional Politics Approach to Social Movements." *Sociological Theory* 26(1):74–99.

Associated Press. 2011. "Sharp Rise in Foreclosures as Banks Move in–Business–Real Estate–Msnbc.com." NBC News. http://www.msnbc.msn.com/id/44885991/ns/business-real_estate/

Aviram, Hadar, and Gwendolyn Leachman. 2015. "The Future of Polyamorous Marriage: Lessons from the Marriage Equality Struggle." *Harvard Journal of Law & Gender* 38:269–336.

Bakunin, Mikhail. 1964. *The Political Philosophy of Bakunin.* Edited by G.P. Maximoff. New York: Free Press.

Balibar, Etinne, and Immanuel Wallerstein. 1991. *Race, Nation, Class: Ambiguous Identities.* Translated by Chris Turner. London: Verso.

Ballard, Richard, Adam Habib, and Imaraan Valodia, eds. 2006. *Voices of Protest: Social Movements in Post-Apartheid South Africa.* Pietermaritzburg: University of KwaZulu-Natal Press.

Baptist, Willie, Mary Bricker Jenkins, and Monica Dillon. 1999. "Taking the Struggle on the Road: The New Freedom Bus–Freedom from Unemployment, Hunger, and Homelessness." *Journal of Progressive Human Services* 10(2):7–29.

Barrett, Michele. 1990. *Women's Oppression Today.* London: Verso.

Bartfeld, Judi. 2000. "Child Support and the Postdivorce Economic Well-Being of Mothers, Fathers, and Children." *Demography* 37(2):203–213.

Barthel, Diane. 1988. *Putting on Appearances: Gender and Advertising.* Philadelphia: Temple University Press.

Beeman, Angie, Davita Silfen Glasberg, and Colleen Casey. 2010. "Whiteness as Property: Predatory Lending and the Reproduction of Racialized Inequality." *Critical Sociology* 37(1):27–45.

Bell, Daniel. 1960. *The End of Ideology: On the Exhaustion of Political Ideas in the Fifties.* New York: Free Press.

Benford, Robert. 1997. "An Insider's Critique of the Social Movement Framing Perspective." *Sociological Inquiry* 67:409–430.

Benjamin, Lois. 1991. *The Black Elite: Facing the Color Line in the Twilight of the Twentieth Century.* Chicago: Nelson-Hall.

Bentley, Arthur. 1967. *The Process of Government*. Chicago: Chicago University Press.

Berkman, Alexander. 2003. *What is Anarchism?* Oakland, CA: AK Press.

Berlin, Loren. 2012. "Foreclosure Crisis is Far from Over, Report Finds." *Huffington Post*, April 4. http://www.huffingtonpost.com/2011/11/17/foreclosure-crisis-center-for-responsible-lending_n_1099120.html

Bernstein, Mary. 2003. "Nothing Ventured, Nothing Gained? Conceptualizing Social Movement 'Success' in the Lesbian and Gay Movement." *Social Science History* 26:531–581.

Blau, Joel. 1999. *Illusions of Prosperity: America's Working Families in an Age of Economic Insecurity*. New York: Oxford University Press.

Block, Fred. 1987. *Revising State Theory: Essays in Politics and Postindustrialism*. Philadelphia: Temple University Press.

Block, Fred, Richard A. Cloward, Barbara Ehrenreich, and Frances Fox Piven. 1987. *The Mean Season: The Attack on the Welfare State*. New York: Pantheon Books.

Bloom, Joshua, and Waldo E. Martin, Jr. 2016. *Black against Empire: The History and Politics of the Black Panther Party*. Oakland, CA: University of California Press.

Blumenfeld, Warren J., ed. 1992. *Homophobia: How We All Pay the Price*. Boston: Beacon Press.

Bock, Gisela, and Pat Thane, eds. 1991. *Maternity and Gender Politics: Women and the Rise of the European Welfare States, 1880s–1950s*. New York: Routledge.

Boggiano, Ann K., and Mary Barrett. 1991. "Strategies to Motivate Helpless and Mastery-Oriented Children: The Effect of Gender-Based Expectancies." *Sex Roles* 25:487–451.

Bogira, Steve. 2011. "Separate, Unequal and Ignored." *Chicago Reader* 10 (February).

Bonacich, Edna. 1972. "A Theory of Ethnic Antagonism: The Split Labor Market." *American Sociological Review* 37:547–559.

———. 1976. "Advanced Capitalism and Black/White Relations in the United States: A Split Labor Market Interpretation." *American Sociological Review* 41:34–51.

Bonilla-Silva, Eduardo. 2013. *Racism without Racists: Color-Blind Racism and the Persistence of Racial Inequality in America*. Lanham, MD: Rowman & Littlefield Publishers. Fourth edition.

Borchorst, Anette. 1994. "The Scandinavian Welfare States: Patriarchal, Gender Neutral, or Woman-Friendly?" *International Journal of Contemporary Sociology* 31:1–23.

Boris, Eileen, and Peter Bardaglio. 1983. "The Transformation of Patriarchy: The Historic Role of the State." In *Families, Politics, and Public Policy*, edited by Irene Diamond, 70–93. New York: Longman.

Bostic, Raphael W., and Breck L. Robinson. 2005. "What Makes Community Reinvestment Act Agreements Work?" *Housing Policy Debate* 16:513–545.

Bourdieu, Pierre. 1992. *Language and Symbolic Power*. Cambridge: Polity.

Bradley, Jeanette. 2000. *The Community Guide to Predatory Lending Research*. North Carolina: Community Reinvestment Association of North Carolina.

Bray, Mark. 2013. *Translating Anarchy: The Anarchism of Occupy Wall Street.* Winchester, UK: Zero Books.

Brecher, Jeremy, Tim Costello, and Brendan Smith. 2000. *Globalization from Below: The Power of Solidarity.* Cambridge, MA: South End Press.

Breslin, Shaun, and Richard Higgot. 2000. "Studying Regions: Learning from the Old, Constructing the New." *New Political Economy* 5(3):333–353.

Brown, Carol. 1981. "Mothers, Fathers, and Children: From Private to Public Patriarchy." In *Women and Revolution,* edited by Lydia Sargent, 239–268. Boston, MA: South End Press.

Brown, Judith M. 1991. *Gandhi: Prisoner of Hope.* New Haven: Yale University Press.

Brown, Michael K. 1999. *Race, Money, and the American Welfare State.* Ithaca: Cornell University Press.

Brown, Wendy. 1995. *States of Injury: Power and Freedom in Late Modernity.* Princeton, NJ: Princeton University Press.

Brush, Lisa D. 2003. *Gender and Governance.* Walnut Creek, CA: AltaMira Press.

Bryant, Bunyan, and Paul Mohai, eds. 1992. *Race and the Incidence of Environmental Hazards.* Boulder, CO: Westview Press.

Bullard, Robert D. 1983. "Solid Waste Sites and the Houston Black Community." *Sociological Inquiry* 53(Spring):273–288.

———. 1993. *Confronting Environmental Racism: Voices from the Grassroots.* Boston: South End Press.

Bunce, Harold L., Debbie Bruenstein, Christopher E. Herbert, and Randall M. Scheessele. 2001. "Subprime Foreclosures: The Smoking Gun of Predatory Lending?" In *Housing Policy in the New Millennium Conference Proceedings,* edited by Susan M. Wachter and R. Leo Peene, 257–272. Washington, DC: U.S. Department of Housing and Urban Development. http://www.huduser.org/publications/pdf/brd/12Bunce.pdf

Burley, Shane. 2014. "No Exit: Transforming Housing through Solidarity and Resistance." In *The End of the World as We Know It? Crisis, Resistance, and the Age of Austerity,* edited by Deric Shannon, 247–266. Oakland, CA: AK Press.

Burnham, James. 1943. *The Managerial Revolution.* London: Putnam.

Burris, Val. 1992. "Elite Policy-Planning Networks in the United States." *Research in Politics and Society* 4:111–134.

Butler, C.T., and Keith McHenry. 2000. *Food Not Bombs.* Tucson, AZ: See Sharp Press.

Calavita, Kitty. 2005. *Immigrants on the Margins: Laws, Race and Exclusion in Southern Europe.* Cambridge: Cambridge University Press.

Capehart, Jonathan. 2015. "Marilyn Mosby's Amazing Press Conference." *Washington Post,* May 1. http://www.washingtonpost.com/blogs/post-partisan/wp/2015/05/01/marilyn-mosbys-amazing-press-conference/

Carey, Sabine C., Mark Gibney, and Steven C. Poe. 2010. *The Politics of Human Rights: The Quest for Dignity.* Cambridge, MA: Cambridge University Press.

Carolan, Michael. 2012. *The Sociology of Food and Agriculture.* New York: Routledge.

Casey, Colleen, Davita Silfen Glasberg, and Angie Beeman. 2011. "Racial Disparities in Access to Mortgage Credit: Does Governance Matter?" *Social Science Quarterly* 92(3):782–806.

Casey, Timothy J. 1998. "Welfare Reform and Its Impact in the Nation and in New York." New York: Federation of Protestant Welfare Agencies, Inc. http://www.wnylc.net/web/welfare-law/resource-material/welrefor.htm

Cashmore, Ellis, and Eugene McLaughlin, eds. 1991. *Out of Order?: Policing Black People*. New York: Routledge.

Cazenave, Noel A. 2011. *The Urban Racial State: Managing Race Relations in American Cities*. Lanham, MD: Rowman & Littlefield.

Cerny, Philip G. 2000. "Paradoxes of the Competition State: The Dynamics of Political Globalization." *Government and Opposition* 32(2):251–274.

Chabot, Sean. 2002. "Transnational Diffusion and the African American Reinvention of the Gandhian Repertoire." In *Globalization and Resistance: Transnational Dimensions of Social Movements*, edited by Jackie Smith and Hank Johnston, 97–114. Lanham, MD: Rowman and Littlefield.

Chomsky, Noam. 2009. *Powers and Prospects: Reflections on Human Nature and the Social Order*. Boston, MA: South End Press.

Chorev, Nitsan. 2007. *Remaking U.S. Trade Policy: From Protectionism to Globalization*. Ithaca, NY: Cornell University Press.

Chou, Rosalind S., and Joe R. Feagin. 2008. *The Myth of the Model Minority: Asian Americans Facing Racism*. Boulder, Colorado: Paradigm Publishers.

Cincotta, Gail. 2000. Testimony before the U.S. House of Representatives Committee on Banking and Financial Services. http://archives.financialservices.house.gov/banking/52400cin.shtml

Clawson, Dan, Alan Neustadtl, and Mark Weller. 1998. *Dollars and Votes: How Business Campaign Contributions Subvert Democracy*. Philadelphia: Temple University Press.

Cleman, Korva. 2011. "New York City Fire Department to Get Court Monitor in Discrimination Case." NPR, October 7. www.npr.org/sections/thetwo-way/2011/10/7/141154592/new-york-city-fire-department-to-get-court-monitor-in-discrimination-case

Clotfelter, Charles T. 2004. *After Brown: The Rise and Retreat of School Desegregation*. Princeton: Princeton University Press.

Collins, J. Michael. 2000. *Analyzing Trends in Subprime Originations: A Case Study of Connecticut*. Washington, DC: Neighborhood Reinvestment Corporation.

Combahee River Collective. 1977. "The Combahee River Collective Statement." http://circuitous.org/scraps/combahee.html

Conlin, Michelle, and Peter Rudegeair. 2013. "Former Bank of America Workers Allege It Lied to Home Owners." Reuters, June 14. http://www.reuters.com/assets/print?aid=USL2N0EQ1KT20130614

Connell, R.W. 1997. "Why is Classical Theory Classical?" *American Journal of Sociology* 102(6):1511–1557.

———. 1999. "The State, Gender, and Sexual Politics." *Theory and Society* 19(5):507–544.

Conrad, Ryan, ed. 2010. *Against Equality: Queer Critiques of Gay Marriage.* Lewiston, ME: Against Equality Press.

Cose, Ellis. 1992. *A Nation of Strangers: Prejudice, Politics, and the Populating of America.* New York: William Morrow and Co.

Cott, Nancy F. 2000. *Public Vows: A History of Marriage and the Nation.* Cambridge, MA: Harvard University Press.

Courchane, Marsha J., Brian J. Surette, and Peter M. Zorn. 2004. "Subprime Borrowers: Mortgage Transitions and Outcomes." *Journal of Real Estate Finance and Economics* 29(4):365–392.

Craven, Julia. 2015. "Black Lives Matter Co-Founder Reflects on the Origins of the Movement." *Huffington* Post, September 30. http://www.huffingtonpost.com/entry/black-lives-matter-opal tometi_us_560c1c59e4b0768127003227

Crenshaw, Kimberle. 1989. "Demarginalizing the Intersection of Race and Sex: A Black Feminist Critique of Antidiscrimination Doctrine, Feminist Theory and Antiracist Politics." *University of Chicago Legal Forum* 1989:139–167.

Culver, John. 1992. "Capital Punishment, 1977–1990: Characteristics of the 143 Executed." *Sociology and Social Research* 76(20):59–61.

Curran, Laura, and Laura S. Abrams. 2000. "Making Men into Dads: Fatherhood, the State, and Welfare Reform." *Gender & Society* 14(5):662–678.

Dahl, Robert A. 1961. *Who Governs?* New Haven: Yale University Press.

———. 1963. *Pluralist Democracy in the United States: Conflict and Consent.* Chicago: Rand McNally.

———. 2000. *On Democracy.* New Haven: Yale University Press.

Davenport, Christian, Hank Johnston, and Carol Mueller, eds. 2005. *Repression and Mobilization.* Minneapolis: University of Minnesota Press.

Davies, James. 1962. "Toward a Theory of Revolution." *American Sociological Review* 27(1):5–19.

———. 1969. "The J-Curve of Rising and Declining Satisfactions as a Cause of Some Great Revolutions and a Contained Revolution." In *Violence in America,* edited by Hugh D. Graham and Ted R. Gurr, 671–709. New York: Signet.

———. 1974. "The J-Curve and Power Struggle Theories of Collective Violence." *American Sociological Review* 39:607–610.

Davis, Kathryn. 2008. "Intersectionality as Buzzword: A Sociology of Science Perspective on What Makes a Feminist Theory Successful." *Feminist Theory* 9(1):67–85.

Day, Richard J.F. 2005. *Gramsci Is Dead: Anarchist Currents in the Newest Social Movements.* Ann Arbor, MI: Pluto Press.

De Cleyre, Voltarine. [1912] 2004. "Direct Action." In *The Voltarine de Cleyre Reader,* edited by A. J. Brigati. Oakland, CA: AK Press.

Deleuze, Gilles, and Felix Guattari. 1987. *A Thousand Plateaus: Capitalism and Schizophrenia.* Minneapolis: University of Minnesota Press.

D'Emilio, John. [1983] 1998. *Sexual Politics, Sexual Communities.* Chicago, IL: University of Chicago Press.

Devine, Joel. 1983. "Fiscal Policy and Class Income Inequality: The Distributional Consequences of Governmental Revenues and Expenditures in the United States, 1949–1976." *American Sociological Review* (48):606–622.

Dicken, Peter. 2003. *Global Shift: Reshaping the Global Economic Map in the 21st Century.* London: Sage.

Dirik, Dilar. 2014. "New World Summit: Stateless State." https://vimeo.com/107639261

———. 2015. "Stateless Democracy: How the Kurdish Women's Movement Liberated Democracy from the State." Recorded talk given at *New World Summit*, catalogued at https://vimeo.com/107639261

Dollard, John. 1949. *Caste and Class in a Southern Town.* New York: Doubleday.

Domhoff, G. William. 1990. *The Power Elite and the State: How Policy is Made in America.* New York: Aldine de Gruyter.

———. 2009. *Who Rules America? Challenges to Corporate and Class Dominance.* New York: McGraw-Hill.

Donnelly, Jack. 1999. "The Social Construction of International Human Rights." In *Human Rights in Global Politics*, edited by Dunne and Wheeler. Cambridge, MA: Cambridge University Press.

———. 2003. *Universal Human Rights in Theory and Practice.* 2nd ed. Ithaca, NY: Cornell University Press.

Duberman, Martin. 1993. *Stonewall.* New York: Dutton.

Dye, Thomas R. 2002. *Who's Running America? The Bush Restoration.* Upper Saddle River, NJ: Prentice Hall.

Eckstein, Rick. 1997. *Nuclear Power and Social Power.* Philadelphia: Temple University Press.

Edelman, Marion Wright. 1988. "Growing Up Black in America." In *Crisis in American Institutions*, edited by Jerome H. Skolnick and Elliott Currie, 143–162. Glenview, IL: Scott, Foresman. Seventh edition.

Edin, Katherine, and Laura Lein. 1996. *Making Ends Meet: How Single Mothers Survive Welfare and Low-Wage Work.* New York: Russell Sage Foundation.

Edwards, Sue Bradford, and Duchess Harris. 2015. *Black Lives Matter (Special Reports).* Minneapolis, MN: Essential Library.

Ehrlich, Carol. 2012. "Socialism, Anarchism and Feminism." In *Quiet Rumors: An Anarcha-Feminist Reader*, edited by Dark Star Collective and AK Press, 55–66. Oakland, CA: AK Press. Third edition.

Eitzen, D. Stanley, and Maxine Baca Zinn. 2000. "The Missing Safety Net and Families: A Progressive Critique of the New Welfare Legislation." *Journal of Sociology and Social Welfare* 27(1):53–72.

Elman, Amy R. 2000. "The Limits of Citizenship: Migration, Sex Discrimination and Same-Sex Partners in EU Law." *Journal of Common Market Studies* 38(5):729–749.

Emens, Elizabeth F. 2004. "Monogamy's Law: Compulsory Monogamy and Polyamorous Existence." *Review of Law and Social Change* 29(2):277–376.

England, Paula. 2000. "Marriage, the Costs of Children, and Gender Inequality." In *The Ties That Bind: Perspectives on Marriage and Cohabitation*, edited by Linda J. Waite, Christine Bachrach, Michelle Hindin, Elizabeth Thomson and Arland Thornton, 320–342. New York: Aldine de Gruyter.

Enloe, Cynthia. 1989. *Bananas, Beaches, and Bases: Making Feminist Sense of International Politics.* Berkeley, CA: University of California Press.

———. 2000. *Maneuvers: The International Politics of Militarizing Women's Lives.* Berkeley, CA: University of California Press.

———. 2013. *Seriously! Investigating Crashes and Crises As If Women Mattered.* Berkeley: University of California Press.

Esping-Andersen, Gosta. 1990. *The Three Worlds of Welfare Capitalism.* Princeton, NJ: Princeton University Press.

Evans, David T. 1993. *Sexual Citizenship: The Material Construction of Sexualities.* New York: Routledge.

Fausto-Sterling, Anne. 1987. "Society Writes Biology/Biology Constructs Gender." *Daedalus* 116(4):61–76.

———. 2000. *Sexing the Body: Gender Politics and the Construction of Sexuality.* New York: Basic Books.

Feagin, Joe R. 1991. "The Continuing Significance of Race: Antiblack Discrimination in Public Places." *American Sociological Review* 56:101–116.

———. 2001. *Racist America: Roots, Current Realities, and Future Reparations.* New York: Routledge.

———. 2006. *Systemic Racism: A Theory of Oppression.* New York: Routledge.

Feagin, Joe R., and Melvin P. Sikes. 1994. *Living with Racism: The Black Middle-Class Experience.* Boston: Beacon Press.

Federal News Service. 1993. "White House Press Briefing: Secretary of the Treasury Lloyd Bentsen." March 10. http://www.presidency.ucsb.edu/ws/?pid=60010

Federal Reserve Bank of New York, 1933. Banking Act of 1933. June 22. https://fraser.stlouisfed.org/scribd/?item_id=15952&filepath=/files/docs/historical/ny%20circulars/1933_01248.pdf

Federici, Silvia. 2012. *Revolution at Point Zero: Housework, Reproduction, and Feminist Struggle.* Oakland, CA: PM Press.

Ferdnance, Tyrone. 1998. "Colonialism and the Economic Demise and Transformation of Northern Nigeria's Slave Fundamental Extractors from1903 to the 1920s." *Journal of Asian and African Studies* 33(3):223–241.

Ferguson, Charles H. 2012. *Predator Nation; Corporate Criminals, Political Corruption, and the Hijacking of America.* New York: Crown Business.

Ferree, Myra Marx. 2005. "Soft Repression: Ridicule, Stigma, and Silencing in Gender Based Movements." In *Repression and Mobilization,* edited by Christian Davenport, Hank Johnston, and Carol Mueller, 138–155. Minneapolis: University of Minnesota Press.

Ferree, Myra Marx, and Elaine J. Hall. 1990. "Visual Images of American Society: Gender and Race in Introductory Sociology Textbooks." *Gender & Society* 4(4):500–533.

Finer, S. 1966. *Anonymous Empire.* London: Pall Mall.

Finlayson, Alan, and James Martin. 2006. "Poststructuralism." In *The State: Theories and Issues,* edited by Colin Hay, Michael Lister, and David Marsh, 155–171. Basingstok, UK and New York: Plagrave Macmillan.

Flank, Lenny. 2007. *Philosophy of Revolution: Towards a Non-Leninist Marxism.* St. Petersburg: Red and Black Publishers.

Fording, Richard C. 2001. "The Political Response to Black Insurgency: A Critical Test of Competing Theories of the State." *American Political Science Review* 95(1):115–130.

Foucault, Michel. 1980. *Power/Knowledge: Selected Interviews and Other Writings, 1982–1977*. New York: Pantheon.

———. 1987. *The History of Sexuality*. Harmondsworth: Penguin.

———. 1991. "Governmentality." In *The Foucault Effect: Studies in Governmentality*, edited by Graham Burchell, Colin Gordon, and Peter Miller. Hemel Hempstead: Harvester Wheatsheaf.

Fraser, Nancy, and Linda Gordon. 1994. "Dependency Demystified: Inscriptions of Power in a Keyword of the Welfare State." *Social Politics* 1:14–31.

Frymer, Paul. 2008. *Black and Blue: African Americans, the Labor Movement, and the Decline of the Democratic Party*. Princeton, NJ: Princeton University Press.

Galbraith, John Kenneth. 1983. *American Capitalism*. Harmondsworth: Penguin.

———. 1985. *The New Industrial State*. Boston: Houghton-Mifflin Co. Fourth edition.

Gamson, Joshua. 1996. "Organizational Shaping of Collective Identity." *Sociological Forum* 11:231–261.

Gamson, William A. 1990. *Strategy of Social Protest*. Belmont: Wadsworth Publishing Company. Second edition.

———. 1992. *Talking Politics*. New York: Cambridge University Press.

Garland, David. 2010. *Peculiar Institution: America's Death Penalty in an Age of Abolition*. New York: Oxford University Press.

Garrow, David J. 1981. *FBI and Martin Luther King, Jr.: From "Solo" to Memphis*. New York: WW Norton & Co.

———. 2016. *MLK: An American Legacy: Bearing the Cross, Protest at Selma, and the FBI and Martin Luther King, Jr.* New York: Open Road Media.

Gaskell, Jane. 1984. "Gender and Course Choice: The Orientation of Male and Female Students." *Journal of Education* 166(1):89–102.

Gates, Henry Louis Jr. 2013. "The Five Greatest Slave Rebellions in the United States." http://www.pbs.org/wnet/african-americans-many-rivers-to-cross/history/did-african-american-slaves-rebel/

Gault, Barbara, and Annisah Um'rani. 2000. "The Outcomes of Welfare Reform for Women." *Poverty and Race* 9(4):1–6.

Gelderloos, Peter. 2007. *How Nonviolence Protects the State*. Cambridge, MA: South End Press.

Gerbauso, Paolo. 2014. "The Persistence of Collectivity in Digital Protest." *Information, Communication & Society* 17(2):264–268.

Gilbert, Jess, and Carolyn Howe. 1991. "Beyond 'State vs. Society': Theories of the State and New Deal Agricultural Policies." *American Sociological Review* 56:204–220.

Gitlin, Todd. 2012. *Occupy Nation: The Roots, the Spirit, and the Promise of Occupy Wall Street*. New York: It Books.

Glasberg, Davita Silfen. 1987a. "Chrysler Corporation's Struggle for Bailout: The Role of the State in Finance Capitalist Society." *Research in Political Sociology* 3:87–110.

———. 1987b. "International Finance Capital and the Relative Autonomy of the State: Mexico's Foreign Debt Crisis." *Research in Political Economy* 10:83–108.

———. 1989. *The Power of Collective Purse Strings: The Effect of Bank Hegemony on Corporations and the State.* Berkeley, CA: University of California Press.

———. 1992. "Race, Class, and Differential Application of Bank Bailouts: An Emerging Sociology of the Politics of Finance." *Critical Sociology* 18(2):51–76.

Glasberg, Davita Silfen, and Dan Skidmore, D. 1997. *Corporate Welfare Policy and the Welfare State: Bank Deregulation and the Savings and Loan Bailout.* New York: Aldine de Gruyter.

Glasberg, Davita Silfen, and Deric Shannon. 2011. *Political Sociology: Oppression, Resistance, and the State.* Thousand Oaks, CA: Sage.

———. 2015. "Some Things Borrowed, Some Things New: Toward a Multi-Sites of Power Approach to State Theory." *Theory in Action* 8(4):1–37.

Glasberg, Davita Silfen, Angie Beeman, and Colleen Casey. 2014. "Predatory Lending and the Twenty-First Century Recession: Preying on the American Dream and Reasserting Racialized Inequality." In *The End of the World as We Know It? Crisis, Resistance, and the Age of Austerity,* edited by Deric Shannon, 55–69. Oakland, CA: AK Press.

Glenn, Evelyn Nakano. 2002. *Unequal Freedom: How Race and Gender Shaped American Citizenship and Labor.* Cambridge, MA: Harvard University Press.

Goldberg, David Theo. 2002. *The Racial State.* Malden, MA: Blackwell Publishers.

Goldstein, Deborah. 1999. *Understanding Predatory Lending: Moving toward a Common Definition and Workable Solutions.* Cambridge, MA: Joint Center for Housing Studies of Harvard University.

Goldstone, Jack A., ed. 2003. *States, Parties and Social Movements.* Cambridge: Cambridge University Press.

Goodwin, Jeff, and James M. Jasper. 1999. "Caught in a Winding, Snarling Vine: The Structural Bias of Political Process Theory." *Sociological Forum* 14:107–125.

Goodwin, Joanne L. 1997. *Gender and the Politics of Welfare Reform.* Chicago: Chicago University Press.

Gordon, Colin. 1991. "Governmental Rationality: An introduction." In *The Foucault Effect: Studies in Governmentality,* edited by Graham Burchell, Colin Gordon, and Peter Miller. Hemel Hempstead: Harvester Wheatsheaf.

Gordon, David M., Michael Reich, and Richard Edwards. 1982. *Segmented Work, Divided Workers: The Historical Transformations of Labor in the United States.* New York: Cambridge University Press.

Gordon, Linda, ed. 1990. *Women, the State, and Welfare.* Madison, WI: University of Wisconsin Press.

———. 1994. *Pitied But Not Entitled: Single Mothers and the History of Welfare.* New York: The Free Press.

Gordon, Robert. 1998. "Some Critical Theories of Law and Their Critics." In *The Politics of Law: A Progressive Critique,* edited by Kairys. New York: Basic Books.

Third edition. As Quoted in *The Bridge*. http://cyber.law.harvard.edu/bridge/CriticalTheory/rights.htm

Gordon, U. 2008. *Anarchy Alive: Anti-Authoritarian Politics from Practice to Theory*. London: Pluto Press.

Gordon, Wayne, John M. Perkins, Richard Mouw, and Dick Durbin, Jr. 2017. *Do All Lives Matter? The Issues We Can No Longer Ignore and the Solutions We All Long For*. Ada, MI: Baker Books.

Gottschalk, Marie. 2006. *The Prison and the Gallows: The Politics of Mass Incarceration in America*. New York: Cambridge University Press.

Gramsci, Antonio. 1971. *Selections from the Prison Notebooks*. Edited and translated by Q. Hoare and G. N. Smith. New York: International Publishers.

Gray, John. 1998. *False Dawn: The Delusions of Global Capitalism*. London: Granta.

Greenberger, Marcia. 1980. "The Effectiveness of Federal Law Prohibiting Sex Discrimination in the United States." In *Equal Employment Policy for Women*, edited by Ronnie S. Ratner, 108–128. Philadelphia: Temple University Press.

Greider, William. 1997. *One World, Ready or Not*. New York: Simon & Schuster.

Gruenstein, Debbie, and Christopher E. Herbert. 2000. "Analyzing Trends in Subprime Originations and Foreclosures: A Case Study of the Atlanta Metro Area." Washington, DC: Neighborhood Reinvestment Corporation. http://www.abtassociates.com/reports/es-20006470781991.pdf

Gustafson, S. 1994. "Childcare and Types of Welfare States" In *Gendering Welfare States*, edited by Diane Sainsbury, 45–61. Thousand Oaks, CA: Sage.

Haglage, Abbey. 2014. "Hate Crime Victimization Statistics Show Rise in Anti-Hispanic Crime." *Daily Beast*, February 20. http://www.thedailybeast.com/articles/2014/02/20/hate-crime-victimization-statistics-show-rise-in-anti-hispanic-crime.html

Hall, Jarvis A. 2003. "Linking Two Theoretical Traditions: Toward Conceptualizing the American Racial State in a Globalized Milieu." *National Political Science Review* 9:173–182.

Haney, Lynne A. 2000. "Feminist State Theory: Applications to Jurisprudence, Criminology, and the Welfare State." *Annual Review of Sociology* 26:641–666.

Haney Lopez, Ian F. 1996. *White by Law: The Legal Construction of Race*. New York: New York University Press.

Hannah-Jones, Nikole. 2014. "Segregation Now…: Sixty Years after *Brown v. Board of Education*, the Schools in Tuscaloosa, Alabama, Show How Separate and Unequal Education Is Coming Back." *Atlantic*, May. http://www.theatlantic.com/magazine/archive/2014/05/segregation-now/359813

Harris, Frederick C. 2014. "Will Ferguson Be a Moment or a Movement?" *Washington Post*, August 22.

Harrison, Frank. 1983. *The Modern State: The Anarchist Analysis*. Montreal: Black Rose Books.

Hartmann, Heidi. 1976. "Capitalism, Patriarchy, and Job Segregation by Sex." *Signs* 3:137–169.

Hassim, Shareen. 2006. *Women's Organizations and Democracy in South Africa: Contesting Authority*. Durban, SA: University of Kwa Zulu Natal Press.

Hay, Colin. 2000. "Contemporary Capitalism, Globalization, Regionalization and the Persistence of National Variation." *Review of International Studies* 26:509–531.

———. 2004. "Common Trajectories, Variable Paces, Divergent Outcomes? Models of European Capitalism under Conditions of Complex Economic Interdependence." *Review of International Political Economy* 11(2):231–262.

Hay, Colin, and David Marsh, eds. 2000. *Demystifying Globalization*. London: Macmillan.

Hay, Colin, and Michael Lister. 2006. "Introduction: Theories of the State." In *The State: Theories and Issues*, edited by Colin Hay, Michael Lister, and David Marsh, 1–20. Basingstok, UK and New York: Palgrave Macmillan.

Hays, Gory, and Richard Hornick. 1990. "No End in Sight: Politicians Hurl Blame as the $500 Billion S&L Crisis Races Out of Control." *Time*, August 13.

Heckert, Jamie. 2010. "Love Without Borders? Intimacy, Identity and the State of Compulsory Monogamy." In *Understanding Non-Monogamies*, edited by Meg Barker and Darren Langdridge, 255–266. New York: Routledge.

Held, David, Aanthony D. McGrew, David Goldblatt, and Jonathan Perraton. 1999. *Global Transformations: Politics, Economics and Culture*. Cambridge: Cambridge University Press.

Herrnstein, Richard J., and Charles Murray. 1994. *The Bell Curve: Intelligence and Class Structure in American Life*. New York: Basic Books.

Hirst, Paul, and Grahame Thompson. 1999. Globalization in Question: *The International Economy and the Possibilities of Governance*. Cambridge: Polity Press.

Hobson, Barbara. 1994. "Solo Mothers, Social Policy Regimes, and the Logics of Gender." In *Gendering Welfare States*, edited by Diane Sainsbury, 170–187. Thousand Oaks, CA: Sage.

Hochschild, Arlie, and Anne Machung. 1997. *The Second Shift: Working Parents and the Revolution at Home*. New York: Viking Penguin.

Hooks, Gregory. 1990. "The Rise of the Pentagon and US State Building: The Defense Program as industrial Policy." *American Journal of Sociology* 96:358–404.

———. 1991. *Forging the Military-Industrial Complex: World War II's Battle of the Potomac*. Urbana: University of Illinois Press.

———. 1993. "The Weakness of Strong Theories: The U.S. State's Dominance of the World War II Investment Process." *American Sociological Review* 58:37–53.

Houppert, Karen. 1999. "You're Not Entitled! Welfare 'Reform' Is Leading to Government Lawlessness." *The Nation*, October 25.

Houston, Brant, and Jack Ewing. 1992 "Racial Inequality Still Evident in Setting of Bail." *Hartford Courant*, May 17.

Howard-Pitney, David. 2004. *Martin Luther King, Jr., Malcolm X, and the Civil Rights Struggle of the 1950s and 1960s: A Brief History with Documents*. Boston and New York: Bedford/St. Martin's Press.

Huber, Evelyne, and John D. Stephens. 2000. "Partisan Governance, Women's Employment, and the Social Democratic Service State." *American Sociological Review* 65(3):323–342.

Huber, Melissa S., and Ellen Ernst Kosser. 1999. "Community Distress Predicting Welfare Exits: The Under-Examined Factor for Families in the United States." *Community, Work and Family* 2(2):173–186.

Hughey, Matthew. 2014. *The White Savior Film: Content, Critics, and Consumption.* Philadelphia: Temple University Press.

Iceland, John, Daniel H. Weinberg, and Erika Steinmetz. 2002. *Racial and Ethnic Residential Segregation in the United States: 1980–2000.* Washington, DC: US Census Bureau.

Ignatiev, Noel. 1995. *How the Irish Became White.* New York: Routledge.

Immergluck, Dan. 2004. *Credit to the Community: Community Reinvestment and Fair Lending Policy in the United States.* Armonk, NY: M.E. Sharpe, Inc.

Immergluck, Dan, and Geoff Smith. 2005. "Measuring the Effect of Subprime Lending on Neighborhood Foreclosures: Evidence from Chicago." *Urban Affairs Review* 40(3):362–389.

Jackson, Mandi Isaacs. 2008. *Model City Blues: Urban Space and Organized Resistance in New Haven.* Philadelphia, PA: Temple University Press.

James, Joy. 1996. *Resisting State Violence: Radicalism, Gender, and Race in U.S. Culture.* Minneapolis: University of Minnesota Press.

———. 2000. "The Dysfunctional and the Disappearing: Democracy, Race and Imprisonment." *Social Identities* 6(4):483–492.

James, Selma. 2012. *Sex, Race, and Class: The Perspective of Winning; A Selection of Writings 1952–2011.* Oakland, CA: PM Press.

Jenkins, J. Craig, and Barbara G. Brents. 1989. "Social Protest, Hegemonic Competition, and Social Reforms." *American Sociological Review* 54:891–909.

Jeppesen, Sandra. 2010. "Queer Anarchist Autonomous Zones and Publics: Direct Action Vomiting against Homonormative Consumerism." *Sexualities* 13(4):463–478.

Jessop, Bob. 1990. *State Theory: Putting the Capitalist State in Its Place.* University Park, PA: Pennsylvania State University Press.

———. 2008. *State Power.* Cambridge, UK: Polity Press.

Jordan, A. 1981. "Iron Triangles, Wooly Corporatisms and Elastic Nets: Images of the Policy Process." *Journal of Public Policy* 1:95–123.

Jordan, A., and J. Richardson. 1982. "The Policy Process in Britain." In *Policy Styles in Western Europe*, edited by J. Richardson. London: Allen & Unwin.

———. 1987a. *Government and Pressure Groups in Britain.* Oxford: Clarendon Press.

———. 1987b. *British Politics and the Policy Process.* London: Unwin Hyman.

Kamerman, Sheila B. 1984. "Women, Children, and Poverty: Public Policies and Female-Headed Households in Industrialized Countries." In *Women and Poverty*, edited by Barbara C. Gelpi, Nancy C. M. Hartsock, Clare C. Novak, and Myra H. Strober, 41–63. Chicago, IL: Chicago University Press.

Kato, Daniel. 2015. *Liberalizing Lynching.* New York: Oxford University Press.

Katz, Jonathan Ned. 1992. *Gay American History: Lesbians and Gay Men in the USA: A Documentary History.* Plume.

Katzenstein, Mary Fainsod. 1995. "Discursive Politics and Feminist Activism in the Catholic Church." In *Feminist Organizations: Harvest of the New Women's*

Movement, edited by Myra M. Ferree and Patricia Y. Martin, 35–52. Philadelphia: Temple University Press.

Kennedy, Duncan. 2002. "The Critique of Rights in Critical Legal Studies." In *Left Legalism/Left Critique*, edited by Wendy Brown and Janet Halley. Durham, NC: Duke University Press.

Kessler, Suzanne. 1990. "The Medical Construction of Gender: Case Management of Intersexed Infants." *Signs* 16(1):3–26.

Kessler-Harris, Alice. 1980. *Women Have Always Worked: A Historical Overview*. New York: Feminist Press.

King, Desmond. 2017. "Forceful Federalism against American Racial Inequality." *Government and Opposition* 52(2):356–382.

Kingsolver, Barbara. 1989. *Holding the Line: Women in the Great Arizona Mine Strike of 1983*. Ithaca, NY: ILR Press.

Kirschenman, Joleen, and Kathryn Neckerman. 1991. "'We'd Love to Hire Them, But. . .': The Meaning of Race for Employers." In *The Urban Underclass*, edited by Christopher Jencks and Paul Peterson, 203–232. Washington, DC: The Brookings Institution.

Klandermans, Bert. 1984. "Mobilization and Participation in a Social Movement: Social Psychological Expansions of Resource Mobilization Theory." *American Sociological Review* 1984; 49:583–600.

———. 1988. "The Formation and Mobilization of Consensus." In *From Structure to Action. Comparing Social Movements across Cultures*, edited by Bert Klandermans, Hanspeter Kriesi, and Sidney Tarrow. Greenwich, CT: JAI-Press.

Klandermans, Bert, Marlene Roefs, and Johan Olivier. 2001. "Grievance Formation in a Country in Transition: South Africa, 1994–1998." *Social Psychology Quarterly* 64(1):41–54.

Klesse, Christian. 2006. "Polyamory and Its 'Others': Contesting the Terms of Non-Monogamy." *Sexualities* 9(5):565–583.

———. 2007. "'How to Be a Happy Homosexual?!' Non-Monogamy and Governmentality in Relationship Manuals for Gay Men in the 1980s and 1990s." *The Sociological Review* 55(3):571–591.

———. 2014. "Polyamory: Intimate Practice, Identity or Sexual Orientation?" *Sexualities* 17(1–2):81–99.

Koopmans, Ruud, and Paul Statham. 1999. "Challenging the Liberal Nation-State? Postnationalism, Multiculturalism, and the Collective Claims Making of Migrants and Ethnic Minorities in Britain and Germany." *American Journal of Sociology* 105(3):652–696.

Korpi, Walter. 2000. "Faces of Inequality: Gender, Class, and Patterns of Inequalities in Different Types of Welfare States." *Social Politics* 7(2):127–191.

Koven, Seth, and Sonya Michel, eds. 1993. *Mothers of the New World: Maternalistic Policies and the Origins of the Welfare State*. New York: Routledge.

Kozol, Jonathan. 1991. *Savage Inequalities*. New York: Crown.

———. 2005. *The Shame of the Nation: The Restoration of Apartheid Schooling in America*. New York: Crown.

Krivo, Lauren, and Robert Kaufman. 2004. "Housing and Wealth Inequality: Racial-Ethnic Differences in Home Equity in the United States." *Demography* 41(3):585–605.

Kuhn, Gabriel, ed. 2010. *Revolution and Other Writings: A Political Reader.* Oakland, CA: PM Press.

Laborde, C. 2000. *Pluralist Thought and the State in Britain and France, 1900–1925.* Basingstok, UK and New York: Palgrave Macmillan.

Laclau, Ernesto. 1996. *Emancipations(s).* London and New York: Verso.

Laclau, Ernesto, and Chantal Mouffe. 1985. *Hegemony and Socialist Strategy: Towards a Radical Democratic Politics.* London: Verso.

Lawson, Steven F. 1997. *Running for Freedom: Civil Rights and Black Politics in America since 1941.* Boston, MA: McGraw Hill Press.

Leira, Arnlaug. 1992. *Welfare States and Working Mothers: The Scandinavian Experience.* New York: Cambridge University Press.

Lenin, V. I. [1917] 2015. *State and Revolution.* Chicago: Haymarket Books.

Levine, Rhonda. 1988. *Class Struggle and the New Deal: Industrial Labor, Industrial Capital and the State.* Lawrence, KS: University of Kansas Press.

Lewis, Jane. 1992. "Gender and the Development of Welfare Regimes." *Journal of European Social Policy* 3:159–173.

Lieberman, Robert. 1998. *Shifting the Color Line: Race and the American Welfare State.* Cambridge, MA: Harvard University Press.

Lipset, Seymour Martin. 1981. *Political Man.* Baltimore: Johns Hopkins University Press. Expanded edition.

Lipsitz, G. 1998. *The Possessive Investment in Whiteness: How White People Profit from Identity Politics.* Philadelphia, PA: Temple University Press.

Lister, Michael and David Marsh. 2006. "Conclusion." In *The State: Theories and Issues,* edited by Colin Hay, Michael Lister, and David Marsh, 1–20. Basingstoke, UK and New York: Palgrave Macmillan.

Lombardi, Kristen. 2015. "'They Figured Our Neighborhood Is Black, So They'll Do It.'" Center for Public Integrity, August 13. http://www.publicintegrity.org/2015/08/13/17759/they-figured-our-neighborhood-black-so-theyll-do-it

Lord, Richard. 2005. *American Nightmare: Predatory Lending and the American Dream.* Monroe, ME: Common Courage Press.

Lowder, J. Bryan. 2015. "The Real Dangers of Same-Sex Marriage." *Slate,* June 25. http://www.slate.com/blogs/outward/2015/06/25/some_unintended_consequences_of_marriage_equality_worth_taking_seriously.html

Luker, Kristin. 1984. *Abortion and the Politics of Motherhood.* Berkeley, CA: University of California Press.

———. 1998. "Sex, Social Hygiene, and the State: The Double-Edged Sword of Social Reform." *Theory and Society* 27(5):601–634.

MacKinnon, Catharine A. 1989. *Toward a Feminist Theory of the State.* Cambridge, MA: Harvard University Press.

Malatesta, Errico. 2015. *Life and Ideas: The Anarchist Writings of Errico Malatesta.* Edited and translated by Vernon Richards. Oakland, CA: PM Press.

Mandel, Ernest. 1975. *Late Capitalism.* London: New Left Books.

Mansbridge, Jane J. 1986. *Why We Lost the E.R.A.* Chicago: University of Chicago Press.

Manza, Jeff, and Christopher Uggen. 2008. *Locked Out: Felon Disenfranchisement and American Democracy.* Oxford, UK: Oxford University Press.

Marable, Manning. 1983. *How Capitalism Underdeveloped Black America: Problems in Race, Political Economy and Society.* Boston: South End Press.

Markham, Tim. 2014. "Social Media, Protest Cultures and Political Subjectivities of the Arab Spring." *Media, Culture & Society* 36(1):89–104.

Marsh, David. 2002. "Pluralism and the Study of British Politics: It Is Always the Happy Hour for Men and Money, Knowledge, and Power." In *British Politics Today*, edited by Colin Hay. Cambridge: Polity Press.

Marsh, David, Nicola J. Smith, and Nicola Hothi. 2006. "Globalization and the State." In *The State: Theories and Issues*, edited by Colin Hay, Michael Lister, and David Marsh, 172–189. Basingstok, UK and New York: Plagrave Macmillan.

Marx, Karl. 1977. *A Contribution to the Critique of Political Economy.* Moscow: Progress Publishers.

Marx, Karl, and Friederich Engels. 1967. *The Communist Manifesto.* Baltimore: Penguin.

Mason, Carol. 2002. *Killing for Life: The Apocalyptic Narrative of Pro-Life Politics.* Ithaca, NY: Cornell University Press.

Massey, Douglas S., and Nancy A. Denton. 1993. *American Apartheid.* Cambridge, MA: Harvard University Press.

McAdam, Doug. 1982. *Political Process and the Development of Black Insurgency, 1930–1970.* Chicago: University of Chicago Press.

———. 1983. "Tactical Innovation and the Pace of Insurgency." *American Sociological Review* 48:735–754.

———. 1988. *Freedom Summer.* New York: Oxford University Press.

———. 1994. "Social Movements and Culture." In *Ideology and Identity in Contemporary Social Movements*, edited by Joseph R. Gusfield, Hank Johnston, and Enrique Larana, 36–57. Phildelphia, PA: Temple University Press.

———. 1996. "Conceptual Origins, Future Problems, Current Directions." In *Comparative Perspectives on Social Movements: Political Opportunities, Mobilizing Structures, and Cultural Framings*, edited by Doug McAdam, John D. MaCarthy, and Mayer N. Zald, 23–40. Cambridge: Cambridge University Press.

McAdam, Doug, and David A. Snow. 1997. *Social Movements: Readings on Their Emergence, Mobilization, and Dynamics.* Los Angeles, CA: Roxbury Publishing Co.

McAdam Doug, John D. McCarthy, and Mayer N. Zald, eds. 1996. *Comparative Perspectives on Social Movements: Political Opportunities, Mobilizing Structures, and Cultural Framings.* New York: Cambridge University Press.

McCall, Leslie. 2001. *Complex Inequality: Gender, Class, and Race in the New Economy.* New York: Routledge.

McCammon, Holly. 1994. "Disorganizing and Reorganizing Conflict: Outcomes of the State's Legal Regulation of the Strike since the Wagner Act." *Social Forces* 72(4):1011–1049.

McCann, Michael W. 1994. *Rights at Work: Pay Equity Reform and the Politics of Legal Mobilization*. Chicago: University of Chicago Press.

McCarthy, Cameron, and Warren Crichlow, eds. 1993. *Race, Identity, and Representation in Education*. New York: Routledge.

McCarthy, John D., and Mark Wolfson. 1996. "Resource Mobilization by Local Social Movement Organizations: Agency, Strategy, and Organization in the Movement against Drinking and Driving." *American Sociological Review* 61(6):1070–1088.

McCarthy, John D., and Mayer N. Zald. 1987. "Resource Mobilization and Social Movements: A Partial Theory." In *Social Movements in an Organizational Society*, edited by Mayer N. Zald and John D. McCarthy. New Brunswick, NJ: Transaction Books.

McIntosh, Mary. 1978. "The State and the Oppression of Women." In *Feminism and Materialism*, 254–289. London: Routledge and Kegan Paul.

McIntosh, Peggy. 1992. "White Privilege and Male Privilege." In *Race, Class, and Gender*, edited by Margaret L. Andersen and Patricia H. Collins, 70–81. Belmont, CA: Wadsworth.

McNally, David. 2011. *Global Slump: The Economics and Politics of Crisis and Resistance*. Winnipeg, Canada: Fernwood Publishing.

Melluci, Alberto. 1989. *Nomads of the Present: Social Movements and Individual Needs in Contemporary Society*. London: Hutchinson Press.

Mepschen, Paul, Jan W. Duyvendak, and Evelien H. Tonkens. 2010. "Sexual Politics, Orientalism and Multicultural Citizenship in the Netherlands." *Sociology* 44(5):962–979.

Merelman, R. 2003. *Pluralism at Yale*. Madison, WI: University of Wisconsin Press.

Merry, Sally Engle. 2006. *Human Rights and Gender Violence: Translating International Law into Local Justice*. Chicago, IL: University of Chicago Press.

Meyer, David S. and Suzanne Staggenborg. 1996. "Movements, Countermovements, and the Structure of Political Opportunity." *American Journal of Sociology* 101(6):1628–1660.

Miliband, Ralph. 1969. *The State in Capitalist Society: An Analysis of the Western System of Power*. London: Weidenfeld & Nicholson.

———. 1973. "Poulantzas and the Capitalist State." *New Left Review* 82:83–92.

Mills, C. Wright. 1956. *The Power Elite*. New York: Oxford University Press.

Mink, Gwendolyn. 1994. *Wages of Motherhood: Inequality in the Welfare State, 1917–1942*. Ithaca, NY: Cornell University Press.

Moore, Robert B. 1995. "Racism in the English Language." In *Race, Class, and Gender in the United States*, edited by Paula S. Rothenberg, 376–386. New York: St. Martin's Press. Third edition.

Moors, Amy C., Jes L. Matsick, Ali Ziegler, Jennifer D. Rubin, and Terri D. Conley. 2013. "Stigma Toward Individuals Engaged in Consensual Nonmonogamy: Robust and Worthy of Additional Research." *Analyses of Social Issues and Public Policy* 13(1):52–69.

Morris, Aldon D. 1984. *The Origins of the Civil Rights Movement: Black Communities Organizing for Change*. New York: Free Press.

————. 1999. "A Retrospective on the Civil Rights Movement: Political and Intellectual Landmarks." *Annual Review of Sociology* 25:517–539.

Morris, Aldon D., and Carol McClurg Mueller, eds. 1992. *Frontiers in Social Movement Theory*. New Haven: Yale University Press.

Muncy, Robyn. 1991. *Creating a Female Dominion in American Reform, 1890–1935*. New York: Oxford University Press.

Myrdal, Gunnar. 1948/1975. *An American Dilemma: The Negro Problem and Modern Democracy*. Vol. I. New York: Pantheon.

Narayan, Anjana, Bandana Purkayastha, and Sudipto Banerji. 2011. "Constructing Virtual, Transnational Identities on the Web: The Case of Hindu Student Groups in the U.S. and U.K." *Journal of Intercultural Studies* 32:495–517.

Nash, Kate. 2002. "Thinking Political Sociology: Beyond the Limits of Post-Marxism." *History of the Human Sciences* 15(4):97–114.

National Community Reinvestment Coalition. 2008. *Income Is No Shield: against Racial Differences in Lending: A Comparison of High-Cost Lending in America's Metropolitan Areas*. http://www.ncrc.org/images/stories/pdf/research/income%20is%20no%20shield%20ii.pdf

National Urban League. 2014. *One Nation: Underemployed: Jobs Rebuild America*. Washington, DC: National Urban League.

Nelson, Barbara J. 1990. "The Origins of the Two-Channel Welfare State: Workmen's Compensation and Mothers' Aid." In *Women, the State, and Welfare*, edited by Linda Gordon, 123–151. Madison, WI: University of Wisconsin Press.

Neubeck, Kenneth J. 2006. *When Welfare Disappears: The Case for Economic Human Rights*. Routledge, New York.

Neubeck, Kenneth J., and Noel Cazenave. 2001. *Welfare Racism: Playing the Race Card against America's Poor*. New York: Routledge.

New York Times. 1989. "Saving Units' Junk Bonds." July 19.

Niemonen, Jack. 1995. "The Role of the State in the Sociology of Racial and Ethnic Relations: Some Theoretical Considerations." *Free Inquiry in Creative Sociology* 23(1): 2727.

O'Connor, James. 1987. *The Meaning of Crisis: A Theoretical Introduction*. New York: Basil Blackwell.

O'Connor, Julia S. 1993. "Gender, Class, and Citizenship in the Comparative Analysis of Welfare State Regimes: Theoretical and Methodological Issues." *British Journal of Sociology* 44:501–518.

O'Connor, Julia S, Ann Shola Orloff, and Sheila Shaver. 1999. *States, Markets, and Families: Gender, Liberalism and Social Policy in Australia, Canada, Great Britain, and the United States*. New York: Cambridge University Press.

Ohmae, K. 1996. *The End of the Nation State: The Rise of Regional Economics*. London: HarperCollins.

Oliver, Pamela E., and Hank Johnston. 1999. What a Good Idea! Frames and Ideologies in Social Movement Research. Paper presented at the annual meeting of the American Sociological Association, Chicago, IL, August 8, 1999.

Omi, Michael. 2001. "The Changing Meaning of Race." In *America Becoming: Racial Trends and Their Consequences,* edited by Neil Smelser, William Julius Wilson, and Faith Mitchell, 243–263. Washington, DC: National Academy Press.

Omi, Michael, and Howard A. Winant. 1986. *Racial Formation in the United States: From the 1960s to the 1980s.* New York: Routledge Chapman & Hall.

———. 1990. *Racial Formation in the United States: From the 1960s to the 1990s.* New York: Routledge.

Orloff, Ann. 1993. "Gender and the Social Rights of Citizenship: The Comparative Analysis of Gender Relations and Welfare States." *American Sociological Review* 58:303–328.

Orloff, Ann. 1996. "Gender and the Welfare State." *Annual Review of Sociology* 22:51–78.

Padavic, Irene, and Barbara F. Reskin. 2002. *Women and Men at Work.* Thousand Oaks, CA: Pine Forge Press.

Pager, Devah, Bruce Western, and Bart Bonikowski. 2009. "Discrimination in a Low-Wage Labor Market: A Field Experiment." *American Sociological Review* 74(5):777–799.

Pannekoek, Anton. 2003. *Workers' Councils.* Oakland: AK Press.

Parekh, Bhikhu. 2001. *Gandhi: A Very Short Introduction.* New York: Sterling Publishing Co.

Parks, Rosa. 1992. *My Story.* New York: Dial Books.

Peattie, Lisa, and Martin Rein. 1983. *Women's Claims: A Study in Political Economy.* London: Oxford University Press.

Peltz, William H. 1990. "Can Girls + Science - Stereotypes = Success?" *Science Teacher* 57(9):44–49.

Penney, Joel, and Caroline Dadas. 2014. "(Re)Tweeting in the Service of Protest: Digital Composition and Circulation in the Occupy Wall Street Movement." *New Media & Society* 16(1):74–90.

Petchesky, Rosalind P. 1984. *Abortion and Woman's Choice: The State, Sexuality, and Reproductive Freedom.* New York: Longman.

Phelan, Shane. 2001. *Sexual Strangers: Gays, Lesbians, and Dilemmas of Citizenship.* Philadelphia, PA: Temple University Press.

Phillips, Kevin. 1990. *The Politics of Rich and Poor: Wealth and the American Electorate in the Reagan Aftermath.* New York: Random House.

Piven, Frances Fox. 1990. "Ideology and the State: Women, Power and the Welfare State." In *Women, the State, and Welfare,* edited by Linda Gordon, 250–264. Madison, WI: University of Wisconsin Press.

Piven, Frances Fox, and Richard Cloward. 1977. *Poor People's Movements: Why They Succeed, How They Fail.* New York: Vintage.

———. 1993. *Regulating the Poor: The Functions of Public Welfare.* New York: Vintage Books. Updated edition.

Poulantzas, Nicos. 1969. "The Problem of the Capitalist State." *New Left Review* 58(Nov/Dec):67–78.

———. 1978. *State, Power, Socialism.* London: Verso.

Prechel, Harland. 1990. "Steel and the State." *American Sociological Review* 55:634–647.

———. 2000. *Big Business and the State: Historical Transitions and Corporate Transformation, 1880s–1990s.* Albany, NY: SUNY Press.

Price, Wayne. 2007. *The Abolition of the State: Anarchist and Marxist Perspectives.* Bloomington, IN: Author House.

Pringle, Rosemary, and Sophie Watson. 1992. "Women's Interests and the Post-structuralist State." In *Destabilizing Theory*, edited by Michelle Barret and Anne Phillips, 53–73. Stanford, CA: Stanford University Press.

Pudrovska, Tetyana, and Myra Marx Ferree. 2004. "Global Activism in 'Virtual Space': The European Women's Lobby in the Network of Transnational Women's NGOs on the Web." *Social Politics: International Studies in Gender, State, and Society* 11:117–143.

Pulido, Laura. 2000. "Rethinking Environmental Racism: White Privilege and Urban Development in Southern California." *Annals of the Association of American Geographers* 90(1):12–40.

———. 1993. *Boiling Point: Republicans, Democrats, and the Decline of Middle Class Prosperity.* New York: Random House.

Quadagno, Jill. 1992. "Social Movements and State Transformation: Labor Unions and Racial Conflict in the War on Poverty." *American Sociological Review* 57:616–634.

———. 1994. *The Color of Welfare: How Racism Undermined the War on Poverty.* New York: Oxford University Press.

———. 2000. "Another Face of Inequality: Racial and Ethnic Exclusion in the Welfare State." *Social Politics* 7(2):229–237.

Quadagno, Jill, and Madonna Harrington Meyer. 1989. "Organized Labor, State Structures, and Social Policy Development: A Case Study of Old Age Assistance in Ohio, 1916–1940." *Social Problems* 36:181–196.

Radelet, Michael L. 1981. "Racial Characteristics and the Death Penalty." *American Sociological Review* 46:918–927.

Raymond, Janice. 1979. *The Transexual Empire.* Boston: Beacon Press.

Reardon, Sean F., Elena Tej Grewal, Demetra Kalogrides, and Erica Greenberg. 2012. "Brown Fades: The End of Court-Ordered School Desegregation and the Resegregation of American Public Schools." *Journal of Public Policy Analysis and Management* 31:876–904.

Reese, Ellen. 2005. *Backlash against Welfare Mothers: Past and Present.* Berkeley, CA: University of California Press.

Reich, Michael. 1981. *Racial Inequality.* Princeton, NJ: Princeton University Press.

Reich, Robert B. 1991. *The Work of Nations: Preparing Ourselves for 21st Century Capitalism.* New York: Knopf.

Renaurt, Elizabeth. 2004. "An Overview of the Predatory Lending Process." *Housing Policy Debate* 15(3):467–502.

Renzetti, Claire M., and Daniel J. Curran. 1992. *Women, Men, and Society.* Boston: Allyn and Bacon. Second edition.

Reskin, Barbara F., and Hartmann, Heidi I., eds. 1986. *Women's Work, Men's Work: Sex Segregation on the Job.* New York: National Academy Press.

Reskin, Barbara F., and Patricia A. Roos. 1990. *Job Queues, Gender Queues: Explaining Women's Inroads into Male Occupations.* Philadelphia: Temple University Press.

Richardson, Diane. 2000. "Constructing Sexual Citizenship: Theorizing Sexual Rights." *Critical Social Policy* 20(1):105–135.

Richardson, J., and A. Jordan. 1979. *Governing Under Pressure.* Oxford: Martin Robertson.

Roberts, Dorothy. 1997. *Killing the Black Body: Race, Reproduction, and the Meaning of Liberty.* New York: Pantheon Books.

Robinson, Margaret. 2013. "Polyamory and Monogamy as Strategic Identities." *Journal of Bisexuality* 13(1):21.

Rocker, Rudolf. [1938] 2004. *Anarcho-Syndicalism: Theory and Practice.* Oakland, CA: AK Press. Sixth edition.

Roschelle, Anne R. 1999. "Gender, Family Structure, and Social Structure: Racial Ethnic Families in the United States." In *Revisioning Gender*, edited by Myra Marx Ferree, Judith Lorber, and Beth B. Hess, 311–340. Thousand Oaks, CA: Sage.

Rose, Peter I. 1997. *Tempest-Tost: Race, Immigration, and the Dilemmas of Diversity.* Oxford: Oxford University Press.

Ross, Stephen L., and John Yinger. 2002. *The Color of Credit: Mortgage Discrimination, Research Methodology, and Fair-Lending Enforcement.* Cambridge, MA: MIT Press.

Rubin, Gayle S. 1984. "Thinking Sex: Notes for a Radical Theory of the Politics of Sexuality." In *Pleasure and Danger: Exploring Female Sexuality,* edited by Carol S. Vance. New York: Routledge & K. Paul.

Ruggie, Mary. 1984. *The State and Working Women.* Princeton, NJ: Princeton University Press.

Rugman, Alan. 2000. *The End of Globalisation.* London: Random House.

Sadker, David, and Myra Sadker. 1988. *Teachers Make the Difference.* New York: McGraw-Hill. Second edition.

———. 1994. *Failing at Fairness: How America's Schools Cheat Girls.* New York: Scribner.

Sainsbury, Diane, ed. 1994. *Gendering Welfare States.* Thousand Oaks, CA: Sage.

———. 1996. *Gender, Equality, and Welfare States.* New York: Cambridge University Press.

Sapiro, Virginia. 1990. "The Gender Bias of American Social Policy." In *Women, the State, and Welfare,* edited by Linda Gordon, 36–54. Madison, WI: University of Wisconsin Press.

Schaeffer, R. 2003. *Understanding Globalization.* New York: Rowman and Littlefield Publishers.

Schattschneider, E. E. 1975. *The Semi-Sovereign People.* Hinsdale, IL: Dryden. Reissued edition.

Schilt, Kristen, and Laurel Westbrook. 2009. "Doing Gender, Doing Heteronor-mativity: 'Gender Normals,' Transgender People, and the Social Maintenance of Heterosexuality" *Gender & Society* 23(4):440–464.

Schmitter, Philippe C. 1974. "Still the Century of Corporatism?" *Review of Politics* 36(1):85–127.

Scholte, J.A. 2000. *Globalization: A Critical Introduction.* Basingstoke and New York: Palgrave Macmillan.

Schram, Sanford F., and Samuel H. Beer, eds. 1999. *Welfare Reform: A Race to the Bottom?* Baltimore: Johns Hopkins University Press.

Schur, Edwin M. 1984. *Labeling Women Deviant: Gender, Stigma, and Social Control.* New York: Random House.

Schwartz, Alex. 1998. "Banking Lending to Minority and Low-Income House-holds and Neighborhoods: Do Community Reinvestment Agreements Make a Difference?" *Journal of Urban Affairs* 20:269–301.

———. 2000. "The Past and Future of Community Reinvestment Agreements." *Housing Facts and Findings* 2:3–7.

Scott, James C. 1985. *Weapons of the Weak: Everyday Forms of Peasant Resistance.* New Haven: Yale University Press.

Scott, John. 1991. *Who Rules Britain?* Cambridge: Polity Press.

Seale, Bobby, and Stephen Shames. 2016. *Power to the People: The World of the Black Panthers.* New York: Harry N. Abrams, Inc.

Seccombe, Karen. 1999. *"So You Think I Drive a Cadillac?" Welfare Recipients' Perspectives on the System and its Reform.* Boston: Allyn & Bacon.

Seidman, Steven. 2001. "From Identity to Queer Politics: Shifts in Norma-tive Heterosexuality and the Meaning of Citizenship." *Citizenship Studies* 5(3):321–328.

Sen, Amartya. 1981. *Poverty and Famines: An Essay on Entitlement and Depriva-tion.* New York: Oxford University Press.

Shannon, Deric. 2012. "Chopping off the Invisible Hand: Internal Problems with Markets and Anarchist Theory, Strategy, and Vision." In *The Accumulation of Freedom: Writings on Anarchist Economics*, edited by Deric Shannon, Anthony J. Nocella, II, and John Asimakopoulos, 276–290. Oakland, CA: AK Press.

———, ed. 2014. *The End of the World as We Know It? Crisis, Resistance, and the Age of Austerity.* Oakland, CA: AK Press.

———. 2016. "Food Justice, Direct Action, and the Human Rights Enterprise." *Critical Sociology* 42(6):799–814.

Sharma, Sohan, and Kumar Surinder. 2003. "The Military Backbone of Globalisation." *Race and Class* 44(3):23–40.

Shaver, Sheila. 1993. "Body Rights, Social Rights, and the Liberal Welfare State." *Criti-cal Social Policy* 13:66–93.

Sheak, Robert. 1990. "Corporate and State Attacks on the Material Conditions of the Working Class." *Humanity and Society* 14(2):105–127.

Sheff, Elisabeth. 2011. "Polyamorous Families, Same-Sex Marriage, and the Slippery Slope." *Journal of Contemporary Ethnography* 40(5):487–520.

Shlay, Anne B. 1999. "Influencing the Agents of Urban Structure: Evaluating the Effects of Community Reinvestment Organizing on Bank Residential Lending Practices." *Urban Affairs Review* 35:247–278.

Sidel, Ruth. 2000. "The Enemy Within: The Demonization of Poor Women." *Journal of Sociology and Social Welfare* 27(1):73–84.

Skidmore, Dan L., and Davita Silfen Glasberg. 1996. "State Theory and Corporate Welfare: The Crisis and Bailout of the Savings and Loan Industry from a Contingency Perspective." *Political Power and Social Theory* 9:149–191.

Sklar, Katherine Kish. 1993. "The Historical Foundations of Women's Power in the Creation of the American Welfare State." In *Mothers of the New World: Maternalistic Policies and the Origins of the Welfare State*, edited by Seth Koven and Sonya Michel, 43–93. New York: Routledge.

Skocpol, Theda. 1985. "Bringing the State Back in: Strategies of Analysis in Current Research." In *Bringing the State Back in*, edited by Peter B. Evans, Dietrich Rueschemeyer, and Theda Skocpol, 3–37. Cambridge, UK: Cambridge University Press.

———. 1992. *Protecting Soldiers and Mothers: The Political Origins of Social Policy in the United States*. Cambridge: Harvard University Press.

Skocpol, Theda, and John Ikenberry. 1983. "The Political Formation of the American Welfare State in Historical and Comparative Perspective." *Comparative Social Research* 6:87–148.

Smith, Dorothy. 1999. *Writing the Social: Critique, Theory, and Investigations*. Toronto: University of Toronto Press.

Smith, Martin. 1990. "Pluralism, Reformed Pluralism and Neopluralism: The Role of Pressure Groups in Policy Making." *Political Studies* 38:302–322.

Smith, Rogers M. 2001. "Citizenship and the Politics of People-Building." *Citizenship Studies* 5(1):73–96.

Snow, David A. 2004. "Social Movements as Challenges to Authority: Resistance to an Emerging Conceptual Hegemony." *Research in Social Movements, Conflicts and Change* 25:3–25.

Snow, David A., and Robert D. Benford. 1988. "Ideology, Frame Resonance, and Participant Mobilization." In *From Structure to Action: Social Movement Participation Across Cultures*, edited by Bert Klandermans, Hanspeter Kriesi, and Sidney Tarrow, 197–217. Greenwich, CT: JAI Press.

Sorrels, Bobbye D. 1983. *The Nonsexist Communicator: Solving the Problems of Gender and Awkwardness in Modern English*. Englewood Cliffs, NJ: Prentice-Hall.

Squires, Gregory, ed. 1992. *From Redlining to Reinvestment: Community Responses to Urban Disinvestment*. Philadelphia, PA: Temple University Press.

———. 1994. *Capital and Communities in Black and White*. Albany: State University of New York Press.

———, ed. 2003. *Organizing Access to Capital: Advocacy and Democratization of Financial Institutions*. Philadelphia, PA: Temple University Press.

Stetson, Dorothy Mcbride, ed. 2005. *Abortion Politics, Women's Movements, and the Democratic State: A Comparative Study of State Feminism*. Oxford: Oxford University Press.

Stevens, Jacqueline. 1999. *Reproducing the State*. Princeton, NJ: Princeton University Press.

Stychin, Carl F. 2000. "'A Stranger to Its Laws': Sovereign Bodies, Global Sexualities, and Transnational Citizens." *Journal of Law and Society* 27(4):601.

Swenson, Peter A. 2002. *Capitalists against Markets: The Making of Labor Markets and Welfare States in the United States and Sweden*. New York: Oxford University Press.

Taguieff, Pierre-Andre. 2001. *The Force of Prejudice: On Racism and its Doubles*. Translated by Hassan Melehy. Minneapolis: University of Minnesota Press.

Taibbi, Matt. 2011. *Griftopia: A Story of Bankers, Politicians, and the Most Audacious Power Grab in American History*. New York: Spiegel & Grau.

Takaki, Ronald. 1982. "Reflections on Racial Patterns in America: An Historical Perspective." In *Ethnicity and Public Policy*, Vol. 1, edited by Winston A. VanHorne and Thomas V. Tonnesen, 1–23. Milwaukee, WI: University of Wisconsin System American Ethnic Studies Coordinating Committee/Urban Corridor Consortium.

Tarrow, Sidney. 1983. *Struggling to Reform: Social Movements and Policy Change During Cycles of Protest*. Ithaca: Cornell University Press.

———. 1998. *Power in Movement: Social Movements and Contentious Politics*. Cambridge: Cambridge University Press.

TATORT Kurdistan. 2013. *Democratic Autonomy in North Kurdistan: The Council Movement, Gender Liberation, and Ecology—in Practice*. Hamburg, Germany: New Compass Press.

Taylor, John, Josh Silver, and David Berenbaum. 2004. "The Targets of Predatory and Discriminatory Lending: Who Are They and Where Do They Live?" In *Why the Poor Pay More: How to Stop Predatory Lending*, edited by Gregory Squires. Westport, CT: Praeger Publications.

Taylor, Keeanga-Yamahtta. 2016. *From #BlackLivesMatter to Black Liberation*. Chicago: Haymarket Books.

Taylor, Verta, and Nancy E. Whittier. 1992. "Collective Identity in Social Movement Communities: Lesbian Feminist Mobilization." In *Frontiers in Social Movement Theory*, edited by Aldon D. Morris and Carol McClurg Mueller, 104–129. New Haven, CT: Yale University Press.

Teeple, Gary. 2005. *The Riddle of Human Rights*. Amherst, NY: Humanity Books.

Temkin, Kenneth, Jennifer E. H. Johnson, and Diane Levy. 2002. *Subprime Markets, the Role of GSE's, and Risk-Based Pricing*. Washington, DC: Urban Institute and the U.S. Department of Housing and Urban Development, Office of Policy Development and Research.

Theoharis, Jeanne. 2013. *The Rebellious Life of Mrs. Rosa Parks*. Boston, MA: Beacon Press.

Thernstrom, Stephan and Abigail Thernstrom. 1997. *America in Black and White: One Nation, Indivisible; Race in Modern America*. New York: Simon and Schuster.

Thomas, William I. 1928. *The Child in America*. New York: Knopf.

Tomaskovic-Devey, Donald. 1993. *Gender and Racial Inequality at Work*. Ithaca, NY: ILR Press.

Touraine, Alaine. 1985. "An Introduction to the Study of Social Movements." *Social Research* 52(4):749–787.

Tremayne, Mark. "Anatomy of Protest in the Digital Era: A Network Analysis of Twitter and Occupy Wall Street." *Social Movement Studies* 13(1):110–126.

Truman, David. 1951. *The Governmental Process*. New York: Alfred A. Knopf.

Tuchman, Gaye, Arlene Kaplan Daniels, and James Benet, eds. 1978. *Hearth and Home: Images of Women in the Mass Media*. New York: Oxford University Press.

Turner, Margery Austin, Michael E. Fix, and Raymond J. Struyk. 1991. *Opportunities Denied, Opportunities Diminished: Racial Discrimination in Hiring*. Washington, DC: Urban Institute Press.

Tweedy, Anne E. 2011. "Polyamory as a Sexual Orientation." *University of Cincinnati Law Review* 79(4):1461–1515.

Uggen, Christopher, and Jeff Manza. 2002. "Democratic Contraction? Political Consequences of Felon Disenfranchisement in the United States." *American Sociological Review* 67(6):777–803.

U.S. Census Bureau. 2015. "Quick Facts." https://www.census.gov/quickfacts/

U.S. Congress: House of Representatives. 1979. Committee on Banking, Finance, and Urban Affairs, Subcommittee on Economic Stabilization. *The Chrysler Corporation Financial Situation*. 96th Congress, 1st Session. Washington, DC: Government Printing Office.

U.S. Congress: House of Representatives. 1989. Committee on Banking, Finance, and Urban Affairs, Subcommittee on General Oversight and Investigations. *Junk Bonds: 1988 Status Report*. 100th Congress, 2nd Session. Washington, DC: Government Printing Office.

U.S. Department of Agriculture. 2015. "Food Security in the U.S.: Key Statistics and Graphics." https://www.ers.usda.gov/topics/food-nutrition-assistance/food-security-in-the-us/key-statistics-graphics.aspx

U.S. Department of Housing and Urban Development. 2000. "Unequal Burden: Income and Racial Disparities in Subprime Lending in America." https://archives.hud.gov/reports/subprime/subprime.cfm

U.S. Department of Housing and Urban Development-U.S. Treasury National Predatory Lending Task Force. 2000. *Curbing Predatory Lending*. Washington, DC.

U.S. Department of Justice. 2016. *After-Action Assessment of the Police Response to the August 2014 Demonstrations in Ferguson, Missouri*. Washington, DC: Government Printing Office.

U.S. Department of Labor. 1991. *A Report on the Glass Ceiling Initiative*. Washington, DC: Government Printing Office.

Useem, Michael. 1984. *The Inner Circle: Large Corporations and the Rise of Business Political Activity in the U.S. and U.K.* New York: Oxford University Press.

Vallochi, Steven. 1989. "The Relative Autonomy of the State and the Origins of British Welfare Policy." *Sociological Forum* 4:349–365.

Van Dijk, Teun A. 1993. *Elite Discourse and Racism*. Newbury Park, CA: Sage Publications.

Wade, Robert. 1996. "Globalisation and Its Limits: Reports of the Death of the National Economy Are Greatly Exaggerated." In *National Diversity and Global*

Capitalism, edited by Suzanne Berger and Ronald P. Dore. London: Cornell University Press.

Waites, M. 2005. "The Fixity of Sexual Identities in the Public Sphere: Biomedical Knowledge, Liberalism and the Heterosexual/Homosexual Binary in Late Modernity." *Sexualities* 8(5):539–569.

Waldschmidt-Nelson, Britta. 2012. *Dreams and Nightmares: Martin Luther King Jr., Malcolm X and the Struggle for Black Equality in America.* Gainesville, FL: University of Florida Press.

Wallach, Lori, and Michelle Sforza. 1999. "NAFTA at 5." *Nation*, January 25.

Warner, Michael. 1999. *The Trouble with Normal: Sex, Politics, and the Ethics of Queer Life.* Cambridge, MA: Harvard University Press.

Weber, Max. [1921] 1978. *Economy and Society: An Outline of Interpretative Sociology.* Berkeley, CA: University of California Press.

Weeks, Jeffrey. 1977. *Coming Out.* London: Quartet Books.

———. 1985. *Sexuality and Its Discontents: Meanings, Myths, & Modern Sexualities.* London and Boston: Routledge & K. Paul.

Weinstein, James. 1968. *The Corporate Ideal in the Liberal State, 1900–1918.* Boston: Beacon Press.

Westra, Laura, and Bill E. Lawson, eds. 2001. *Faces of Environmental Racism: Confronting Issues of Global Justice.* Lanham, MD: Rowman and Littlefield.

Whitt, J. Allen. 1979. "Toward a Class Dialectic Model of Power: An Empirical Assessment of Three Competing Models of Political Power." *American Sociological Review* 44:81–100.

———. 1982. *The Dialectics of Power: Urban Elites and Mass Transportation.* Princeton: Princeton University Press.

Whittier, Nancy. 2002. "Meaning and Structure in Social Movements." In *Social Movements: Identity, Culture, and the State*, edited by David S. Meyer, Nancy Whittier, and Belinda Robnett, 289–307. Oxford: Oxford University Press.

Wilkins, Amy C., and Cristen Dalessandro. 2013. "Monogamy Lite: Cheating, College, and Women." *Gender & Society* 27(5):728–751.

Williams, Richard, Reynold Nesiba, and Eileen Diaz McConnell. 2005. "The Changing Face of Inequality in Home Mortgage Lending." *Social Problems* 52(2):181–208.

Willis, Abbey S. 2013. "Negotiating Non-Monogamies: Narratives of Resistance to the Reproduction of Compulsory Monogamy in Everyday Life." Master's Thesis, Paper 516, University of Connecticut. http://digitalcommons.uconn.edu/gs_theses/516

Wilson, Carter A. 1996a. *Racism: From Slavery to Advanced Capitalism.* Thousand Oaks, CA: Sage Publications.

Wilson, William Julius. 1987. *The Truly Disadvantaged.* Chicago: University of Chicago Press.

———. 1996b. *When Work Disappears: The World of the New Urban Poor.* New York: Knopf.

Winant, Howard. 1994. *Racial Conditions: Politics, Theory, Comparisons.* Minneapolis: University of Minnesota Press.

————. 2000. "Race and Race Theory." *Annual Review of Sociology* 26:169–185.

Witte, Edwin E. 1972. "Organized Labor and Social Security." In *Labor and the New Deal*, edited by Milton Derber and Edwin Young, 241–274. New York: DeCapo Press.

Wolf, Naomi. 1991. *The Beauty Myth*. New York: Morrow.

Wright, Erik Olin. 1978. *Class, Crisis, and the State*. London: Verso.

Yanow, Dvora. 2003. *Constructing 'Race' and 'Ethnicity' in America: Category-Making in Public Policy and Administration*. Armonk, NY: M.E. Sharpe.

Yuval-Davis, N. 1997. *Gender and Nation*. Thousand Oaks, CA: Sage.

Zeitlin, Maurice, and Richard E. Ratcliff. 1975. "Research Methods for the Analysis of the Internal Structure of Dominant Classes: The Case of Landlords and Capitalists in Chile." *Latin American Research Review* 10(3):5–61.

Zeitlin, Maurice, Lynda Ann Ewen, and Richard E. Ratcliff. 1974. "New Princes for Old? The Large Corporation and the Capitalist Class in Chile." *American Journal of Sociology* 80:87–123.

Zolberg, Aristide R. 1990. "Reforming the Back Door: The Immigration Reform and Control Act of 1986 in Historical Perspective." In *Immigration Reconsidered: History, Sociology, and Politics*, edited by Virginia Yans-McLaughlin, 315–339. Oxford: Oxford University Press.

Zong, Jie, and Jeanne Batalova. 2016. "Mexican Immigrants in the United States." *Migration Policy Institute*. http://www.migrationpolicy.org/article/mexican-immigrants-united-states

Zucchino, David. 1999. *Myth of the Welfare Queen*. New York: Simon and Schuster.

Zweigenhaft, Richard L., and G. William Domhoff. 1998. *Diversity in the Power Elite: Have Women and Minorities Reached the Top?* New Haven: Yale University Press.

————. 2006. *Diversity in the Power Elite: How It Happened, Why It Matters*. Lanham, MD: Rowman & Littlefield.

Zylan, Yvonne. 2000. "Maternalism Redefined: Gender, the State, and the Politics of Day Care, 1945–1962." *Gender & Society* 14(5):608–629.

————. 2009. "Passions We Like…And Those We Don't: Anti-Gay Hate Crime Laws and the Discursive Construction of Sex, Gender, and the Body." *Michigan Journal of Gender & Law* 16(1):1–48.

Zysman, J. 1994. "How Institutions Create Historically Rooted Trajectories of Growth." *Industrial and Corporate Change* 3(1):243–283.

Index

"abnormal." *See* "naturalness"
abortion, 41, 49–51, 58, 162
ACORN. *See* Association of
　Community Organizations for
　Reform Now
affirmative action, 32–33, 41, 42, 52,
　56, 97, 98, 102, 103
African Americans, 28, 33, 42, 46, 52,
　54, 70–71, 89, 98–100, 104, 105,
　108–9, 111, 112, 122–23, 128,
　147, 148, 149.
　See also Black Lives Matter; Black
　Panthers; National Association
　for the Advancement of Colored
　People; people of color
agriculture, 55, 127, 150
Americans With Disabilities Act, 17
anarchism, 3, 39, 48, 113–16, 131, 133,
　136, 156, 157, 163
anti-capitalism, 3, 110, 114
anti-miscegenation. *See* miscegenation
anti-statism, 3, 132, 136, 157, 163
Argentina, 74–75, 131
Asians, 54, 102–3.
　See also people of color
assimilation, 32, 97
Association of Community
　Organizations for Reform Now
　(ACORN), 67–68, 72, 73–74
austerity, 1, 18, 74, 133, 152–53, 162

balance of class forces. *See* balance of
　political forces
balance of gendering forces. *See* balance
　of political forces
balance of political forces, 2, 28, 30,
　31, 35, 39, 43, 45, 47–56, 59–77,
　79, 80–82, 87, 91, 95–96, 101–2,
　103, 116, 117–24, 127–36, 139,
　141–42, 145, 152, 153, 156, 157,
　160–61, 163
balance of racial formation forces. *See*
　balance of political forces
balance of sexuality forces. *See* balance
　of political forces
banking, 14, 18, 140;
　predatory lending, subprime lending,
　and foreclosures, 68–72, 73, 76,
　99, 121–24, 151, 158, 160.
　See also Glass-Steagall Act; savings
　and loans bailout
Banking Act of 1933. *See* Glass-Steagall
　Act
bathrooms. *See* restrooms
BDSM, 27, 29, 30
bisexuality, 27, 41, 44, 47, 83, 84, 88,
　90.
　See also lesbian, gay, bisexual, and
　transgender and queer (LGBTQ)
　people
bisexual rights. *See* rights

blacks. *See* African Americans
Black Lives Matter, 1, 51, 96, 108, 109,
    111, 113, 116
Black Panthers, 115, 116
bureaucracies, 18, 19, 116
business dominance state theories, 11,
    12–19, 25
business leaders. *See* capitalists

capital accumulation, 7, 13–17, 19–21,
    24, 38, 41, 72, 138–39, 141, 151
capitalists, 12–14, 16, 18–20, 138–40,
    146, 151
capitalist state structuralism, 11, 15–18,
    80
challenges from below. *See* resistance
    from below
Chrysler, 61–66, 117, 151
cisnormativity, 57–58n1, 58
citizenship, 27, 38, 42, 47, 54, 144.
    See also sexual citizenship
citizenship rights. *See* rights
civil rights. *See* rights
civil unions, 28, 90
claims process, 32, 40, 44, 49, 51, 53,
    95–96, 101, 144, 160
class. *See* class-based analyses of race;
    class-based domination; class-
    based policy; class-based theories
    of the state; class consciousness;
    class dialectic theories; class
    oppression; class relations; class
    struggle
class-based analyses of race, 32–33,
    97–98
class-based domination, 160
class-based policy, 21, 47, 56, 83, 153,
    162
class-based theories of the state, 37–38,
    83, 88.
See also class dialectic theories
class consciousness, 16, 32–33, 97, 110
class dialectic theories, 19–21, 25,
    34–35, 80, 115, 138
class forces. *See* balance of political
    forces

class oppression, 24–25, 138
class relations, 12, 15, 21, 24, 31,
    38–39, 41, 56, 81, 96, 137,
    141–42, 153, 158, 162
class struggle, 12, 16, 20
coercion, 3, 4, 20, 30
collective bargaining, 15, 16, 17, 20, 41,
    139–40
colonialism, 55, 73, 75, 77, 158
common good, 6–10, 15, 19, 151, 157
Community Reinvestment Act of 1977
    (CRA), 67–68, 70–72, 76, 123
complex globalization theory, 23–24
Congress of Racial Equality (CORE),
    52, 102, 105, 108
CORE. *See* Congress of Racial Equality
corporations, 4, 9, 11–16, 19–23, 41,
    60–67, 75, 104, 117, 140–42,
    145–47, 150–52.
    See also business dominance state
    theory
Council on Foreign Relations, 13–14
CRA. *See* Community Reinvestment
    Act of 1977
critical race theory. *See* race theory
critical state theory, 3, 55, 79, 118, 136,
    155–56, 162–63

Defense of Marriage Act (DOMA), 28
deregulation. *See* regulation
Diagnostic and Statistical Manual of
    Mental Disorders (DSM), 30–31
direct action, 104, 112–16, 124,
    127–36
disabilities, 17, 19, 149–51
discourse, 5, 24–26, 29–31, 33, 38, 43,
    48, 87, 90, 98, 130, 131–33, 136,
    144, 156–57, 162
discrimination, 8, 28, 30–32, 46, 51–52,
    69, 85–86, 88, 90, 96–97, 101–3,
    108–9, 115, 149, 159, 162
DOMA. *See* Defense of Marriage Act
domestic partners, 28.
    See also civil unions
DSM. *See* Diagnostic and Statistical
    Manual of Mental Disorders

eco-feminist stateless confederalism, 1
education, 6, 22, 28, 42, 45–47, 49, 51,
      62, 73, 99–100, 103, 115, 127,
      138, 141, 145, 147, 149, 161
electoral politics, 4, 6, 10, 13, 111,
      114–15.
      See also political action committees;
      voting
electoral processes. *See* electoral politics
electoral strategies. *See* electoral politics
elites, 6–7, 10–13, 16, 19, 24–26,
      34–35, 39, 95, 103–4, 110–11
elitist state theories, 24–26, 34
endangered species, 17, 19
environmental laws, 19, 22
equality, 9, 30, 39, 42, 47, 52, 102.
      See also Congress of Racial
      Equality; inequality
ethnicity-based theories of race. *See*
      race theory

families, 12, 28, 41, 44–46, 49, 66,
      80–81, 83, 90, 119, 124, 129,
      138–39, 142–44, 146–49, 159.
      See also kinship; marriage
feminist state theories, 5, 24, 30–32, 33,
      38, 56, 96, 142–45, 153, 156, 161.
      See also intersectionality
finance. *See* banking
FNB. *See* Food Not Bombs
food. *See* Food Not Bombs; food
      security; state projects
Food Not Bombs (FNB), 129–36, 161 163
food security, 128–29
foreign affairs. *See* foreign policy
foreign policy, 10, 13–14
foreign relations. *See* foreign policy

gay rights. *See* rights
gays, 13, 17, 19, 27, 28, 31, 41, 44, 47,
      80, 87–89, 158.
      See also lesbian, gay, bisexual, and
      transgender and queer (LGBTQ)
      people
gender, 2, 3, 6, 10, 21, 24–25, 27–34,
      37–45, 47–51, 53–57, 57–58n1,
      80–90, 92, 96, 99, 101, 128–29,
      137–38, 142–45, 149, 153–54,
      157–62.
      See also intersex people; lesbian,
      gay, bisexual, and transgender
      and queer (LGBTQ) people;
      nonbinary people; queer people;
      transgender people; trans men;
      trans women; women
gendered state process analyses, 144–45
gendered state subsystem analyses,
      143–44
gendering forces. *See* balance of
      political forces
genderqueer people. *See* nonbinary
      people
Glass-Steagall Act, 60–77, 117–18, 121
GLBA. See Graham-Leach-Bliley Act
globalization, 22–24.
      See also complex globalization
      theory; ideational global theory;
      skeptical theory
"governmentality," 25
Graham-Leach-Bliley Act (GLBA),
      117–18
Great Depression, 60, 72, 76, 140, 146
Great Recession, 59, 72–76

healthcare, 22, 51, 141, 146
heteronormativity, 9, 27, 29, 37–40,
      42, 44–45, 58, 77, 79–92, 137,
      158–60
heterosexuality, 9, 37, 41, 44, 46–47,
      80, 83–85, 90, 92, 158–60
hierarchy, 10, 39, 46, 89, 100, 114, 132,
      135, 143
Hispanics. *See* Latinxs
homelessness, 9, 67, 132, 146–47, 149,
      152–53
homonormativity, 31, 84, 89
House Bill 2, 85
housing, 22, 51, 55, 68–72, 101, 118,
      120–24, 133, 139, 142, 149, 152,
      160, 162–63.
      See also homelessness
human rights. *See* rights

ICESCR. *See* International Covenant on Economic, Social, and Cultural Rights

ideational globalization theory, 24

identities, 25–27, 29–33, 41, 44, 79–81, 83–84, 86–91, 97, 109–10, 123, 157–60, 162–63

immigrants. *See* immigration

immigration, 27, 32, 42, 54–56, 97, 98, 102–3, 119–20, 138, 162

imperialism, 38, 55, 75, 77, 158

Industrial Revolution, 54, 138

industrial unions. *See* unions

inequality, 2–3, 8, 23, 24, 32–34, 39, 41–43, 51, 54–55, 67, 77, 80, 92, 96–99, 101, 113, 115, 117, 119–20, 123–24, 127–29, 142, 150, 155, 158–60.
    See also equality

instrumentalism, 12–17, 80

interest groups, 5–10, 18, 38, 50

International Covenant on Economic, Social, and Cultural Rights (ICESCR), 121, 127, 129

intersectionality, 24, 38, 54–55, 84–85, 155–56, 159

intersex people, 30, 82

Jessop, Bob, 2, 4–5, 39–40, 43, 47–48, 54, 56–57, 80–81, 88, 91, 118, 120, 153, 156–57, 162

kinship, 27–28, 41, 44, 55, 77, 81, 84, 87.
    See also families; marriage

labor. *See* workers

labor rights. *See* rights

labor unions. *See* unions

laissez-faire, 60, 63, 118, 138–39

language, 44, 46, 79, 87, 91, 100, 118–19, 127, 138, 163

Latinxs, 33, 98, 100, 102, 119, 120, 122–23, 128, 147, 149.
    See also people of color; race

leaders. *See* leadership

leadership, 5–8, 10, 14, 16, 45, 62–63, 66, 105, 107–8, 112, 114, 117, 120

legislative processes. *See* political action committees; policy formation

legitimacy, 3–8, 13–15, 20, 28, 34, 39, 45–46, 49, 52, 87, 90, 92, 101, 113, 119, 121, 133, 136

legitimation. *See* legitimacy

lesbian, gay, bisexual, and transgender (LGBT) people, 29, 85.
    See also sexual orientation; transgender people; trans men; trans women

lesbian, gay, bisexual, and transgender and queer (LGBTQ) people, 9.
    See also queer people; queer theory; sexual orientation; transgender people; trans men; trans women

lesbian rights. *See* rights

lesbians, 13, 17, 19, 27–28, 41, 44, 47, 88–89.
    See also lesbian, gay, bisexual, and transgender and queer (LGBTQ) people

LGBT. *See* lesbian, gay, bisexual, and transgender (LGBT) people

LGBTQ. *See* lesbian, gay, bisexual, and transgender and queer (LGBTQ) people

marriage, 27–29, 41, 44, 46, 55, 56, 82–85, 87–90, 92, 159, 162.
    See also kinship; families

Marx, Karl. *See* Marxism

Marxism, 11–12, 105–7, 110, 113–14, 131, 155–56, 163–64.
    See also business dominance state theories; capitalist state structuralism; class dialectic theories

meaning-making, 5, 24–26, 30, 79, 90, 109, 158

military-industrial complex, 12

minimum wage, 17, 21, 106, 146–47, 149–50, 152
minorities, 27, 29, 42, 47, 88–90, 102–3, 122, 129
miscegenation, 28, 55, 84–85
monogamy, 81–82, 84, 90–91. *See also* non-monogamy
movements from below. *See* resistance from below
MSP. *See* multi-sites of power
multi-partnered relationships, 28–29, 44, 87
multi-sites of power (MSP), 2–3, 35, 37–39, 47, 52–57, 76–77, 84–92, 95, 115–16, 118, 121, 124, 136, 154, 156, 157, 159, 163

NAACP. *See* National Association for the Advancement of Colored People
NAFTA. *See* North American Free Trade Agreement
NARAL. *See* National Abortion and Reproductive Rights Action League
National Abortion and Reproductive Rights Action League (NARAL), 50
National Association for the Advancement of Colored People (NAACP), 52, 102, 105, 108, 109
National Labor Relations Act. *See* Wagner Act
National Organization for Women (NOW), 50
"naturalness," 3, 9, 26, 28–32, 34, 44–46, 49, 51, 83, 89–90, 95–96, 100, 116,118, 120, 134, 143–45, 159–60
neoliberalism, 63, 75, 77, 117–20
New Deal, 2, 137
New Federalism, 145–52
nonbinary people, 27, 30, 80, 83, 86, 159. *See also* queer people

nonelites, 12, 34–35, 95, 103
non-monogamy, 29, 82, 87–88, 90–91. *See also* monogamy
"normal." *See* "naturalness"
"normalcy." *See* "naturalness"
North American Free Trade Agreement (NAFTA), 23, 119, 141
NOW. *See* National Organization for Women
nutrition, 22, 135, 142

Occupy movements, 1, 107, 124, 136, 152–53
oppression, 9, 15, 25, 27–28, 31–35, 37, 45, 48, 53–56, 80, 85, 90, 92, 95–99, 104–6, 108, 115–16, 129, 138–39, 142, 144–45, 153–54, 156, 159, 161–62

patriarchy, 1, 9, 24, 40, 44–45, 49, 92, 143, 159
people of color, 9, 13, 32–33, 42–43, 46–47, 51–52, 55, 67, 70–71, 77, 97–103, 108, 111, 119, 122–24, 145, 147, 149–52, 158. *See also* African Americans; Asians; Latinxs; National Association for the Advancement of Colored People
Personal Responsibility and Work Opportunity Reconciliation Act of 1996, 66–67, 148–50
police, 16, 22, 29, 33, 51, 55, 57, 62, 101–2, 108–9, 111–13, 115, 134, 140, 153
political action committees, 13, 14
political economy, 1, 5, 11, 15–16, 18–20, 48, 55, 105, 118, 135–36
political opportunity structures, 110–13
political participation. *See* electoral politics
political process theory, 110
political socialization, 14
political stability. *See* stability
polyamory, 27, 84, 87–90

poststructuralism, 5, 25–26, 27
poverty, 21, 23, 46, 56–57, 66–67,
    68, 100, 115, 127–28, 131–32,
    141–52, 154, 161–62
pluralism. *See* pluralist theory
pluralist theory, 5–11, 18, 25, 39, 80;
    U.S. version of, 5–7;
    U.K. version of, 7
political, social, and economic rights.
    See rights
pressure from below. *See* resistance
    from below
queer people, 9, 31, 84, 89.
    See also lesbian, gay, bisexual, and
    transgender and queer people;
    nonbinary people; queer theory

queer theory, 3, 27–31, 34, 38, 56,
    88–89, 156, 157, 162–63

race, 2, 3, 6, 10, 38, 40, 42–43, 46–48,
    51–56, 69, 71, 77, 84, 122–23,
    128–29, 158, 160
    racial formation and the state,
    95–116.
    See also balance of political forces;
    miscegenation; racial formation
    theory; race theory; racism
race theory, 56, 96;
    critical race theory, 31–34, 156;
    ethnicity-based theories of race,
    32–33, 97–98
racial formation forces. *See* balance of
    political forces
racial formation theory, 31–34, 38
racism, 9, 33–34, 39–43, 46–47, 51, 52,
    96, 98–103, 104–6, 108–9, 111,
    113, 115, 120–24, 125n1
regulation, 8, 13, 14, 16, 22, 40, 41, 53,
    119–21, 123–24, 144, 146–47,
    151, 160;
    Glass-Steagall Act, 60–77, 117–18,
    121;
    Graham-Leach-Bliley Act (GLBA),
    117–18;
    House Bill 2, 85

"relative autonomy," 17, 40, 48, 53
religion, 6, 10, 45, 162
reproductive rights. *See* rights
resistance from below, 1, 4, 16, 18–20,
    23, 25, 34–35, 39–40, 48, 53–54,
    56, 59, 67, 72, 79, 95–96, 98,
    104, 119, 130, 134, 136, 153,
    156–58, 160–61
resource mobilization theory, 108
restrooms, 30, 80, 83, 85–87, 111, 159
revolution, 6, 105–8, 114, 132, 153.
    See also Industrial Revolution
"rhizome," 25
rights, 32, 33, 41, 45, 96, 124, 127, 128,
    130–34, 136, 142, 145;
    bisexual rights, 47;
    citizenship rights, 27, 42;
    civil rights, 17, 19, 32, 42, 50, 52,
    96–97, 98, 102, 105–6, 108–12,
    115–16, 123, 145;
    gay rights, 17, 19, 47;
    human rights, 109, 121, 123–24,
    127–36, 152, 160;
    labor rights, 17, 22, 141;
    lesbian rights, 17, 19, 47;
    of married partners, 27, 28, 90;
    of people with disabilities, 19;
    of the disadvantaged, 131;
    of the poor, 67;
    political, social, and economic rights,
    31, 32, 96, 97, 133;
    reproductive rights, 17, 50;
    to collective bargaining, 41;
    to housing and food, 121, 130;
    transgender rights, 31;
    voting rights, 102;
    welfare rights, 152;
    women's rights, 17, 50, 145.
    See also International Covenant
    on Economic, Social, and
    Cultural Rights; Universal
    Declaration of Human Rights

Savings and loans bailout, 64–68,
    150–51
schools. *See education*

SCLC. *See* Southern Christian
Leadership Conference
selectivity filters, 2, 29–31, 39, 41,
43–49, 53, 55, 59, 77, 79–82,
84–88, 90–92, 95, 100–101, 103,
116, 120, 143–44, 152, 156,
158–60, 162–63
"selective globalization," 75
sexual citizenship, 27, 38
sexuality, 2, 3, 24, 25, 27, 29–30,
38–45, 47–48, 53–56, 77, 80–85,
87–90, 92, 157, 159, 162–63
sexuality forces. *See* balance of political
forces
sexual minorities, 27, 29, 42, 47, 88, 90
sexual orientation, 27, 29, 31, 44, 80,
83–84, 87–90, 158–59
sex work, 27, 29
skeptical theory, 22–23
social movement theories, 38, 56,
95–116
Southern Christian Leadership
Conference (SCLC), 105, 108
stability, 6–8, 60, 110
standpoint theory, 54, 56
state-centered structuralism, 11, 18–19,
80, 114
state managers, 10, 15–16, 18–19
state policies, 3, 15, 17–20, 23–24, 27,
29–31, 33, 39–40, 49, 51, 54, 57,
59, 61, 72, 79, 81, 90–91, 98–99,
101, 115–16, 119–21, 123–24,
127, 129, 136, 150, 153–54,
156–57, 160.
See also state projects
state power, 2, 22, 24, 37, 40, 115, 120,
132, 134, 157, 163
state projects, 2, 43, 48, 52–53, 156–62;
and economic intervention, 44, 56,
59–77, 117, 124, 138–41, 154,
157–58, 160, 161;
and gender, 49–51, 56, 87–88, 99,
138, 142–45, 154, 161;
and heteronormativity, 27, 77,
79–92, 159–60;
and kinship and marriage, 27–28, 55;

and multi-sites of power and the
welfare state, 137–54, 161;
and race, class, and gender, 54–55,
137, 145;
and social movements, 95–116;
and the human right to food, 127–36,
160, 163;
and the human right to shelter,
117–25, 160, 163;
and the surveillance state, 55;
of capitalist globalization, 130;
of economic intervention, 138–41;
of gender, sexuality, and racial
formation, 44, 47;
of militarization of the domestic
police force, 55;
of monogamy, 90;
of race, class, and nation, 158;
of racial formation, 34, 46, 56, 57,
85, 91, 95, 96–103, 115–16, 138,
142, 154, 160–62;
of racial formation, gendering,
sexuality, and class relations,
38–43, 55;
of sexuality, 56, 87–88, 163
state-society relationship, 2, 37, 43, 82,
88, 156, 161, 163
stereotypes, 42, 46, 99–100, 102
strategic selectivity, 4–5
strike, 17, 20–21, 41, 49, 112, 140–41,
153
Supreme Court, 10, 41–43, 49–50, 52,
99, 102, 103

taxation, 9, 22, 41, 75, 145–47, 150
Taylor Law, 16–17, 140
theory of power, 5
Thomas Theorem, 24
"too big to fail," 63, 65, 66, 124
trade, 22–24, 104, 119, 129, 141
trade unions. *See* unions
transgender people, 9, 27, 30–31, 41,
44, 57–58n1, 80, 85, 159.
See also lesbian, gay, bisexual, and
transgender and queer (LGBTQ)
people; trans men; trans women

transgender rights. *See* rights
trans men, 58, 86.
   See also lesbian, gay, bisexual,
     and transgender (LGBT) people;
     lesbian, gay, bisexual, and
     transgender and queer (LGBTQ)
     people
trans women, 58, 86.
   See also lesbian, gay, bisexual, and
     transgender (LGBT) people;
     lesbian, gay, bisexual, and
     transgender and queer (LGBTQ)
     people

UDHR. *See* Universal Declaration of
   Human Rights
unions, 20–21, 52, 102, 108, 139–41,
   147
Universal Declaration of Human Rights
   (UDHR), 121, 123, 127
"unnatural." *See* naturalness

violence, 6, 20, 23, 33, 41, 46, 51, 57,
   98, 100, 101, 102, 105, 108,
   111–15, 119, 132–34, 136, 139
voters. *See* voting
voting, 6–11, 33, 42, 50, 98–99, 102,
   108, 111, 112.
   See also electoral politics

Wagner Act, 139–40
Weber, Max, 3–4
welfare, 18, 42–45, 52, 55–57, 64,
   66–67, 74–75, 99, 102, 136,
   137–54, 161, 163.
   See also Personal Responsibility and
     Work Opportunity Reconciliation
     Act of 1996
whites, 9, 28, 32–33, 38, 42–43,
   46–47, 51, 54, 57, 67, 70, 77, 92,
   96–103, 106, 108–9, 111, 115,
   119, 120, 122–23, 147–50, 152,
   154, 158–59, 162.
   See also race
women, 1, 9, 13, 41, 44, 47, 49–50,
   57–58n1, 83, 85–86, 128, 135,
   142–45, 150–52, 162;
   and poverty, 44–46, 51, 56, 142–44,
   146, 148–49, 154, 161;
   of color, 42–43, 51, 57, 99, 148–49,
   154, 162
women's rights. *See* rights
workers, 13, 15–17, 19–21, 34, 41,
   54–55, 61, 63, 67, 73, 74, 77,
   97, 105–6, 113–15, 119–20, 124,
   133–34, 138–41, 143, 147–53,
   158
workers' rights. *See* labor rights
working class. *See* workers

About the Authors

Davita Silfen Glasberg is interim dean of the College of Liberal Arts and Sciences at the University of Connecticut, and a professor of sociology. She has taught both undergraduate and graduate courses and authored or coauthored twelve books and dozens of scholarly journal articles on issues of power and oppression, human rights, finance capital and the state, predatory lending, and inequality and diversity. Her latest books are *Political Sociology: Oppression, Resistance, and the State,* coauthored with Deric Shannon (Sage/Pine Forge Press); William T. Armaline, Davita Silfen Glasberg, and Bandana Purkayastha. 2015. *The Human Rights Enterprise: The State, Resistance, and Human Rights* (Polity Press); and *Human Rights in Our Own Back Yard: Injustice and Resistance in the United States,* coedited with William T. Armaline and Bandana Purkayastha (University of Pennsylvania Press) (Hirabayashi Book Award for Best Book, 2012, American Sociological Association Human Rights Section).

Abbey S Willis is a PhD candidate in sociology at the University of Connecticut. Her scholarly work includes investigations into sexuality, the family form, political theory, and social movements. She has been published in *Sexualities Journal* and *Educational Studies.*

Deric Shannon is a former line cook, cashier, and fast food worker, now an Associate Professor of sociology at Emory University's Oxford College. His work largely focuses on political economy, food, social theory, ecology, and experiential learning. His peer-reviewed work has appeared in *Educational Studies, Qualitative Report, Critical Sociology, Sexualities, Peace Studies Journal*, and *Theory in Action*. He has edited, coedited, and coauthored seven books and his work has been translated into over a half dozen different languages. He has led and accompanied students on global travel courses in the United States, South America, and Europe, typically looking at the intersections of political life and ecology. He is currently working on his first single-authored monograph, *Eating: Adventures in the Sociology of Being Human.*

Lightning Source UK Ltd.
Milton Keynes UK
UKOW04n0950151217
314520UK00001B/33/P